Being Interrupted

Being Interrupted

*Re-imagining the Church's Mission
from the Outside, In*

Al Barrett and Ruth Harley

with illustrations by Ally Barrett

scm press

Published in 2020 by SCM Press
Editorial office
3rd Floor, Invicta House,
108–114 Golden Lane,
London EC1Y 0TG, UK
www.scmpress.co.uk

SCM Press is an imprint of Hymns Ancient & Modern Ltd
(a registered charity)

H
Y
M
N Ancient
S &Modern

Hymns Ancient and Modern® is a registered trademark of
Hymns Ancient & Modern Ltd
13A Hellesdon Park Road, Norwich,
Norfolk NR6 5DR, UK

British Library Cataloguing in Publication data
A catalogue record for this book is available
from the British Library

978-0-33405-862-5

Typeset by Regent Typesetting
Printed and bound by
CPI Group (UK) Ltd

Contents

If we have more power
than the people we are with,
we need to remember to listen
as much as we talk.
And if we have less power,
we need to remember to talk
as much as we listen.
Both are difficult.
Gloria Steinem

Foreword

ANTHONY REDDIE

The mission of the Church in post-war Britain has been carried out against the backdrop of Church decline and the seeming marginalization of the historic mainline churches, in particular.

Churches in Europe are facing a major existential crisis; some even fearing for their very existence. This is evidenced by: falling numbers in the congregations of their respective churches; diminishing human resources with a shortage of willing people to participate in God's mission via the Church; and when people do participate it is as volunteers and not disciples (that is, people often do what fits their free time and not what their faith demands).

Falling numbers, diminishing financial resources, tired, dispirited and depleted numbers of ministers and laypeople are but the symptom. It can be argued that an underlying problem is a Christological one: it is an age-old missiological challenge. The primary casualty in this present epoch is that the old certainties of a 'Church Triumphant' have disappeared. The identity of white majority historic churches was predicated on the three Cs – namely, Christendom, Colonialism and (a white) Christ. Church growth in Europe reached its zenith during the high watermark of European expansion. Church mission was predicated on a Jesus that reinforced white, European notions of exceptionalism, manifest destiny and superiority.

British churches have responded to this definitional and missiological challenge by developing a range of commodified and market-driven strategies to arrest decline. They have sought to attempt to reconnect with a Jesus that speaks to the cultural contexts in which the Church is currently immersed – trying to share a new image of Christ for changing times.

This can be seen in initiatives such as fresh expressions – new ways of being church, pioneer ministry and renewed forms of lay discipleship.

The rise of popularist, right-wing nationalism as evidenced in the USA, Brazil and Europe represents a major challenge for Christian mission.

White nationalism, in particular, is often a reassertion of former impulses that gave rise to empire, white exceptionalism and notions of superiority.

Sadly, the attempt to reinvigorate the Church by means of the afore-mentioned has done nothing to deconstruct the philosophical and theological certainties that have remained an unacknowledged problem for centuries. The relationship between empire and colonialism, in many respects, remains the 'elephant in the room' in much academic theological discourse in the UK. The major theological and ethical challenge for the Church post-Brexit is how the Church can be in solidarity with black and minority ethnic people and vulnerable migrants, asylum seekers and refugees. Given that Brexit has emboldened groups on the political right such as Britain First and the English Defence League, the sharp challenge is: where is the church leadership that will face down the rise in white English nationalism?

The conflation of white privilege and entitlement alongside notions of election that are derived from a deep-seated theology of exceptionalism that is buttressed and exacerbated by the triumphs of empire has seen many historic churches remain somewhat ambivalent to the increased significance of black and minority ethnic people to the future mission and ministry of their churches. Given that British Christianity has been one of the greatest beneficiaries of post-war migration from the Caribbean and Africa, one might have hoped for a greater resolve to oppose the very concept of Brexit, given the ways in which this phenomenon traduced the very multi-ethnic and multicultural paradigms that have benefited the Church in Britain. It is my contention that this apparent ambivalence is a result of the continuing need to placate white sensibilities and the fragility of whiteness that has little agency once it is shorn from its moorings of privilege, entitlement and superiority.

It is in the midst of these wider cultural and social changes, and the lack of any substantive missiological response to it, that I wish to com-mend *Being Interrupted*. The authors of this very fine text have sought to dig deep and go beneath the surface of the missiological problems facing the Church, especially the Church of England. The authors recog-nize the neo-colonial edifice that is the Anglican Church in England and that simply devising new strategies and marketing gimmicks for arresting decline will not get to the heart of the disconnect between this venerable institution and the wider socio-cultural milieu.

Being Interrupted is a searingly honest and challenging 'insider account' written by two committed practitioners who are serious about asking critical questions about the Church's engagement with those who are on the margins. Gone is the seemingly axiomatic trope of 'hospitality' as the panacea for all ecclesial ills. The authors recognize the fundamental challenge that faces powerful institutions like the Church of England whose formative identity occurred under the aegis of empire and patrician forms of control.

Simply seeking to be nicer to people will not do. Creating more attractive forms of worship will certainly be an advantage as historic ecclesial bodies like the Church of England seek to arrest their numerical decline. But as *Being Interrupted* so clearly demonstrates, this in itself will not cure the neo-colonial habitus that has seen the Church assume for itself an indispensable position in God's gracious economy. Something more substantive and theologically astute is needed; I say this in the knowledge that so much of the top-down institutional attempts to revitalize the Church have exuded little in the way of theological acumen to underpin their various strategies.

This text is, I believe, an important first. In *Being Interrupted*, Al Barrett and Ruth Harley have written what is demonstrably an important and significant text that will command the interest of practitioners, denominational educators, missiologists and church leaders, who will benefit from engaging with a challenging, insightful and hopeful text that encourages us to seek the generous God we serve in the other. Gone is the assumption that the locus of authority lies within the orbit of the Church, with God moving from the Church to those beyond it. *Being Interrupted* challenges us to pause and reverse the flow of the traditional missiological direction of grace, away from the Church and towards the often powerless others. This requires a massive change in identity, focus and intent. *Being Interrupted* offers important reflective tools for effecting this change and I for one look forward to seeing who is willing to follow in its lead.

Professor Anthony Reddie
Oxford Centre for Religion and Culture
Regent's Park College, Oxford University and
The University of South Africa

Foreword

LYNNE CULLENS

I've never been asked to write a foreword for a book. So, before I began, I googled 'how to write a foreword for a book' and was given the following guidance: be honest, use your unique voice, discuss your connection to the story and the author, mimic the style of the book, sign off.

I think I've ticked the be honest part and possibly gone some way towards using my unique voice, so my connection to this story, and to one of the authors in particular, is where I'll begin.

Several years ago, I began to blog. One of my first attempts was a short piece called 'Voiceless' and in it I sought to capture something of the sense of frustration I felt in being unheard as a working-class woman in the Church. It marked the culmination of many years of being within church congregations and structures where I felt demeaned, placated and 'spoken for'.

I'm a single mum, born to a single mum, and we have had many times of struggle. I'm also someone with a fairly strong academic and professional background and I had the firm conviction that I – and many others like me – had gifts to offer the Church that were being ignored. I also had the strongest sense that I was loved, called and affirmed by God in all of those things, that I had a role to play and that I was called to be, as you'll see the authors describe, part of the 'invasion of the inside by the outside'.

But though that blog received some degree of acknowledgement, nothing changed. I attended conferences where the presentation of the working class within the Church, given always by middle-class voices, was something akin to a study in cultural anthropology. We were case studies, we were 'the poor', our voices were to be curated, filtered and sanitized to be deemed acceptable to the wider Church.

And into this, fairly bleak, picture stepped Al. Two conscious decisions that he took proved to be game changers.

The first was an invitation from a national journalist to provide a quote on the experience of the working class within the Church. That invitation was extended to Al himself, as an academic and acknowledged and respected practitioner in ministry in working-class contexts. He could have taken up that opportunity himself, but chose not to. He chose instead to use his status, platform and privilege to give me, as a working-class woman, a voice. That incident, and the subsequent article, are referenced here in this book.

The second was at a conference more recently, with a break-out group consisting of middle-class men and women, including Al, where the discussion centred on mission to those from working-class communities. During that session, I attempted to speak on several occasions and was ignored or spoken over. After some time, Al spoke and, as the group fell immediately silent, he said 'I think Lynne has been trying to speak'. Again, he used his agency to give me voice.

It's hard to convey quite how powerfully affirming I found both of those incidents. Not only was I enabled to speak, but Al had recognized the need to interrupt the flow of the power dynamic in each case, and to step aside from taking the platform himself, in order for me to do so.

So, when he and Ruth asked me to write a foreword for this book I immediately said yes. Without having seen it. And then it arrived. All 300-plus pages delivered to a self-confessed non-reader. In saying that, I should stress that I can read; I feel obliged to clarify that since expectations of the working class can be so spectacularly low within the Church. I mean that I don't read for pleasure. This, therefore, was going to be a 'reading for work' exercise, except it turned out to be very far from that.

This is not merely a book to be read, it is an experience. In fact, more like an adventure. It's the unfolding of a story; the story of allowing ourselves and our churches to be carried deeper into the mystery of incarnation; a relaxation, an abandonment into grace. A story of what can happen when we cease to 'do' church, when we hold a mirror up to our own privilege and when we allow ourselves to be transformed by the divine intervention of interruption (and, Reader, I read it for pleasure!).

In the early part of this book you will 'meet' both authors. I found this section to be an unexpected delight. From Al's early experiences growing up in military camps, with the strict segregation of rank and status, to Ruth's working-class roots and later studies at university in Oxford (giving her a foot in both of those worlds, 'I am now bi-lingual but middle class will never be my mother tongue'), Al and Ruth lay bare their own backgrounds in a way that embraces their vulnerability, and which encourages each of us to do the same.

Then we are invited by consistent, gracious 'beckoning' to go ever deeper into this story of interruption, encounter and transformation.

But this book is also part manual, part workbook. There are 'questions' and 'wonderings' to reflect on at the end of each chapter, there are tableaus of experience gained in the authors' contexts and set against wider wisdom; there are practical exercises. This book will challenge you, as it's challenged me, in ways that mean you come away from it changed.

One key change for me lay in this book articulating so much of my lived experience that I had no prior framework to express. Another was that I came to it with some degree of certainty as to who I was, the nature of my ministry and the place of the Church. I believed I had my understanding reasonably well thought through and defined. But now, looking back from the other side of reading it, I feel I was in something of a Hall of Mirrors, seeing a series of distortions and that now I am invited to gaze with something of a truer lens.

Like the child who makes a sandcastle at the edge of the seashore, only to have the tide gradually erode its structure, I was gradually taken back (or forward?) by the ebb and flow of wave upon wave of encounter, suggestion and challenge; by the constant gracious 'beckoning' and invitation to think differently, to live differently, to listen to and encounter others and God differently, that Al and Ruth's writing embodies; in their own words, 'by allowing room within ourselves for wild, uncontrolled flourishing'.

Now to the sign off. Do more than read this book. Open yourself to it. Encounter the Christ who was challenged and changed by interruption; revel in the beauty of seed bombs, of dining tables and chandeliers set up in a patch of woodland at the heart of an estate, of community parties and talent shows, of the gifts of children. Take on the risk of embracing vulnerability. Take on the risk of stepping into the power of story, of interruption and of 'disruptive grace'. And, in the love and mercy of God, go well.

Revd Lynne Cullens
St Mary's Rectory, Stockport

Foreword

RACHEL MANN

I dislike being interrupted. 'Who doesn't?' you might say. After all, 'inter-ruption', so often, entails someone seeking to cut across one's speech or action. It is a signal that another voice or agent wishes to claim power or space or position and deprive one of agency. One only needs to witness the state of discourse in our parliamentary or televisual politics, or on social media sites, to recognize how 'interruption' is so often framed as a crass kind of power game, a sign of a damaged discourse.

Perhaps one reason I dislike being interrupted is I've had to put up with quite a lot of it. Being a woman, as well as being trans, disabled and of working-class heritage to boot, means one encounters considerable interruption. It is rarely much fun to have one's voice, subjectivity or body devalued by dominant, fragile and insistent narratives. One does rather want to be permitted to speak, act, or be heard with a little less interruption.

Nonetheless, I also hold profound privilege. I am white and educated. Within the Church, as a priest, I hold power and authority. As a writer (even one with a modest-to-vanishingly small audience!), I have influence. I have also learned to 'take up' space and claim power. As a powerful person in the Church, who is authorized to preach and lead, I often need to be interrupted. I may dislike it, but interruption is surely necessary. For who do I silence when I deploy my bumptious confidence and licensed surety?

One of the reasons I think Al and Ruth's book is both necessary and important is because it is unafraid to draw attention (forgive the jargon-laden phrase) to the 'missional necessity' of interruption. I like to think that, as priest and theologian, I am committed, in the company of others, to discern the *missio dei*. Where that discernment has been at its liveliest and most fruitful is in contexts of interruption. At parish, diocesan and national level, I've encountered 'interruption' as a site of wonder, shock, bewilderment and conversion. What especially excites me about Ruth and Al's work is its preparedness to frame interruption as both multivalent and multidirectional. Their work reminds me, and I hope you, that Jesus and his agents were not and are not simply the privileged 'disrupters-in-chief'. Jesus' work and ministry was interrupted and changed by the interruptions, action and bodies of those coded as 'subaltern'. Crucially, Al and Ruth remind me that without such interruptions Jesus could not be the Christ. They show, then, how interruption is biblical. If Jesus is 'Saviour' he doesn't get to be so without interruption, as if 'God' is simply one-way traffic. If mission is, genuinely, to be grounded, real and transformative for everyone and each one, it needs to be biblical in the ways Al and Ruth indicate.

I also commend *Being Interrupted* for its grit and grace. What I mean is that this a book one can 'use', without tumbling into utilitarian ideas about value or meaning. It's a kind of workbook and workbooks are among my favourite kinds of things. Why? Because they remind theologians like me that if I do get excited about 'doctrine' or 'ecclesiology' or whatever, humans are creatures thrown into a world of mess and limit. Workbooks keep people like me honest. Indeed, they invite people of faith to value craft as much as art and science. In short, Ruth and Al know that there is dignity in work. *Being Interrupted* is an invitation to be present to the potentialities of 'work together', but most of all, not to be afraid when our places of comfort are disrupted. Grace meets us in the grit. If I've long been convinced one can't really find the one without the other, *Being Interrupted* underlines this point.

Finally, a related matter. *Being Interrupted* strikes me as an honest book. Honesty, right now, seems important. I can't be alone in feeling trauma, bewilderment and, well, occasional rage in the face of structures and institutions which no longer seem to be load-bearing, if they ever were. While Al and Ruth, rightly, are unafraid to bring sophisticated theological, cultural and sociological ideas to bear in their interrogation of human economies, ecologies and ecotones, they keep ever close to stories. In a world sometimes characterized as 'post-truth', I understand why some suspect 'story' is a feeble way to frame accountability. Ruth and Al resist that suspicion, and then some. They remind their readers that the promises of mission, which is one way of talking about the promises of God, surely lie in honest, sometimes exhausting wrestling with the power and cost of human story.

Canon Rachel Mann
Priest, poet and theologian

PART I

Where Are We?

Act 1

An Interrupted Nativity

It was the annual Street Nativity play: one of those rare occasions where there are more adults wearing tea towels on their heads than children. The story had begun at the Hub, our shop-front youth and community centre, with the surprise news to teenage Mary that she was going to have a baby. From there we walked – through the wind and rain, this year – with our real, live donkey (on loan for the evening from a nearby stables), along the puddle-strewn streets of our estate, a small crowd of the excited, curious and slightly-too-cold-for-comfort adding themselves to the performers, the latter mostly clutching their soggy scripts with one hand, and making sure their makeshift head-coverings didn't blow away with the other.

Out of the darkness of Comet Park appeared the angel Gabriel, complete with 4-foot wings, light-up halo and a megaphone to ensure her voice was heard by not just the shepherds, and the crowd, but most of the residents of the adjacent tower block too. Turning up Chipperfield Road, we were joined by the magi (approaching from the east end of Bromford Drive), and a young star-bearer led us up the hill known locally as Mount Chipper.

So, it was something of a relief for all of those in the procession when we stopped, for the next scene, in the relative shelter outside Sonny's chip shop, Atlantis Fish Bar. Sonny, not known for flamboyant performances, had had his arm twisted to play King Herod. Having heard from the magi, he delivered his line responding to them, telling them to go and find the new king and report back to him when they had done so. He then removed his crown and robe (with visible relief) and, in a much more confident voice, invited everyone into the chippy for free fish and chips.

It was at this point that the vicar (Al, also in robe-and-tea-towel attire) reached nervously into his pocket for his mobile phone, to ring those waiting up at the church building, to let them know that the mulled wine and mince pies they were busy warming up wouldn't be needed for at least another half an hour; that our crowd of people, when we arrived, might well be cold, but not half as hungry as we'd thought; and that those arriving at church expecting the Carol Service to start promptly at

6.30 p.m. should be plied with refreshments in the hope that this might encourage them as they waited for our arrival.

Introduction

The (true) story you've just read is a parable: of the kin-dom of God,[1] in the hands of our neighbours, interrupting the plans, expectations and flow of the Church's life and mission, with an undreamt-of abundance that grabs our attention, expands our horizons and reorients our sense of direction and purpose.

When we say 'us', we mean, primarily, we who are used to calling ourselves 'the Church'. We also mean, as a sub-group of the above, we whom the structures of society, and the Church – at least as both of those entities are right now – have given an undue proportion of power, prominence and privilege. In this book we will try to be alert to such unjust structures, and to bring them into greater visibility. We will focus most sharply on the ways human beings have been divided down lines of race,[2] class and gender, and the ways in which each of those divisions has assumed a relationship of superiority and inferiority: privileging, in particular, those

---

1 While we have tried as much as possible to avoid technical jargon in this book, we also try to be very careful with our words. Kin-dom: most readers will be familiar with the idea of 'the kingdom of God', used by Jesus repeatedly in the Gospels. It's a term that is used deliberately, ironically, to subvert, turn on their heads, our usual understandings of 'kingdoms' (hierarchical societies ruled over by a powerful monarch), and most specifically the Roman emperor of Jesus' time. But as a term, even used ironically, it's still very hard to imagine its meaning beyond a male-centred, patriarchal world – something that we'll explore in some depth as this book unfolds. We've opted for the term, 'kin-dom', used by some feminist theologians, to retain the subversive sense of Jesus' term, but within an expansive idea of how we – human and other-than-human (see footnote below) creatures – might discover transformed ways of relating to each other as 'kin'.

2 Race: when we use the term 'race' throughout this book, we are referring to something that is *socially constructed* rather than an innate characteristic of any human being's identity. Counter-intuitively perhaps, 'race' is a product of *racism*, and more specifically, a product of an entrenched but often unspoken ideology of white supremacy. Through racist social processes, we are *racialized*, divided into 'identity boxes' primarily on the basis of skin tone (although other factors, such as nationality, language or cultural heritage, are often also at play). Various kinds of 'other' are named, usually in relation to a 'whiteness' that goes unnamed because it is assumed to be 'normal'. In a British context, for example, these might include 'black, 'Asian' and what are often lumped together as other 'minority ethnic' groups – sometimes, not necessarily helpfully, referred to collectively as 'BAME'.

who find themselves identified as white, middle-class (and 'higher') and male. We will also explore the ways in which children have been pushed to the edges of an adult-centred world, and the other-than-human world[3] has been exploited, abused and destroyed by many – but not all – of those who call ourselves 'human'.

While it was far from an easy decision to make, we have chosen not to reflect in detail here on some of the other dividing lines and hierarchies that distort our relationships, especially those that privilege non-disabled people (however temporarily they might be so) over disabled people; heterosexual people over gay, lesbian and bisexual people, and people who are in relationships with someone of the opposite sex over those who are either in same-sex relationships or single; and cis people (those whose gender identity aligns with that given them at birth) over trans and non-binary people. The book would simply have become even more complex, and even longer, than it is already – and we needed to set ourselves a relatively finite, coherent and achievable task! Nevertheless, we have written this book in solidarity with all those who suffer the pain of those divisions that we have not attended to here, and we have done our best both to point to reflection that has been done in those areas already, and also to be 'creatively disruptive' in ways that might just inspire or encourage others to do some of the work that still needs doing.

We will assume in these pages not only that these divisions, coupled with an unequal distribution of power, are sinful, signs of humanity's falling short of what we are created to be; but we will also explore some of the ways in which the Church (particularly when it is dominated by Christians who benefit from the status quo, whether unwittingly or not) all too often colludes with and reinforces those divisions, rather than seeking to break them down. And we will suggest, through sharing stories from our own experience, the analysis of others, and rereadings of Gospel texts, that another way is possible: a way that begins with being interrupted – which means also disrupted, challenged and changed – by our neighbours who, in all kinds of different ways, are 'other' than us, but always come bearing gifts – wonderful, strange and sometimes even difficult gifts – that we are invited, with curiosity, wild patience, delight and humility, to receive.

---

3 Other-than-human: we have chosen to use the term 'other-than-human' in this book where some others would say 'non-human' or, more problematically, 'nature' – remembering that we humans are inextricably part of the world we often call 'natural', and also preferring to name our creature-kin as 'other' rather than what they are 'not'. We realize all of these are tricky and contested terms, but hope you can bear with the choices we have made!

We will also argue in this book that although these divisions have long histories which can be traced back centuries, there is also something critical about this moment, particularly in the national context of the United Kingdom within which both of us are living and writing, that makes an attention to divisions of race, class, gender and age – and our 'other-than-human' relationships – of critical importance. We have written this book in the tumultuous four years between the UK's referendum on membership of the European Union in 2016, and the COVID-19 global pandemic which reached the UK in 2020. But both 'Brexit' and COVID-19 have exposed divisions in our society that go much deeper than an abstract question of international politics and economics (EU membership), and which have had – and continue to have – as profound an impact as the coronavirus that has killed hundreds of thousands of people worldwide.[4] These deeper divisions have come to public visibility through other crises in our national and global life. All four of them 'broke' in the year 2017 – the 'Windrush scandal' (race), the Grenfell Tower tragedy (class), the #MeToo movement (gender), and 15-year-old Greta Thunberg's solo school strike (climate change) – and all four of them, at the time of writing, are anything but resolved.

Windrush

In November 2017, *Guardian* journalist Amelia Gentleman reported the story of 61-year-old Paulette Wilson, who had been living and working in Britain for 50 years when she received a letter informing her that she was an illegal immigrant and was going to be removed to Jamaica, a country she left when she was ten.[5] Wilson's story, Gentleman revealed, was just one among tens of thousands, stories from the sharp end of the British government's attempt to detain and deport people from Commonwealth territories who had arrived in the UK before 1973 and did not have documentary evidence of their right to remain in the country.

Dubbed the 'Windrush scandal' for its apparent focus on post-war arrivals from the Caribbean (on the *Empire Windrush* and subsequent ships), estimates suggested up to 57,000 citizens from all over the

---

4 At the time of writing this (May 2020), the UK has seen almost 50,000 deaths from COVID-19, and one of the highest death rates per head of population in the world – including a disproportionately high death rate among people from lower-income communities and from black, Asian and minority ethnic backgrounds.

5 Amelia Gentleman, '"I can't eat or sleep": the woman threatened with deportation after 50 years in Britain', *Guardian*, 28 November 2017, www.theguardian.com/uk-news/2017/nov/28/i-cant-eat-or-sleep-the-grandmother-threatened-with-deportation-after-50-years-in-britain, accessed 5 March 2020.

Commonwealth might be affected, and links were quickly made to the stated aim, in 2012, of home secretary Theresa May, creating a 'hostile environment' for 'illegal immigrants', with a 'deport now, appeal later' policy. Part of 'an arsenal of measures aimed at curtailing immigration, facilitating deportation, and maintaining hierarchies of status for those who are resident', the 'hostile environment' was shown to be both explicitly legitimizing sanctions against those deemed 'foreign criminals' and suspects in the 'War against Terror', while also quietly rendering huge numbers of 'black and brown British citizens in a perpetual state of precarity'.[6]

In April 2018, 64-year-old Renford McIntyre was homeless and sleeping on a sofa in an industrial unit in Dudley. He has lived in the UK for almost 50 years since arriving from Jamaica in 1968 at 14, to join his mother who had moved here to work as a nurse. He has worked and paid taxes here for 48 years, as an NHS driver and a delivery man, but in 2014 a request for updated paperwork from his employers revealed he did not have documents showing he had a right to be in the UK. He was sacked; the local council told him he was not eligible for housing support or any benefits, so he became homeless. He gathered together paperwork showing 35 years of national insurance contributions but the Home Office returned the application requesting further information. 'I can't tell you how angry and bitter it makes me feel. I've worked hard all my life, I've paid into the system. I've sent them details of my NHS pension, and HMRC records going back 40 years. They've got all my documents. What more do they want?' he said. 'How do they expect me to live? How am I expected to eat or dress myself?'[7]

Grenfell Tower

In the early hours of 14 June 2017, a 24-storey tower block in west London caught fire. The fire spread with terrifying speed and ferocity, and despite a massive fire-fighting operation, 71 people lost their lives: people from many different nationalities, many different backgrounds,

---

6 Nisha Kapoor, 'On Windrush, Citizenship and its Others', *Verso Books blog*, 1 May 2018, www.versobooks.com/blogs/3774-on-windrush-citizenship-and-its-others, accessed 5 March 2020.

7 Amelia Gentleman, 'The children of Windrush: "I'm here legally, but they're asking me to prove I'm British"', *Guardian*, 15 April 2018, www.theguardian.com/uk-news/2018/apr/15/why-the-children-of-windrush-demand-an-immigration-amnesty, accessed 5 March 2020.

but almost all of them, in financial terms, among the least well-off in British society.

In the days that followed the Grenfell Tower tragedy, we discovered that residents of the Tower, members of the Grenfell Action Group, had been issuing repeated warnings for several years, that 'only a catastrophic event will expose the ineptitude and incompetence of our landlord ... and bring an end to the dangerous living conditions and neglect of health and safety legislation that they inflict upon their tenants' (Grenfell Action Group 2016). Tragically, those warnings were not heard or heeded by their landlord, by Kensington and Chelsea Borough Council, or by anyone else in a position to put pressure on those bodies to do what was necessary to ensure the safety of the Tower's residents. The gaping chasm between the affluent and the poorest in our society, widened and intensified by years of 'austerity' as government policy – with drastic cuts in public services, investment, and the social security safety net, and an accompanying stigmatization of the poorest as 'scroungers' – was exposed, in the Grenfell fire, in all its deadliness.

At the time of writing, in early 2020, the official inquiry into the tragedy is ongoing; but it opened, in May 2018, with verbal 'pen portraits' of those who had died – at the request of the bereaved families. Among so many stories of gifted human beings, loving and beloved, consider Khadija Saye's as an example:

> Khadija Saye was 24 years old, born in London, and lived with her Gambian mother in a flat on the 20th floor of the tower. At the age of 16, already recognised as a talented photographer, she won a scholarship to the prestigious Rugby school.
>
> 'She was incredibly grateful for the experience,' says Nicola Green, an artist and mentor of Khadija's, 'but she told me it was one of the most difficult things she had done. It was a completely different world to the one she was part of – she was living at the top of Grenfell Tower and the school was full of privileged people ... it gave her an understanding that confidence is a mysterious thing – I think maybe it gave her the tenacity and determination to find it in herself.'
>
> Saye went on to the University for the Creative Arts, pursuing her artistic career despite the financial barriers in her way. On the cusp of widespread recognition, her work was exhibited at the Venice Biennale in 2017. One of her fellow artists described her as 'one of the most remarkable people I have ever, and probably will ever, meet'.[8]

---

8 'The lives of Grenfell Tower', *Guardian*, 14 May 2018, www.theguardian.com/uk-news/ng-interactive/2018/may/14/lives-of-grenfell-tower-victims-fire, accessed 8 May 2020.

#MeToo

A third moment, between the first two, began in the USA but quickly spread – at the wildfire speed of social media – to the UK and across the world. Although the phrase 'Me Too' was being used 11 years earlier by American activist Tarana Burke in a campaign to promote 'empower-ment through empathy' among women of colour from marginalized communities who had experienced sexual abuse, #MeToo exploded as a social media hashtag in October 2017 when actress Alyssa Milano shared her own experience of sexual abuse by Hollywood producer Harvey Weinstein, and encouraged other women to do likewise – to 'give people a sense of the magnitude of the problem'.[9] Within days, millions of women had shared, via Twitter, Facebook and Instagram, their own experiences of harassment and abuse, and sparked an international conversation about 'socially-accepted' norms of male behaviour, and imbalances of power between men and women at all levels of society. Here's just one of a multitude of testimonies now in the public domain:

> When I saw the #MeToo hashtag I was just coming to terms with my sexual assault. It happened when I was in middle school by one of my teachers. It took me a while to come forward with what had happened to me and then when I went to the administration I was told I didn't have enough evidence to prove anything and I should just keep quiet about it because I and the school could be sued for slander if I went public with the experience. It was really silencing because when I was being assaulted it was that stereotypical line of 'let's keep this between me and you'. And then when I found the courage to come out I was told again 'let's keep this quiet'. So for me too, it was a way to have a voice and it was a way for me to see that I'm not the only one that has gone through this and that women all around the world have all experienced the same thing. It was really unifying (Samantha Hanahentzen, 17).[10]

The concept of 'toxic masculinity' – the traditional and stereotypical behaviour of the 'alpha male', socially dominant, misogynist, emotionally repressed and externally aggressive – was, of course, nothing new to the millions of women now sharing their stories online, or the billions of

---

9 Nadia Khomani, '#MeToo: how a hashtag became a rallying cry against sexual harassment', *Guardian*, 20 October 2017, www.theguardian.com/world/2017/oct/20/women-worldwide-use-hashtag-metoo-against-sexual-harassment, accessed 8 May 2020.

10 Talia Lakritz, 'These 15 women opened up about their sexual assault experiences thanks to the #metoo campaign', *Insider*, 1 October 2018, www.insider.com/me-too-hashtag-sexual-harassment-assault-2017-11, accessed 8 May 2020.

women who have always shared with each other their stories of abusive and predatory male behaviour, warning each other about which men to watch out for, and who to avoid being alone with. But now this previously 'hidden' reality entered the mainstream, male-centred[11] public conversation, so much so that the razor makers Gillette cited it, and the #MeToo movement, in their rebranding campaign that changed their slogan from the assertive, individualistic, acquisitive, 'The best a man can get' to the more communal, self-reflective, 'The best men can be'.[12] The backlash was depressingly predictable and, if anything, underlined the point.

School Strike for Climate

In August 2017, a 15-year-old Swedish schoolgirl called Greta took a day off school to sit outside the parliament building in Stockholm with a simple hand-written placard: 'skolstrejk för klimatet' ('school strike for climate'). Her parents had tried to dissuade her, and none of her classmates chose to join her.

In January 2019, Greta Thunberg was addressing the World Economic Forum of international business and government leaders in Davos, Switzerland:

> Our house is on fire ... According to the IPCC (Intergovernmental Panel on Climate Change), we are less than 12 years away from not being able to undo our mistakes. In that time, unprecedented changes in all aspects of society need to have taken place, including a reduction of our CO_2 emissions by at least 50% ...
>
> We are facing a disaster of unspoken sufferings for enormous amounts of people. And now is not the time for speaking politely or focusing on what we can or cannot say. Now is the time to speak clearly ...
>
> We all have a choice. We can create transformational action that will safeguard the living conditions for future generations. Or we can continue with our business as usual and fail ...
>
> We must change almost everything in our current societies. The bigger your carbon footprint, the bigger your moral duty. The bigger your platform, the bigger your responsibility.

---

11 Some feminists use the term 'malestream' to indicate the extent to which the 'mainstream' is centred around the needs, desires and experiences of men.

12 Isaac Stanley-Becker, 'Gillette ad takes on "toxic masculinity" in #MeToo-era rebrand, provoking a backlash', *Washington Post*, 15 January 2019, www.washington post.com/nation/2019/01/15/gillette-takes-toxic-masculinity-new-ad-rebranding-me too-era-inviting-backlash/, accessed 8 May 2020.

Adults keep saying: 'We owe it to the young people to give them hope.' But I don't want your hope. I don't want you to be hopeful. I want you to panic. I want you to feel the fear I feel every day. And then I want you to act. I want you to act as you would in a crisis. I want you to act as if our house is on fire. Because it is.[13]

In September 2019, the 'global climate strike', led by schoolchildren and students, took place across 4,500 locations in 150 countries, and drew over 6 million people to the streets. In just over two years, Greta Thunberg's one-girl school strike had energized a worldwide movement for radical change in the face of the climate emergency and mass species extinction – change not just in an individual's lifestyle habits, but in our *systems*: of production and consumption, of economics and finance, of government and democracy.

She has also sparked a backlash of remarkable ferocity, among some of the most powerful and influential people in the world – especially some of those who happen to be white and male, something that, as this book unfolds, will become increasingly unsurprising. Little of the reaction seeks to challenge Thunberg's arguments, or the robust and ever-growing body of scientific knowledge she seeks to highlight. Instead, it tends to go for the personal attack approach, belittling her for being young (and therefore clearly naive), a girl (who should really be softly spoken and more concerned about her appearance than the future of the planet), or labelling her a 'freak' or a 'weirdo' (usually referring to aspects of her personality associated with her Asperger's syndrome, which she herself claims as a 'superpower'). When she was named *Time* 'Person of the Year' in December 2019, US President Donald Trump tweeted: 'So ridiculous. Greta must work on her Anger Management problem, then go to a good old fashioned movie with a friend! Chill, Greta, Chill!'

It was clearly inconceivable to Trump that Thunberg's fiery, and some-times tearful, seriousness reflects the seriousness of the climate emergency itself. Thunberg, on the other hand, has done her best to deflect attention away from her and back on to the planet:

---

13 See www.fridaysforfuture.org/greta-speeches. It is important to note here that Greta is by no means alone as an inspiring young leader of the climate action movement – and that it is hardly coincidental that others, especially young people of colour and from among indigenous peoples, have received less media attention. See for example Leah Ashmelash, 'Greta Thunberg isn't alone. Meet some other young activists who are leading the environmentalist fight', *CNN World*, 29 September 2019, https://edition. cnn.com/2019/09/28/world/youth-environment-activists-greta-thunberg-trnd/, accessed 8 May 2020.

Some people have chosen not to listen to us, and that is fine, we are after all just children. You don't have to listen to us, but you do have to listen to the science, the scientists. And that is all we ask, just unite behind the science![14]

Windrush, racism and the 'hostile environment'. Grenfell, class inequality and the deadliness of austerity. #MeToo, toxic masculinity, and gender-based violence and abuse. Climate change and mass species extinction. Any one of these crises could easily overwhelm us, let alone the combination of all of them together. Although they are our starting point for this book's journey, for most of the pages that follow we will 'zoom in' to the level of our interactions as individual human beings, as Christians with our neighbours (both human and other-than-human). Through attending carefully to those interactions, attending carefully to our day-to-day encounters with others, and seeking to do those interactions, receive those encounters, *differently*, we are engaged in nothing less, we will argue here, than creating together what Pope Francis has called 'our common home' – creating in the world a dwelling place for God.[15]

Further reading

On the Windrush scandal:

- Amelia Gentleman, *The Windrush Betrayal: Exposing the Hostile Environment* (London: Guardian Faber, 2019)
- Maya Goodfellow, *Hostile Environment: How Immigrants Became Scapegoats* (London: Verso, 2019)
- Nisha Kapoor, *Deport, Deprive, Extradite: 21st Century State Extremism* (London: Verso, 2018)

On Grenfell Tower:

- Dan Bulley, Jenny Edkins and Nadine El-Enany, *After Grenfell: Violence, Resistance and Response* (London: Pluto, 2019)
- Alan Everett, *After the Fire: Finding Words for Grenfell* (Norwich: Canterbury Press, 2018)

---

14 Greta Thunberg, speech at the National Assembly in Paris, 23 July 2019, www.fridaysforfuture.org/greta-speeches.

15 *Laudato Si': On Care for our Common Home*, Pope Francis, Encyclical Letter, 24 May 2015, https://cafod.org.uk/content/download/25373/182331/file/papa-francesco_20150524_enciclica-laudato-si_en.pdf.

On #MeToo:

- Carly Gieseler, *The Voices of #MeToo: From Grassroots Activism to a Viral Roar* (London: Rowman and Littlefield, 2019)
- Jodi Kantor and Megan Twohey, *She Said: Breaking the Sexual Harassment Story that Helped Ignite a Movement* (London: Bloomsbury, 2019)

On School Strike for Climate:

- Lily Dyu, *Earth Heroes: 20 Inspiring Stories of People Saving our World* (London: Nosy Crow, 2019)
- Greta Thunberg, *No One is Too Small to Make a Difference* (Harmondsworth: Penguin, 2019)

Questions for reflection/discussion

- How did you experience the events/movements described here?
- How has your experience of these events been shaped by your own circumstances and life history?
- How might these events have been experienced differently by someone whose life and circumstances are different from yours?

I

Who are 'We'?

The word 'we' is so often used in statements: 'we have decided …', 'this is the way we do things …', 'we know …'

But 'we' should always involve at least three questions:

- Who are the 'we', we are talking about?
- Who is the 'we' doing the talking?
- Who is (implicitly or explicitly) *not* included in 'we'?

For both Al and Ruth (the 'we' writing this book), we much prefer asking these kind of questions in conversation, face to face, when we can see each other, who else is in the room, who is doing the talking and who isn't, and honestly wrestle together with the question of who is *not* in the room.

In writing, it's more difficult. We, the authors, have a good sense of who *we* are. But you, the readers, might well know very little about us – and we can hardly even guess who you might be. You and we are missing the kind of *encounters* with each other that fill the pages of this book. So, if we, the authors, start using the word 'we' in a broader sense – to include you, the readers – then we're on dangerous ground! Who are we imagining you to be? Who are we in danger of *forgetting*, in our imagined 'we'?

All this risks getting very complicated, very quickly. So, we will do three things. First, we're going to invite you to spend a bit of time reflecting on who *you* are! Second, we will make a promise to you: in the rest of this book, whenever we use 'we', we will attempt to be as specific as we can: either we'll be clear that we're talking about us, the authors, Ruth and Al; or we'll try and define what group we're talking about ('those of us who are racialized as white', for example). Third, we will tell you a little bit about ourselves, and how we came to be writing this book.

Who am I? – You

This exercise is taken from black theologian Anthony Reddie's book, *Is God Colour-blind? Insights from Black Theology for Christian Ministry*, offered there as 'something of a diagnostic tool ... a way of helping people to reflect on how they understand themselves' and 'what it means to be human'.[1] Done on your own, or in conversation with others, it can help highlight to us some of the characteristics that make you uniquely *you*, some of the characteristics you share with *some* other people, and some of the characteristics you share with *all* other people. It will also help you think about some of the ways in which your particular identity brings with it certain aspects of *privilege*: unearned advantages that you bring with you into social interactions, because of the way your society values some characteristics of identity over others. We will explore that in more detail in the following chapters.

For now, we invite you to think about the different components or elements that make up your identity – that make you who you are. On an A4 piece of paper (or larger if you can get it!), you'll need to draw five concentric circles (see below). Then, fill in those circles as follows:

- In the innermost circle, write down just one or two words (or very short phrases) that define who you are. These should be the words that feel most central to how you see and understand yourself at this precise moment. They can be nouns (e.g. man), adjectives (e.g. female), relational terms (e.g. sister), roles (e.g. teacher), or even verbs (e.g. loves music). There are no 'wrong' answers – what you put down is entirely your own choice, and deeply personal to you.
- In the next circle outwards, write down the next three or four words to describe yourself. These are not quite as central, for you, as those in the innermost circle, but they're still very important.
- Work your way outwards, with four or five words in the next circle, and so on, until you've written words in all the circles – around 20 altogether.

---

1 Anthony Reddie, *Is God Colour-blind? Insights from Black Theology for Christian Ministry* (London: SPCK, 2009), pp. 39–42.

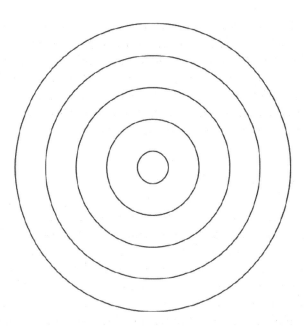

Figure 1: Concentric circles of identity

- Once you've finished writing, have a look at what you've written, and where you've written it. What is close to the centre, and why? What is closer to the periphery?
- If you are with other people, you might want to share *some* of what you've written, in conversation with someone else. Don't feel under any pressure to show them your whole diagram – there may be some things you've written that you want to keep to yourself. But if you're able to share something together, you might want to reflect on where your similarities and differences are – both in *what* you've written, and *where* you've located it.
- If you're doing it on your own, you could repeat the exercise a few days, or weeks, later – or even longer – and see what's changed between the two versions. What do those changes say about you, and the 'places' where you were at when you did the exercise each time?

As Anthony Reddie himself reflects on the exercise, one of the many things it can highlight is that 'we all have multiple selves' – there are many different aspects to who we are, and at different times, in different contexts, one or more of those aspects might be more central. There might also be some characteristics of our identity that we don't think of mentioning, and we might only notice their absence when we are in conversation with someone whose identity is significantly different to ours. For some of us, those 'invisible' identity characteristics might well include things like 'male', 'white', 'middle class', 'heterosexual', 'able-bodied', and 'adult' – 'invisible' precisely because they are markers of *privilege*. In the rest of this chapter, we will both describe some of our moments of 'waking up' to aspects of privilege in our own identities – and also to areas where we have found ourselves on the 'other side' of those lines.

Who Am I? – Al

I'm an only child, born in 1975, and grew up mostly between west London and Newbury, a market town in Berkshire. My dad was an officer in the Royal Air Force for his entire working life, and at times in my childhood we lived on an RAF base, a community divided down lines of rank: the officers lived in the big houses in one section, and socialized in one building ('the mess'); sergeants and 'airmen' lived in smaller houses in other sections of the base, and had other buildings where they would socialize together. 'Socializing', I would learn much later in life, doesn't just mean 'hanging out together'; it also means being formed by the people and structures around you, in particular ways of seeing, behaving in and interacting with the world. Being an RAF child had its socializing effect on me, but even as a child I remember feeling that this way of ordering the world was odd, if not actually a bit wrong.

Two years into secondary school, I moved from a west London, mixed-sex comprehensive school, to a Berkshire, boys-only grammar school. Despite passing the entrance exam with flying colours, I was put in bottom set for every subject. Coming from a 'comp', my teachers had low expectations of my academic abilities. I started off simply being a bit puzzled by this, but over my first year there developed a steely determination to prove them wrong. After coming third in the end-of-year physics exam, and being told I could move up one set (to the second lowest) for the following year, I remember trying to ask my physics teacher to explain, and being embarrassed by the tears running down my face. I realize, as I write this, that this moment was more formative for me than I have, over the years since, remembered. I have, for all the reasons I'm exploring here, rarely been on the receiving end of prejudice – but this was one of those moments. However fleeting, it gives me a tiny window into the experience that, for many of my fellow human beings, is a constant, unavoidable aspect of daily life.

After three years at Cambridge University studying maths and astrophysics, and with a growing sense of call to ordained ministry in the

Church of England, I found myself in a terraced house in a run-down part of Salford, Greater Manchester, committed to a year of sharing life with three other young Christian housemates, being part of the local Methodist church, and getting to know the neighbours who lived around us. The four of us had been prepared well: whatever our particular gifts or more-or-less privileged backgrounds, we knew that we had moved to our statistically 'deprived' neighbourhood in Salford not to 'save' it or 'transform' it but instead, with empty hands, to seek out friendship with our new neighbours, to learn from them, and to learn what it might mean to love each other – what theologian Sam Wells, in more recent years, has called '*being with*' in sharp contrast to '*doing for*'.[2]

If Salford was my first serious schooling in forming meaningful relationships across class divides, the following three years at theological college in Birmingham (with placements in inner-city Glasgow and multi-ethnic Handsworth) opened my eyes to questions particularly of race, gender and sexuality. I discovered liberation theology, black theology, feminist theology and queer theology, and the first glimpses of what has more recently been called 'intersectionality': the complex ways in which, for some people, multiple dimensions of inequality and oppression can overlay each other (so that a black, lesbian woman, for example, is triply excluded from structures dominated by straight, white men) – and conversely, that others of us (white, middle-class, heterosexual, able-bodied men like me, most particularly) are multiply privileged by the societal structures in which we are all caught up. Through my eye-opening reading in feminist theology especially, I began to realize how much the ways I see and experience the world is different, because of *my* gender, to the ways half the human race see and experience the world, because of *their* gender; how much the world has been set up to assume *male* experience as the 'norm'; and how much this is true also of other identity markers besides gender.

One of the pennies that has taken longer to drop for me is the question of *how* I might be able to think, speak and write, conscious and critical of the ways in which I'm privileged by societal structures. Reading feminist theology was eye-opening and world-changing for me – but could *I*, as a male, be a feminist theologian? I've spent some years believing I can, as a male committed to sharing in the work of dismantling patriarchal structures. But I have had to remember I can only share in that work *as a man*, and that requires a different kind of participation to that of a female feminist theologian. For a while after discovering the class-based liberation theologies of Latin America and from some urban corners of

2 Samuel Wells, *A Nazareth Manifesto: Being With God* (Chichester: Wiley Blackwell, 2015).

19

the UK, I would imagine that I was doing liberation theology, in solidarity with my economically marginalized neighbours. But now I'm more convinced that trying to do liberation theology on behalf of my neighbours is much less valid than supporting my neighbours to do liberation theology, and – even less glamorous – trying to do some kind of self-conscious, self-critical theology as someone entangled in the economic and social trappings of 'middle-classness', but wanting to receive, and be changed by, the gifts and challenges that my neighbours present to me.

That was the central question of my PhD research. I hadn't expected, in those early days of writing and rewriting research proposals, that by the other end of writing my thesis a vital strand of it would be acknowledging, and critically teasing out the implications of, my whiteness. But that was what happened, and that strand emerged through a combination of reading – discovering the still-infant discipline of critical white theology, alongside Robin DiAngelo's laying bare of 'white fragility' (see Chapter 3) – and encounter, with the lived realities and stories of people of colour in my church congregation in Hodge Hill. All of these will unfold as this book goes on, but their impact on the way I now see the world can't be understated.

The most recent revolution in my life and thinking has been entangled with parenthood. Becoming a parent in my mid-30s was another of those profound 'penny-drop' moments! Sharing life with two other human beings who, for at least the first few years of their lives, have been smaller, slower and less articulate than me, and utterly dependent on us adults in almost every way, has been an ongoing lesson in how inattentive I am, how little I know, how much they are able to teach me, and how rich the utterly unexpected, entirely unearned, and often mentally, emotionally and spiritually stretching gifts I receive from them both every day we spend together. And in the last year or so, it has been my 11-year-old son who has led me into an ecological conversion: taking me with him to a School Strike for Climate day, challenging our church community to take action on ecological issues, and reminding me – along with his eight-year-old sister – that their future is, right now, more precarious and fearful than that of perhaps any previous generation of human beings.

As I write this, I've been vicar of Hodge Hill for just over ten years. Much of the rest of this book is the fruit of the 'schooling' I've received, over this time, within this particular neighbourhood, and with this particular church community – and alongside wise and provocative travelling companions on the journey, like Ruth.

Who Am I? – Ruth

Born in 1987, I grew up in a small coastal town in east Kent with a declining fishing fleet and surrounded by closed collieries. Another major local employer left the area when I was a child, and opportunities for employment were limited, centring around the docks in the neighbouring town. It was, and still is, a very static community – out of the 60 children in my year at primary school, I was one of only three whose Mum had not gone to a local secondary school. As a child, I knew my neighbours and played out in the street.

I passed the 11-plus and went to the grammar school in a neighbouring town. This was my first experience of noticing an 'us and them' divide, and finding myself – by virtue of being 'a brainy swot' – placed squarely in the 'them' category by my friends and neighbours. It was also my first experience of having unearned privilege. There were opportunities I got which my peers did not, simply because my mind happened to work in a particular way. Some of those opportunities would change the course of my life.

There were clear expectations placed on us as 'grammar school girls', summed up in our headmistress's phrase: 'girls, you *can* have it all'. But I realized early on that this did not square with my experience. The women I knew, including the former grammar school girls, did not seem to have it all (whatever that might mean!). What they seemed to have was an unending struggle to balance everybody's competing needs, with their own needs always coming bottom of the heap. This was not a struggle which seemed to be shared in quite the same way by the men in our community. It marked the beginning of a process of feminist awakening, which I experienced from a young age as an acute sense of unfairness, but for which I would only find language when I got to university.

The other dominant narrative of my later teenage years was the idea of 'getting out'. I desperately wanted to 'get out' and perceived – rightly – that I could do so through education. It was only years later that I would question this highly individualized narrative. Why should I have to distance myself – physically and metaphorically – from the community I grew up in, in order to 'succeed'? If I was 'getting out', did that mean others were 'trapped', 'left behind'? And how could any of us resist that narrative?

One of the things that helped me explore those and other questions was recognizing that I was working class. I only realized this when I got to Oxford University (the ultimate in 'getting out'). Growing up, I had subconsciously divided the world into 'normal people' (who lived in flats, maisonettes or terraced houses and played out) and 'posh people' (who lived in detached houses and did things like ballet lessons). Arriving at Oxford was an indescribably huge culture shock. I rapidly understood first that there were people much, much posher than I had ever previously imagined (and suddenly I was surrounded by them!), and that for them the world was divided not into 'normal people and posh people' but 'normal people and poor people'. This brought home to me the realization of how much of a fundamental difference our location makes to our worldview.

Flung into a very alien world, which I had no idea existed until I was immersed in it, I struggled to adapt, and retain a sense of who I was. I emerged from my time at Oxford feeling deeply uncomfortable in both the working-class world from which I had come, and the middle-class world into which my education had pushed me. I have often likened it to becoming bilingual – I speak fluent 'middle class', and through the choices I have made about education and work that is often the world I inhabit – but it is not, and never will be my mother tongue. Yet, because of the ways in which I have been formed by my life experience, there are ways in which I can never again 'pass' as authentically working class.

By my mid-twenties I had thought a lot about issues of class and gender, and also sexuality. As a lesbian woman from a working-class background, these were the issues that affected me. They were also the areas in which I felt, more or less keenly, my lack of privilege in comparison to my straight, male, middle-class counterparts.

It was only when I came to work as a youth and children's minister in a diverse town, whose schools contained cohorts which were much less than 50 per cent white British, that I began to think seriously about race. I had been aware of racism growing up – in our town at that time it was usually directed against asylum seekers from the Balkans – but I had not given much thought to my own white privilege. Gradually, through the lives of my black Caribbean, Pakistani and Eastern European neighbours, I came to realize that I was walking through life with an enormous amount of privilege of which I had previously been unaware. I continue to be confronted by the ways in which my whiteness has protected and benefited me, and challenged by the work I still need to do in order to move into greater solidarity with my neighbours and friends who are people of colour.

As my awareness of the intersecting aspects of privilege and oppression in my own life grew, so did my commitment both spiritually and politically to addressing issues of race, class and gender within the Church and beyond. This was sometimes met with support, and sometimes with resistance. It would take me some time to understand how often the resistance I encountered was because people were having their worldview challenged, sometimes for the first time.

A 'penny drop' moment for me came when I read Marjorie Procter-Smith's book *Praying With Our Eyes Open: Engendering Feminist Liturgical Prayer*.[3] In it she describes the experience of women (and other oppressed groups) having to 'pray between the lines' because so often the Church's liturgy does not account for the reality of our lives, or sometimes even for the fact that we exist at all. My first reaction was one of recognition: yes, this is how it is for me. But my second, and more profound, reaction was one of discovery: hang on, do you mean to say there are some people who *don't* need to read between the lines? For whom the liturgy (and church, and society) just *works*? I realized that who does and does not need to read between the lines is a good indicator of privilege. In terms of race, I never need to read between the lines. That is my white privilege at work. In terms of gender, class, or sexuality, I do. And that had so affected my worldview, that it hadn't really occurred to me that it could be otherwise.

Further reading

• Anthony Reddie, *Is God Colour-blind? Insights from Black Theology for Christian Ministry* (London: SPCK, 2009)
• Alison Webster, *You are Mine: Reflections on Who We Are* (London: SPCK, 2009)
• Samuel Wells, *A Nazareth Manifesto: Being With God* (Chichester: Wiley Blackwell, 2015)

Questions for reflection/discussion

• How might your perception of yourself/your 'multiple selves' affect your perception of the world you live in?
• How might your perception of yourself affect your reaction to 'current affairs' such as the events described in the Introduction?

---

3 Marjorie Procter-Smith, *Praying With Our Eyes Open: Engendering Feminist Liturgical Prayer* (Nashville, TN: Abingdon Press, 1995).

2

Finding Our Place in Brexit Britain

The writing of a book happens at a particular *time*, but also in a particular *place*. The place that gave birth to this book is the Firs and Bromford estate, in the district of Hodge Hill, on the eastern edge of the city of Birmingham, in England – part of what is currently known as the United Kingdom of Great Britain and Northern Ireland. 'Currently', because the times we are living in are, as the Chinese curse would have it, 'interesting'. Who we are, and *where* we are, in 'interesting times', turn out to be profoundly interrelated.

This estate we're in

The Firs and Bromford was built in the 1950s and 60s, rehousing people from the back-to-backs of inner-city Birmingham in a wonderful new world of open spaces, three-floor maisonettes, and the new high-rise tower blocks they were calling 'streets in the sky'. In one corner of the estate, close to where the M6 motorway rumbles past on its concrete pillars, three of those tower blocks immediately started sinking into the mud. They had been built, incomprehensibly, on a flood-plain, where the River Tame once meandered before it was diverted into a rigid channel underneath the motorway. Within ten years these three sinking blocks were demolished, and the land around them – car parks, streets, green spaces – was abandoned.

Fifty years on – and still counting – what locals have often called 'the wasteland' has come to symbolize one of the true stories that can be told about our neighbourhood: a place abandoned, overlooked, forgotten about by those in the wider world and those in power; a place with a history of being 'done to'; a place where organizations with funding have repeatedly turned up, promised the earth, and then left again, a couple of years later, when their funding ran out; a place which over time has been stripped of most of the (relatively few) community assets it ever had (community centres, council offices, pubs and residents' clubs), as well as most of the factories in the surrounding area that once employed many local people; a place where people have often been 'dumped' from other parts of the city, and from which people have often wanted to move away; the kind of place which politicians and the media have so often labelled a 'broken ghetto' or a 'sink estate', its residents 'work-shy' or 'scroungers'.

The Church Urban Fund – the organization set up by the Church of England in the 1980s to tackle poverty across England – helpfully describes what it calls 'the web of poverty' in terms of a poverty of *resource*, a poverty of *relationship*, and a poverty of *identity* (see Figure 2). Poverty is much more than just 'not having enough money'. And what is true for individuals is also true for *communities*: a neighbourhood feels the effects of poverty not only in the lack of resources, community assets and financial investment in it; but also in a lack of trusting, life-giving relationships between neighbours, and in a profoundly negative sense of collective identity, shaped both by local history and by the way people from other places talk about 'neighbourhoods like ours' – we're 'not good enough', 'deficient', a 'problem'. And if you hear people say it often enough, you begin to believe it about yourselves.

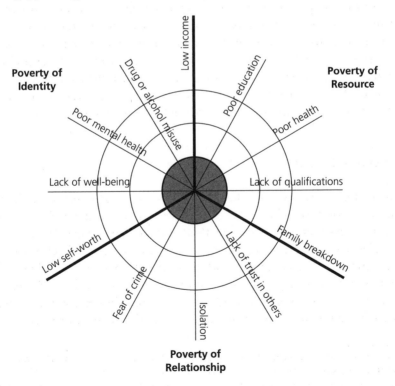

Figure 2: The Web of Poverty (Church Urban Fund, used by permission)

'Left behind' or 'left out'?

When political commentators talk about why the EU referendum result swung narrowly to 'Leave' rather than 'Remain', they often point at neighbourhoods like ours. The 'traditional working class' in 'post-industrial' communities, the 'disenfranchised', the 'left behind': all of these descriptive terms were used for the people that politicians were referring to when they announced, repeatedly, that 'the people have spoken'. The polar opposite of the so-called 'cosmopolitan elite', these were – we were told – the 'ordinary' people who wanted, in the slogan of the Conservative Party's 2019 general election campaign, to 'get Brexit done'.

And from conversations that Al has had with neighbours in the Firs and Bromford, the commentators and politicians are certainly on to something. In the days after the 2016 referendum, many of my neighbours were feeling happy, optimistic about the future, proud to be British and, most crucially, delighted that, for once, their voices had been heard. Things were going to change – and their votes had made a difference.

Those local conversations resonate with much of the post-referendum analysis of people's reasons for voting Leave and we will explore some of those reasons most commonly cited by Leave-voters themselves, and those seeking to listen attentively to their voices – which all cluster around a sense of being left behind or left out by economic, cultural and political changes. In the next section, we will seek to dig a little bit deeper, into some of the possible drivers of the Leave vote that are less often articulated in public – to do with race, national identity and empire.[1]

Economic reasons

The first set of reasons are the most obvious in neighbourhoods like the Firs and Bromford, where Al lives. We live in a 'post-industrial' economy. The factories that used to employ thousands of people have either closed, or relocated to other parts of the world (where labour is cheaper), or dramatically downsized their workforce with the help of the technologies of automation. In many areas like ours, there is less work available; and what there is, is often low-paid, insecure ('zero-hours contracts' mean you have to take whatever hours you're offered, from week to week), and

---

1 What we won't consider here, because it is something of a tangent to the direction of this book, is the evidence that the Leave vote was at least partly engineered by strategic campaigns of disinformation and manipulation, especially via social media. See for example Martin Moore, *Democracy Hacked: How Technology is Destabilising Global Politics* (London: Oneworld, 2018).

demeaning. People who used to proudly make things now find themselves 'servicing a system' – and 'the system' treats its workers less like human beings, and more like utterly expendable, replaceable resources.

Without paid work, and more often now *alongside* poorly paid work, the 'benefits' system once intended to be the 'safety net' is now full of holes. Successive governments have repeatedly 'frozen' benefits levels, tightened the criteria for qualifying, and intensified the punitive sanctions for non-compliance. Add to that an increasingly inadequate supply of affordable social housing, few regulations and restraints on private land-lords, and the 'choice' for those on low incomes is often between scraping by in inadequate housing, or teetering on the brink of homelessness. This at the same time that the income gap between the poorest and the richest in the UK is not only one of the widest among the world's so-called 'developed' countries, but has been steadily increasing since the mid-1980s. All of these factors together meant that, for many people who voted Leave, despite warnings that Brexit would seriously damage the UK economy, they genuinely felt they had nothing to lose.

Political reasons

A second cluster of reasons, not remotely disconnected to the economic reasons outlined already, focus on a dissatisfaction with, and distrust of, politics and politicians. We live, some theorists suggest, in a post-democratic society.[2] Despite the rhetoric of 'the will of the people', politics has become largely a game of persuasion, of 'media presentation', even simply another form of entertainment: a consumer choice, like voting for your favourite act on *Britain's Got Talent*. Another aspect of 'post-democracy' is that politics has become reduced to economics: a competition for who can 'run the economy' best, who is 'best for business'.

Related to these two aspects is what has been called a 'crisis of representation': the workings of government have become increasingly opaque and distanced (the charge of 'unelected bureaucrats' that has gained emotional traction, especially in relation to the EU), and often – covertly or overtly – in the interests of wealthy, powerful individuals and corporations. Post-democratic theorists point to a 'social atomism' that has not just turned 'citizens' into 'consumers', but has also seen the demise of what used to be 'intermediate' institutions between people and government – community groups, unions, churches and the like – and of spaces for dialogue and disagreement between people from different

---

2 See Colin Crouch, *Post-Democracy* (Cambridge: Polity, 2003) and *Post-Democracy after the Crises* (Cambridge: Polity, 2020).

backgrounds and opinions. Lastly, as political theologian Anna Rowlands has pointed out, 'austerity' is understood not just as an economic regime, but as a profoundly political worldview. Where resources are presented as being in short supply, their allocation becomes a 'zero-sum' game: *either* EU membership *or* adequate public services; *either* middle-class financial security *or* a welfare safety net for the most vulnerable. When money is – apparently – tight, the possibility of '*both/and*', of mutual benefit, becomes unimaginable.[3]

'A howl of anger'

> For a brief moment in 2016 the apathy of the British working-class electorate subsided and gave way to a howl of anger ... revealing the levels of pain and hurt of those who had been left out of the successes and rewards that capitalism had created for a cosmopolitan middle class in parts of the United Kingdom.[4]

These words were written by Lisa McKenzie, a sociologist with working-class roots, reflecting on a sustained piece of listening to working-class Leave voters in east London and the ex-mining towns of Nottinghamshire. The term 'left behind', she says, suggests a group of people in society dismissed as 'old fashioned' and 'nostalgic', digging in their heels as the world moves forward around them. It's a suggestion we'll return to in a moment, but for now, we need to stay for just a bit longer with the voices McKenzie seeks to hear and amplify.

We've just explored a whole combination of factors that have resulted in significant numbers of people in the UK being economically marginalized and politically disenfranchised. On one level, this has led to swathes of the population feeling discarded, unvalued, invisible and powerless to change anything. On another level, that has at times been a *visible* invisibility, with working-class communities being demonized as anti-social 'chavs', lazy 'scroungers' and 'stupid' racists. Nowhere has that 'visible invisibility' been felt more intensely than on the issue of immigration – placed front and centre of the EU referendum debate by the Leave

---

3 Anna Rowlands, 'An uprooted nation: From Brexit to a Christian vision of the common good', 9 December 2019, *ABC Religion and Ethics*, www.abc.net.au/religion/uprroted-nation-brexit-and-a-christian-vision-of-common-good/11776698, accessed 8 May 2020.

4 Lisa McKenzie, '"It's not ideal": reconsidering "anger" and "apathy" in the Brexit vote among an invisible working class', *LSE Research Online*, July 2017, https://core.ac.uk/download/pdf/84146282.pdf, accessed 8 May 2020.

campaign. But who was that campaign really about, and what deeper concerns were lurking under the surface issue of immigration? It is to those questions that we now turn.

Immigration, race and national identity crisis?

On 16 June 2016, just a week before the EU referendum polling day, the Labour MP for Batley and Spen in West Yorkshire was murdered, in a busy street, by 53-year-old Thomas Mair, who was heard to shout 'Britain first'. Just a few days before, UKIP leader Nigel Farage had released an anti-immigration poster with the slogan 'Breaking Point', depicting a long queue of people – visibly darker-skinned people – stretching back into the distance, and calling for Britain to 'take back control of its borders'. Commentators with an eye to twentieth-century history noted the stark similarity between UKIP's poster and a Nazi propaganda film from the 1930s – and wondered how much Jo Cox's murderer had been emboldened by the strident anti-immigration messages of the Leave campaign.

The 'zero-sum game' that Anna Rowlands identified as central to the 'austerity worldview', here gets deployed as a powerful argument against immigration: there are not enough resources to go around, the argument goes, for existing British citizens *and* new arrivals both to have enough. Not enough housing, not enough jobs, not enough money for benefits, not enough health care provision, and so on. For people on the sharp end of those limits – struggling to find employment, stuck in inadequate housing, trying to make ends meet with paltry benefits, waiting for ages for medical treatment – the 'not enough' message is a lived reality, and the 'zero-sum game' presented to them by the politicians strikes a chord.

Cathy Milligan is a 53-year-old community activist from Castlemilk, a Glasgow housing estate. 'The root of racism is austerity', she says. 'People on benefits turn against others on benefits. If you're backed into a corner it brings out the worst in you. As human beings, we know how to make things better for each other but the economics of austerity stops all that. We're under the cosh and we're fighting for our lives.'[5] Cathy highlights the way austerity economics, and an austerity worldview, *exacerbate* racism and bring it to the surface. But the *roots* of racism go a whole lot deeper – as we'll explore further in the rest of this chapter.

---

5 Darren McGarvey, *Poverty Safari: Understanding the Anger of Britain's Underclass* (London: Picador, 2019), p. 159.

Cultural change

While the austerity worldview has profoundly shaped political arguments about resources and services, and undergirded an *economic* dimension to anti-immigration politics, a parallel scarcity-imagination lies underneath the so-called 'hostile environment's' *cultural* aspects. Slogans like 'Britain is full' alongside references to the country as a 'small island', and vociferous attacks on 'multiculturalism', bring to the surface the 'not enough' assumption in relation to *space* or *territory*, and also to *cultural identity*. The zero-sum game decrees that the national cultural geography, and even more local geographies within the country (crudely pitting 'working-class towns' against the 'cosmopolitan elite', for example) can be *either* 'British' *or* 'multicultural', but not both. The latter, in this way of thinking, is in direct competition with the former, and vice versa.

Anna Rowlands identifies various elements of this sense of cultural defensiveness, all clustering around feelings of attachment, loss and being 'uprooted' – and affecting older generations with a particular sharpness. The economics of global capitalism coupled with the ever-accelerating evolution of communications technology have created a world of hyper-individualism and 'place-lessness'. Where you live is no longer of great significance. If you can't find work here, then either move, or go virtual: remote working – in 'tech' jobs especially – means a company can have employees scattered across the world, just as social media has enabled us to develop virtual friendships with no reference to geographical closeness.

But our globalized, virtual world has also seen the crumbling of traditional institutions of belonging. As we've already considered as an aspect of political change, those 'intermediate associations' – workplaces and unions; neighbourhoods and community organizations; political parties, uniformed organizations, locally-rooted faith groups and clubs based around shared interests and shared geography – all of these have seen dramatic declines in membership over the last few decades. And the loss of these more local sources of collective identity and belonging has meant, for many people, that *national* identity has to do more of that work for them.

Brexit, class and whiteness

Much post-Brexit analysis, we've noted, has focused on the so-called 'left behind' of 'traditional working-class' communities like the Firs and Bromford estate where Al lives. And 'traditional working class' has usually been a euphemism for '*white* working class'. Sometimes, politicians and media commentators have been more explicit about it: the Brexit vote was a clash of worldviews between the 'white working class' and the 'cosmopolitan elite', and these two groups' polar opposite views on 'immigrants'. But this crude, polarized triangle hides some realities that are vital to acknowledge.

First, 'the working class' is not just 'white'. As Reni Eddo-Lodge has pointed out, a more subtle understanding of contemporary class divisions breaks down 'the working class' into 'traditional working class' (mostly older, 91 per cent white), 'emergent service workers' (often children of 'traditional working-class' parents, including 21 per cent people of colour), and the 'precariat' (the poorest level of British society, making up 15 per cent of the population, and including 13 per cent people of colour).[6] More people of colour fall into the 'emergent service workers' grouping than into any other class category. To talk about the 'working class' without paying attention to the experiences and opinions of people of colour, then, is to ignore a whole swathe of the British population, who are often *doubly* marginalized by both class and race. It is also, as politicians have often done, to play an intentional or unintentional game of 'divide and rule', pitting the interests of white working-class people and working-class people of colour against each other, when there is potential solidarity between them in their common experiences of work, income, housing and geographical marginalization.

Second, to pin responsibility on 'white working-class' voters for the vote to leave the EU is to ignore the facts emerging from more careful analysis of the referendum result. Just 24 per cent of Leave voters were classified as 'working class' or 'non-working', while around 60 per cent of Leave votes came from voters classed as among the elite and middle classes.[7] As sociologist Danny Dorling puts it, 'it was not people who were poorer who voted Leave in high numbers, but people who found the propaganda that immigrants created problems believable. They tended to live in areas of low immigration. In poorer areas of high immigration, everyone was likely to vote Remain.'[8]

---

6 Reni Eddo-Lodge, *Why I'm No Longer Talking to White People about Race* (London: Bloomsbury, 2017), p. 191.

Figures are from the Great British Class Survey 2011, see for example www.bbc.co.uk/news/magazine-34766169, accessed 8 May 2020. For comparison, 2011 census statistics recorded 87.1% of the population identifying as 'white' or 'white British', with 12.9% identifying with other ethnic categories.

7 In Akala, *Natives: Race and Class in the Ruins of Empire* (London: Two Roads, 2018), p. 297.

8 Danny Dorling and Sally Tomlinson, *Rule Britannia: Brexit and the End of Empire* (London: Biteback, 2019), p. 306.

Third, the Leave vote was overwhelmingly white. While 53 per cent of white voters voted Leave, 67 per cent of those describing themselves as Asian voted to remain, as did 73 per cent of black voters.[9] Concerns about immigration, and worries about multiculturalism and its threat to national identity, are largely (while not exclusively) concerns not just among the 'white working class', but for many *white* Britons across the class spectrum, and those who identify as both white and *English* more specifically.[10] Whatever 'being English' used to mean, the concern being expressed, however articulately or otherwise, is that it is being lost in our increasingly multicultural society.

Post-imperial melancholia

There is a huge irony in where we've got to, however. Talk to many people who lament a loss of Britishness or Englishness, and often what comes up in conversation before too long are the things that, we're told, made Britain 'great': 'two world wars and one world cup' (a chant often heard at England's football matches against Germany) and, going back further, 'Rule Britannia! Britannia rule the waves!' Victory, conquest, empire. The irony, to spell it out, is that contemporary British multiculturalism is a direct result of the history of British imperialism. As Ambalavaner Sivanandan, Sri Lankan-born director of the Institute of Race Relations from 1973 to 2013 put it succinctly, speaking for all those British citizens who trace their roots to other parts of the empire: 'we are here, because you were there'.[11]

Post-colonial theorist Paul Gilroy argues that white Britons' current 'xenophobic responses to the strangers who have intruded' upon 'their' country are rooted in what he calls a 'post-imperial melancholia' which has been at the heart of British political and cultural life since at least the 1950s. Melancholia, as Sigmund Freud defined it, is a grieving for what is lost, but unlike *mourning*, it happens largely in the unconscious mind – those grieving are unable to fully comprehend or identify what they are grieving for. For Gilroy, Britain's collective melancholia has a two-fold object: first, that the British empire, and the pride and prestige that came

---

9 https://lordashcroftpolls.com/2019/02/how-the-uk-voted-on-brexit-and-why-a-re fresher/, accessed 8 May 2020.

10 Of those who see themselves as 'English not British', 79% voted Leave, 21% voted Remain; 60% of those who see themselves as 'British not English' voted Remain, 40% Leave.

11 Sivanandan died in 2018. See www.theguardian.com/world/2018/feb/07/ambala vaner-sivanandan for his obituary.

with it, has actually *ended*; second, that our imperial history is far from proud – there is, in Gilroy's words, a 'hidden, shameful store of imperial horrors' that have rarely been acknowledged, let alone addressed in meaningful, reparative ways.[12]

This is not a book about empire and colonialism. It is, primarily, a book about the mission of the Church in twenty-first-century Britain. But Gilroy's point – highlighting Britain's post-imperial melancholia – is a vital one for the broad sweep of our argument here, and it contains within it at least five entangled threads that you can trace through this book.

First, empire was about race. The British empire was founded and sustained on the premise that the British – again, more specifically *English* – way of life was objectively better, more 'civilized' than the cultures of the places Britain colonized. And more than that, the oppression of colonized peoples, and their dehumanization and enslavement, was itself dependent on the invention of 'race' as an idea to justify and perpetuate the supremacy of white bodies over black and brown bodies.

Second, empire was about class. It was the British upper classes that got rich from the natural resources, slave labour and trade that empire unearthed, captured and set in motion. As some back in Britain observed in the 1800s, those profiting from India, and ruthlessly suppressing uprisings in Jamaica, were the same people who displayed 'hard indifference' and 'haughty neglect' towards 'the working men of England'.[13]

Third, empire also had a strongly gendered dimension to it – empire was, as one recent writer puts it 'an essentially masculine project'.[14] It was not just men, among the affluent elite, who were the primary beneficiaries of empire's 'business', but the willing recruits to the empire's cause were also mostly men, drawn in by typically masculine images of the bold, resourceful, pioneering explorer or, in more dangerous times, the strong, stoical and, if necessary, ruthless soldier. And if the primary *agents* of empire were the epitome of masculinity, then those on the receiving end were invariably cast as feminine: 'old world peoples upon coming to the

---

12 Paul Gilroy, *After Empire: Melancholia or Convivial Culture?* (London: Routledge, 2004), p. 98. Anthony Reddie's *Theologising Brexit: A Liberationist and Postcolonial Critique* (Abingdon: Routledge, 2019) has also been profoundly helpful in informing both this chapter and much of this book.

13 The words are from philosopher Richard Congreve in 1857 and historian Edward Beesly in 1865. See the article by Priyamvada Gopal, 'The British empire's hidden history is one of resistance, not pride', *Guardian*, 28 July 2017, www.theguardian.com/commentisfree/2017/jul/28/british-empire-hidden-history-solidarity-truth-resistance, accessed 8 May 2020.

14 Clare Midgley, quoted in John Tosh, *Manliness and Masculinities in Nineteenth-Century Britain: Essays on Gender, Family and Empire* (London: Routledge, 2004), p. 193.

new worlds imagined them and looked on them as virgin and ready to be taken'.[15]

Fourth, then, empire was ecological violence, plundering planet Earth in all places other than 'home', extracting from its common wealth *resources* to drive so-called 'human progress' (the ever-expanding empire itself), and *commodities* to enrich the powerful individuals and corporations most invested in the empire project. As Anthony Reddie reminds us, drawing on the work of climatologist Leon Sealey-Huggins, 'the slave trade was underpinned by rampant greed and profit, the displacing and exploiting of bodies. Once we'd done that, we moved on the environment, grabbing fossil fuels to drive growth. The impact of climate change on black and brown-skinned people comes on the back of 500 years of exploitation of their bodies … It's a compound disaster, adding one injustice to another.'[16]

And last, empire was entangled with Christian mission. Missionaries travelled on the same ships as the colonizers and slave traders, theologians legitimized colonialism as bringing not just civilization but *salvation* to the 'heathen', and British churches – most especially the Church of England – benefited from both the wealth and the slave labour of empire *and* the 'compensation' paid out by the government to slave-owners when emancipation finally arrived.

All of these five dimensions we have phrased in the past tense. But if empire is officially 'over', its effects are still clear to see, and continue to unfold in ways that are destructive for our relationships across race, class and gender, for our relationship with the earth, and for our understanding and practice of Christian mission. Again quoting Anthony Reddie, the 'collective dis-ease' of Brexit is but the latest outbreak of 'shingles' in Britain's body politic, exposing the fact that the toxic 'chickenpox' virus of Empire has been persistently present in the body all the time – it's just been less visible to those of us who have not known what we were looking for.[17]

---

15 Historian Carolyn Merchant, quoted in Willie James Jennings, 'Reframing the World: Toward an Actual Christian Doctrine of Creation', *International Journal of Systematic Theology* 21:4, October 2019, p. 395.

16 Anthony Reddie, 'This monstrous shadow – race, climate and justice', in Jeremy Williams (ed.), *Time to Act: A resource book by the Christians in Extinction Rebellion* (London: SPCK, 2020), p. 75.

17 Reddie, *Theologising Brexit*, pp. 29–30.

Beyond Brexit

This chapter started in an abandoned corner of an east Birmingham outer estate, and ended with an examination of our selective memory about the history of the British empire. If the 'drivers' behind the Brexit vote were to do with our post-industrial economy, our post-democratic society, our uprooted and fragmenting sense of culture, and a post-imperial melancholia, then we urgently need to find ways of acknowledging those root causes and addressing them.

In the past, we might have often looked to the centres of power, to our political leaders, to set our collective direction, for the rest of us to follow. But in a post-democratic society like ours, that is unlikely to be fruitful – not in terms of the patience, kindness and goodness that we Christians count as among the 'fruit of the Spirit', anyway. So we must look elsewhere: we must look inwards, seeking honestly to acknowledge the needs, anxieties and desires often hidden deep within ourselves; we must look outwards, to examine critically the fabric and structures of our society, and our churches; and we must look to the edges, to those whom those structures tend so often to exclude, silence and render invisible.

Further reading

- Akala, *Natives: Race and Class in the Ruins of Empire* (London: Two Roads, 2018)
- Colin Crouch, *Post-Democracy* (Cambridge: Polity, 2003) and *Post-Democracy after the Crises* (Cambridge: Polity, 2020)
- Danny Dorling and Sally Tomlinson, *Rule Britannia: Brexit and the End of Empire* (London: Biteback, 2019)
- Reni Eddo-Lodge, *Why I'm No Longer Talking to White People about Race* (London: Bloomsbury, 2017)
- Paul Gilroy, *After Empire: Melancholia or Convivial Culture?* (London: Routledge, 2004)
- Séverine Kodjo-Grandvaux, 'Colonialism, the Hidden Cause of our Environmental Crisis', *Le Monde, English Edition Worldcrunch*, 14 February 2020, www.worldcrunch.com/culture-society/colonialism-the-hidden-cause-of-our-environmental-crisis
- Darren McGarvey, *Poverty Safari: Understanding the Anger of Britain's Underclass* (London: Picador, 2019)
- Martin Moore, *Democracy Hacked: How Technology is Destabilising Global Politics* (London: Oneworld, 2018)

- Anthony Reddie, *Theologising Brexit: A Liberationist and Postcolonial Critique* (Abingdon: Routledge, 2019)
- Robbie Shilliam, *Race and the Undeserving Poor: From Abolition to Brexit* (Newcastle upon Tyne: Agenda Publishing, 2018)
- Hannah Strømmen and Ulrich Schmiedel, *The Claim to Christianity: Responding to the Far Right* (London: SCM Press, 2020)

Questions for reflection/discussion

- How does the particular time and place in which you are reading this affect your understanding and perception of current political realities, including Brexit?
- What impact has 'empire' had on you? Your neighbours? Your community?
- How do the factors identified in this chapter play out in your neighbourhood?

3

What are We Not Seeing?

The late Uruguayan author Eduardo Galeano once expressed his deepest concern that 'we are all suffering from amnesia ... [that makes us] blind to small things and small people'. Who, I asked him, was responsible for this forgetfulness. 'It's not a person,' he explained. 'It's a system of power that is always deciding in the name of humanity who deserves to be remembered, and who deserves to be forgotten.'[1]

In the previous chapter, we traced the roots of Brexit back to two clusters of issues: the first cluster were to do with economic and political exclusions that render many people invisible, or voiceless; the second cluster were to do with an inability to face the end of empire, and to grapple with its lasting effects. In this chapter, we'll explore different dimensions of a widespread *obliviousness*, that prevents us – or *some* of us, in fact – from seeing and acknowledging aspects of reality, including multitudes of our human kin and other non-human creatures.

To begin this part of our exploration though, we want to invite you to do a little exercise in self-awareness.[2] For some of you, the results will come as no surprise. For others, it may be the most eye-opening thing you've ever done. So please, grab a pen or pencil, and either scribble on these pages, or find something else to write on, as you respond as honestly as you can to the questions that follow. To end up with a 'score', start at zero, and add or take away points depending on your answers.

---

1 Gary Younge, writing in *The Guardian*, 22 May 2017. See Gary Younge, 'Eduardo Galeano: "My great fear is that we are all suffering from amnesia"', *Guardian*, 23 July 2013, www.theguardian.com/books/2013/jul/23/eduardo-galeano-children-days-interview, accessed 8 May 2020.

2 Adapted from 'Breaking the mirror image – privilege quiz', Pensions and Lifetime Savings Association, www.plsa.co.uk/portals/0/Documents/0621a-Privilege-quiz.pdf. The privilege quiz content is an adaptation of the content included in: P. McIntosh, 'White privilege and male privilege: A personal account of coming to see correspondences through work in women's studies', Working paper No. 189 (Wellesley, MA: Wellesley Centres for Women, 1988).

1 If you are reasonably sure you would be hired for a job based on your ability and qualifications, add one point.

2 If you ever went on a family holiday, add one point.

3 If you were born in the country you live in, add one point.

4 If you have ever felt like there was NOT adequate or accurate representation of your racial group, gender group, sexual orientation group, socio-economic group and/or dis/ability group, in the media, take away one point.

5 If your parents or guardians were educated to degree level, add one point.

6 If you feel comfortable walking home alone at night, add one point.

7 If you can legally marry the person you love, regardless of where you live, add one point.

8 If you or your parents have ever gone through a divorce, take away one point.

9 If you have ever been the only person of your ethnicity/gender/socio-economic status/sexual orientation in a classroom or workplace setting, take away one point.

10 If you felt you had adequate access to healthy food growing up, add one point.

11 If you feel comfortable being emotionally expressive/open, add one point.

12 If you can go anywhere in the country, and easily find the kinds of hair products you need, or cosmetics that match your skin colour, add one point.

13 If you can see a doctor whenever you feel the need, add one point.

14 If you have ever been misdiagnosed as having a physical or mental illness / dis/ability, take away one point.

15 If you feel confident that your parents would be able to financially help/support you if you were going through a financial hardship, add one point.

16 If you would never think twice about calling the police when trouble occurs, add one point.

17 If you get time off for your religious holidays, add one point.

18 If you have ever been bullied or made fun of based on something you can't change, take away one point.

19 If there were more than 50 books in your house growing up, add one point.

20 If you were ever offered a job/work because of your association with a friend or family member, add one point.

21 If you are able to move through the world without fear of assault, add one point.

22 If your parents worked nights and weekends to support your family, take away one point.

23 If you can show affection for your romantic partner in public without fear of ridicule or violence, add one point.

24 If the primary language spoken in your household growing up was not English, take away one point.

25 If you came from a supportive family environment, add one point.

26 If you have ever tried to change your speech or mannerisms to gain credibility, take away one point.

27 If you were embarrassed about your clothes or house while growing up, take away one point.

28 If you can make mistakes and not have people attribute your flaws to your ethnic/gender/socioeconomic group, add one point.

29 If you took out loans for your education, take away one point.

30 If you had a job during your school and college years, take away one point.

31 If you have ever travelled outside the UK, add one point.

32 If you studied the culture or history of your ancestors in primary school, add one point.

33 If you can buy new clothes or go out to dinner when you want to, add one point.

34 If one of your parents was ever laid off or unemployed not by choice, take away one point.

35 If you have ever felt uncomfortable about a joke or statement about your ethnicity, class, gender, appearance, or sexual orientation but felt you couldn't confront it, take away one point.

Still on your own, spend some time noticing what (if anything) surprised you in the questions, and in your answers to them.

If you are reading this with others, spend some time talking together about the experience of doing this exercise, what you noticed in your reflections, and how you're feeling now.

There's a good chance that the higher your 'score', (that is, the more privileged you are; +23 is the highest possible score), the more surprised you may be right now. Your feelings may well go beyond surprise – into the territory of shock, even guilt. It's also likely that if your score was lower (-13 is the lowest possible score), little of this will be surprising or shocking.

Privilege is powerful precisely because it tends to be invisible to those who have it. As Peggy McIntosh, one of those who first coined the term, puts it, privilege is 'an invisible package of unearned assets that I can count on cashing in each day, but about which I was "meant" to remain oblivious'.[3] Theologian Mary McClintock Fulkerson talks about such obliviousness as a *'power-related willingness not-to-see'*.[4] When the way my society is structured favours me because of aspects of my identity – my 'race' or 'ethnicity', class, gender, age, dis/ability and sexual orientation – there are some parts of reality that those structures have trained me not to see, not to hear, not to be consciously aware of. And often that training, as we shall see, creates a 'bubble' around me, with quite resilient defences against other parts of reality breaking through.[5]

In the sections that follow, we'll tease out some of these different dimensions of privilege. In reality, they're entangled: the dynamics that operate in one dimension (for example, the inability of middle-class people to hear challenging working-class voices) can often be recognized in other dimensions (for example the defensiveness of 'white fragility'), and when multiple dimensions are overlaid together, the issues described are multiplied, compounded – the challenge that is called 'intersectionality'. But it helps to consider each dimension separately, because each does also have its own distinctive dynamics, and for each of us, in our complex identities, some will be more significant, or more visible, than others.

Windrush, 'white fragility' and race

In February 2014, the black British journalist Reni Eddo-Lodge published a blog post entitled 'Why I'm No Longer Talking to White People about Race'. It began:

3 Peggy McIntosh, 'White Privilege: Unpacking the Invisible Knapsack' (1990), www.racialequitytools.org/resourcefiles/mcintosh.pdf, accessed 5 March 2020.

4 Mary McClintock Fulkerson, *Places of Redemption: Theology for a Worldly Church* (Oxford: Oxford University Press, 2007), p. 17.

5 For a participative exercise highlighting the way this 'obliviousness' works in practice, particularly in relation to racism, see Anthony Reddie's 'What can you see?' in *Black Theology: SCM Core Text* (London SCM Press 2012, pp. 13ff.).

I'm no longer engaging with white people on the topic of race. Not all white people, just the vast majority who refuse to accept the legitimacy of structural racism and its symptoms. I can no longer engage with the gulf of an emotional disconnect that white people display when a person of colour articulates their experience. You can see their eyes shut down and harden. It's like treacle is poured into their ears, blocking up their ear canals. It's like they can no longer hear us.

This emotional disconnect is the conclusion of living a life oblivious to the fact that their skin colour is the norm and all others deviate from it. At best, white people have been taught not to mention that people of colour are 'different' in case it offends us. They truly believe that the experiences of their life as a result of their skin colour can and should be universal. I just can't engage with the bewilderment and the defensiveness as they try to grapple with the fact that not everyone experiences the world in the way that they do. They've never had to think about what it means, in power terms, to be white, so any time they're vaguely reminded of this fact, they interpret it as an affront. Their eyes glaze over in boredom or widen in indignation. Their mouths start twitching as they get defensive. Their throats open up as they try to interrupt, itching to talk over you but not really listen, because they need to let you know that you've got it wrong.

The journey towards understanding structural racism still requires people of colour to prioritise white feelings. Even if they can hear you, they're not really listening. It's like something happens to the words as they leave our mouths and reach their ears. The words hit a barrier of denial and they don't get any further.[6]

The 2017 Windrush scandal exposed for all to see, through the particularly sharp lens of UK immigration policy, the racism that goes deep within British society, that treats people of colour as 'second-class citizens' at best, and refuses to acknowledge their citizenship or their full humanity at worst. As we've already noted in Chapter 2, in the 'Great British Class Survey' based on the 2011 census, people of colour in the UK were significantly over-represented in the poorest-but-one class category, that of 'emergent service workers'. Much that is true of *class* divisions is often true, therefore, in the experience of people of colour – geographical segregation, territorial stigma, silenced voices.

But race brings other forms of othering too. People of colour are all too used to being 'fixed' by white onlookers as *simply this*, carrying a 'sticky' identity less tied to where they are from, but instead inextricable from the

---

6 Reni Eddo-Lodge, *Why I'm No Longer Talking to White People About Race* (London: Bloomsbury, 2017), pp. ix–x.

colour of their skin. And the same, it seems, often doesn't apply the other way round. When Jon Snow, reporting on a 2019 pro-Brexit rally outside the Houses of Parliament, observed that he'd 'never seen so many white people in one place', he stirred up a barrage of angry responses to what was, apparently, a calmly objective comment. But as another journalist, Myriam François, noted after the incident, 'despite habitually racializing others, [it seems] we [white people] generally don't take well to being racialized ourselves. Acknowledging our "whiteness" means accepting that our worldview isn't universal or objective.'[7]

Picking up on Reni Eddo-Lodge's profound articulation of her frustrations, white American author Robin DiAngelo observes that, even in the most self-consciously 'progressive' of white people, any challenge or questioning of our anti-racist credentials can 'trigger a range of defensive moves' which all serve to reinstate the racial status quo. This dynamic of defensiveness she names 'white fragility' – although in reality it is more a desperate effort at white invulnerability, deploying and hanging on to the power and privilege that comes with being racialized as 'white'.[8]

It is critical to remember, DiAngelo reminds us, that racism is not just defined to 'mean people who intentionally dislike others because of their race', or blatant acts of insult or hatred. 'Racism is a structure, not an event,' she says: 'individual whites may be "against" racism, but they still benefit from a system that privileges whites as a group'. Racism is 'a system of advantage based on race' – and, for those of us who are white, it's when our complicity in the system is pointed out to us, when our inability to *see* it is highlighted, that we can suddenly feel profoundly uncomfortable.

Helpfully, DiAngelo identifies some of the ways in which white 'fragility' manifests itself in both internal feelings and external behaviours. Internally, it might include feeling 'singled out, attacked, silenced, shamed, guilty, accused, insulted, judged, angry, scared, [or] outraged'. Externally, defensive behaviours include crying, physically leaving or emotionally withdrawing from an uncomfortable situation, arguing, denying, focusing on the intentions behind our actions (rather than on our actions themselves), seeking forgiveness, or avoiding confrontation or interaction. She also identifies some alternative behaviours and responses, which those of us who are white people can practice to begin to overcome our defensiveness. We'll explore those later on, in Chapter 15.

---

7 Myriam François, 'The fury of "white people" with Jon Snow shows a total lack of self-awareness on race', *Guardian*, 12 April 2019, www.theguardian.com/comment isfree/2019/apr/12/jon-snow-white-people-brexit-rally, accessed 8 May 2020.

8 Robin DiAngelo, *White Fragility: Why It's so Hard for White People to Talk about Racism* (Boston, MA: Beacon, 2018), pp. 20, 118–19.

Grenfell Tower and class

The deaths of 71 people in the Grenfell Tower fire were a desperate tragedy. But what was just as shocking, to the world beyond that small, tight-knit west London neighbourhood, was that residents *knew* the Tower was unsafe, and had been expressing their concerns and warnings to those with power, in the strongest of terms, for at least two years before.

Why had their warnings not been heeded? Why had their voices not been heard? In a lecture two months after the fire, journalist Jon Snow articulated the profound and dangerous 'disconnect' between those who are part of 'the elite' (within which he includes himself and his journalist colleagues), and 'the lives, concerns, and needs of those who are not':

Amid the demonstrations around the tower after the fire there were cries of 'Where were you? Why didn't you come here before?' Why didn't any of us see the Grenfell action blog? Why didn't we know? Why didn't we have contact? Why didn't we enable the residents of Grenfell Tower – and indeed the other hundreds of towers like it around Britain, to find pathways to talk to us and for us to expose their story? ... We can accuse the political classes for their failures, and we do. But we are guilty of them ourselves. We are too far removed from those who lived their lives in Grenfell and who, across the country, now live on amid the combustible cladding, the lack of sprinklers, the absence of centralised fire alarms and more, revealed by the Grenfell Tower.

For Snow, from a profession of communicators, the pressing issue was one of being 'out of touch'. Rather than seeing their role as simply 'communicating *to*' the wider population, journalists – as part of what Snow calls the 'narrow elite' – should be bridging divides of class and background to get to *know* their audience – not as two-dimensional stereotypes, as victims or villains, but in all their three-dimensional complexity as fellow human beings. 'So casually written off as nameless migrants, scroungers, and the rest,' Snow remarks, 'actually, and it should be no shock to us, the Tower was *full* of talent'.[9]

The story of Khadija Saye (in the Introduction) is just one example of the talented human beings who lived in Grenfell Tower. But what is it about our society that meant that she and her neighbours are so often 'written off', that the warnings of the Grenfell Action Group went unheeded – and that similar voices continue to go unheard?

---

9 Jon Snow, McTaggart Lecture 2017, *inews*, 23 August 2017, https://inews.co.uk/news/uk/jon-snow-speech-full-i-know-nothing-ive-experienced-lot-521181, accessed 5 March 2020.

One reason is to do with *distance* – 'we are too far removed', says Jon Snow of his profession. And his words are echoed by none other than Pope Francis, who suggests that the inability of the affluent and the powerful to see and to hear, and their 'tendentious analyses which neglect parts of reality' that result, are products, ultimately, of geographical distance, and the 'lack of physical contact and encounter'.[10] Housing in our society is often segregated so that rich and poor rarely live side by side. And when we do rub up close against each other, 'bumping spaces' shared by neighbours across the class divides are often hard to find. In 2019, a new 'mixed' housing development in central London included an impenetrable hedge separating a playground accessible from the owner-occupied housing, from the social and 'affordable rented' housing in the same block.[11] And one of the reasons given for fitting the cladding to Grenfell Tower (cladding which turned out to be lethally flammable) was to improve the views from the adjacent 'Conservation Areas' – some of the most expensive neighbourhoods in London.

For Alastair McIntosh, theologian and member of the first Scottish Poverty Truth Commission, this distancing between rich and poor is not just geographical. Poverty is *structural*, he reminds us, 'being systemic to the distribution of power, resources and educational opportunities in society'. It is also 'a form of *violence* that comes from a *deficit of empathy* between those who have much and those who have little', and 'sustained by blindness to the full humanity of one another'. Poverty is 'a pathology of the rich and not just a deficit of the poor'.[12]

This leads us into a second, related reason why the residents of Grenfell Tower, and countless others on low incomes in our society, have been 'written off' and 'unheeded' – and that is to do with *identity*, and how that identity is publicly represented. As Al said of his own neighbourhood in Chapter 2, when people with power – politicians and the media especially – talk about neighbourhoods like ours with negative labels, or through negative statistics about crime, employment or education, it's hard not to take that negativity personally, to believe that you are 'not good enough', 'deficient', a 'problem'. But it's also the experience of many of my neighbours that when – when you're applying for a job, say

---

10 Pope Francis, *Laudato Si'*, p. 35.

11 Harriet Grant, 'Too poor to play: children in social housing blocked from communal playground', *Guardian*, 24 March 2019, www.theguardian.com/cities/2019/mar/25/too-poor-to-play-children-in-social-housing-blocked-from-communal-playground, accessed 8 May 2020.

12 Alastair McIntosh, 'A systemic challenge', The Poverty Truth Community blog, 14 February 2012, https://povertytruthcommission.blogspot.com/2011/05/systemic-challenge.html, accessed 7 July 2020.

– someone finds out you're from 'the Bromford', those negative labels can 'stick' to you, and you find yourself landing in the 'No' pile. The sociologist Loïc Wacquant calls this 'territorial stigma' – a prejudice against you, because of where you're from. The now firmly established TV genre of 'poverty porn' – Channel 4's *Benefits Street* being a particularly striking example – portrays people on low incomes as 'skivers' and 'scroungers', 'fixing' their identity as *simply this*, and allowing the viewer to distance themselves, in all their viewerly complexity, as *not that* – a process that is often termed '*othering*'.

A third dimension is to do with *voice*. If the camera is pointed away from the so-called 'socially excluded' and towards the mechanics of exclusion; if the microphone is taken from the distanced observer, into the hands of those with direct experience of poverty and marginalization, then another dynamic kicks in. As Darren McGarvey puts it:

> You are cast out the second you offend the people who're in charge of your empowerment ... The minute you start telling your story in service of your own agenda and not theirs, you're discarded. Your criticism is dismissed as not being constructive. Your anger is attributed to your mental health problems and everything about you that people once applauded becomes a stick they beat you with. Look out for these people. The people who pay wonderful lip service to giving the working class a voice, but who start to look very nervous whenever we open our mouths to speak.[13]

#MeToo and gender

Just as white privilege which sees itself as normative is challenged by acknowledging racism, and middle-class perceptions are challenged by engaging with working-class voices, so too the privilege of male perspectives and voices is challenged by engaging with some of the damaging effects, for people of all genders, of living in a society dominated by patriarchy.[14]

One of the paradoxes of the #MeToo movement is that it is perceived simultaneously as expressing a near-universal experience, and as exposing something previously unknown or unacknowledged. This paradox is, in itself, a demonstration of the misogynistic society in which the movement

---

13 Darren McGarvey, *Poverty Safari* (London: Picador, 2019), p. 123.

14 'Patriarchy' describes social and political systems that are characterized by male dominance over women (and children), reinforced by gendered social roles and stereotyping, and by actual and threatened male violence against women and girls.

45

arose. As with each of the areas we are highlighting, much depends on your perspective.

All her life, Ruth has heard and participated in conversations among women about the sort of male behaviour exposed by the #MeToo movement. Every woman recognized the stories which were suddenly being shared publicly – they echo our own, or our sisters', friends', neighbours', colleagues', mothers', aunts'. In every space in which women gather, stories are shared of unacceptable male behaviour against women, ranging from suggestive remarks and unwanted touch, to violent assault and rape. Warnings are shared about which men are not safe to be alone with, to get in a car with, to give your phone number to. There is nothing new about this reality.

So, what was new about the #MeToo movement, that made something so pervasive yet hidden suddenly so visible? It was that the private conversations and hidden experiences of women had transgressed an unspoken boundary and moved into the public sphere. One of the features of patriarchy is to uphold a binary division between male and female, and with that a whole host of other binaries: mind and body, strong and weak, thinking and feeling, leader and follower, active and passive, public and private.

The last binary in that list is particularly relevant here: under patriarchy, 'women's problems' belong in the private sphere. By placing male violence against women firmly in the public sphere, the #MeToo movement challenged and began to dismantle that construct. Not only was the behaviour it revealed no longer private, hidden (at least to the male, public gaze) and therefore ignorable, it was also no longer a women's problem.

Instead the problem was located firmly where, in truth, it had always been – in male perceptions of gender and therefore of women, and the resulting male behaviour. Toxic masculinity – the toxic way in which men perceive themselves in relation to the female 'other' – has its roots in constructs of gender, and of male dominance and superiority, which owe their origins in no small part to notable Christian theologians, such as Thomas Aquinas, who in the fifteenth century described women as 'defective men'.[15] The same system of binary thinking that relegates women to the passive and the private also creates harmful expectations for men, which lead to male behaviour which is harmful to everyone.

One of the harmful effects of patriarchy is the amount of space – literal and metaphorical – it encourages men to take up, at the expense of women. Many readers may be familiar with the cartoon which depicts a boardroom full of men, and one woman, with the caption, 'That's an

---

15 Thomas Aquinas, *Summa Theologiae* (1a, q. 92, a. 1, obj. 1).

excellent suggestion, Miss Triggs, perhaps one of the gentlemen present would like to make it.' It produces a reaction because it depicts a situation with which most women are all too familiar, and in which most men – perhaps unwittingly – are at least sometimes complicit.

In a patriarchal society, boys and men are socialized to believe that their voice is worth hearing, and girls and women to believe that theirs are not. Many studies have been conducted which show that even when women speak less than men, they are perceived to be dominating the conversation, and that men interrupt women twice as frequently as women interrupt men.[16] And the scenario of Miss Triggs has also been shown to be depressingly common.

None of this is due to any innate difference between the sexes. Rather, it is the product of a society so deeply in thrall to patriarchy that we have largely ceased to be aware of it. When feminists point out the profound gender inequalities which still exist, and the structures and attitudes which perpetuate them they are very often – ironically – shouted down by male voices denying the very existence of the problem to which they are contributing.

What is required in order to start to dismantle the patriarchy and its harmful social effects is a change of perspective. That can come when a movement like #MeToo breaks into the public (male-dominated) sphere and reframes the public (male-dominated) narrative. It can also come when individual men are willing to listen to the voices of women and to allow their worldview, and therefore their attitudes and behaviour, to be reshaped by the female 'other'.

Children in an adult-centred world

If we continue to live in a male-centred world (and we do) in which the experience of men is considered normative, and anything else a deviation from it, then we live even more in an adult-centred world. Thanks to the work of feminists, the male-centred nature of our society has been increasingly revealed, critiqued, challenged and disrupted in recent decades, though there is still a great deal of work to do. Meanwhile, the adult-centred nature of our society remains largely unexamined and unchallenged.

There are many ways in which children are individually and collectively dehumanized, from custody battles which are reported as if children are property, to certain strands of behaviourism which focus almost solely

---

16 Caroline Criado-Perez, *Invisible Women: Exposing Data Bias in a World Designed for Men* (London: Vintage, 2019), pp. 277–9.

on how to 'control' children. Public space is usually organized with little thought for the needs of children (as anyone who has helped a small child wash and dry their hands in a public toilet can attest).

Children are very frequently seen primarily in terms of their impact on adults. For example, in debates around the provision of childcare and parental leave, politicians on all sides frame the question primarily in economic terms or, more rarely, in terms of the impact on parents, but very rarely in terms which centre children and their well-being.

When Ruth was a teenager, there was an embryonic movement to 'empower' young people though the creation of youth councils and youth parliament. Although that movement has continued, and there are some isolated examples of very good practice, it has remained on the fringes of public life, and is still often experienced by young people (as it was by Ruth and her peers) as tokenistic – more a project for adults to be able to say they are listening, than a platform where young people are actually able to wield any power.

The way children are viewed and treated – as an add-on to 'proper grown up' society, or as adults-in-waiting – goes a long way to explaining the reactions when young people do manage to find power and a voice for themselves. The suggestions that young people cannot know what they are asking for, are naive and idealistic, and the refusal to acknowledge young people as leaders – as we will clearly see in the next section – all stem from a collective dismissal of children's agency and full humanity.

Climate change denial and cultural trauma

> Is this microphone on? Can anybody hear me? Is my English OK? I am starting to wonder ... You don't listen to the science because you are only interested in the answers that will allow you to carry on as if nothing has happened. (Greta Thunberg, speaking to UK politicians, 23 April 2019)

What is it that has stopped us, for several decades now, from hearing and heeding the increasingly urgent warnings of scientists and environmentalists that climate change is real, and happening and dangerous – quite possibly to the point of bringing the human race (along with countless other species) to extinction? What is it that allows even many of us who, on one level of our hearts and minds, are passionately committed to creation care and climate justice, to continue jumping into our cars in the morning to pump a few more gallons of CO_2 into the air?

The ways in which Greta Thunberg's powerful testimony has been attacked by those with much more privilege and power than her, exposes the widespread obliviousness to the need to change our behaviours and our systems, and the ways in which that obliviousness is reinforced by – if not in fact *rooted in* – the gendered dualisms of patriarchy. 'Saving the planet' is too easily dismissed and sidelined as 'women's work' within structures that divide the world into 'male/female', 'mind/body', 'spirit/ world', 'strong/weak', and so on – and where the voices of women, and the young, are all too often talked over and silenced (as Ruth has high-lighted above).[17]

Like class and race, climate change denial is also exacerbated by *distance*. In the global South, the effects of climate change are a daily, deeply felt reality: floods, droughts and ever-more-intense storms are already ripping away livelihoods and taking lives on a mammoth scale. In the rich global North, our exposure to the changing climate is lessened, not just by geography, but by the more robust infrastructure that comes with accumulated wealth. For most of us in the global North, hotter summers do not mean starvation, fiercer winds do not mean homelessness. Climate change is something that happens to people 'elsewhere' – or a threat that is looming but has not yet arrived.

But geography is relevant to climate denial in other ways too. In the previous chapter, we touched briefly on the connection between eco-logical violence and empire – the insidious Western worldview which has seen the Earth merely as a store of resources and commodities for human use and enrichment; a worldview 'in which the world sits silently, pas-sively, waiting to give itself up and give up what lies within it'.[18] If Brexit is a product of British 'post-imperial melancholia', a refusal to acknow-ledge and mourn the end of empire, and empire's inglorious reality – then there is surely a parallel sickness at work in relation to human-induced ecological breakdown.

Climate psychologist Glenn Albrecht seeks to wake us up to our 'environmental generational amnesia', the way in which each generation takes an increasingly degenerated world as their 'new normal', forgetting what has gone before. Albrecht has coined the term 'solastalgia' for 'the distress that is produced by environmental change impacting on people while they are directly connected to their home environment' – a 'home-sickness' while your home is falling apart around you, coupled with a

---

17 See for example Elle Hunt, 'The eco gender gap: why is saving the planet seen as women's work?', *Guardian*, 6 February 2020, www.theguardian.com/environment/ 2020/feb/06/eco-gender-gap-why-saving-planet-seen-womens-work, accessed 8 May 2020.

18 Willie James Jennings, 'Reframing the World', *International Journal of Systematic Theology*, 21:4, October 2019, p. 397.

sense of powerlessness to resist what feels unavoidable.[19] Conversely, sociologists Robert Brulle and Kari Marie Norgaard[20] have argued that the changes – on individual, institutional and societal levels – needed to avert ecological catastrophe are practically possible, but feel in themselves so dramatic that even anticipating them is to touch on a kind of collective 'cultural trauma' so intense that our dominant tendency – on individual, institutional and societal levels – is to resist and seek to maintain the status quo, whether consciously or unconsciously.

There are those who overtly deny the reality of climate change, whose vested interests in the status quo are often plain to see. But there are many more of us who are aware of the reality but are unable to fully face it head-on, barely able to acknowledge our grief at the changes happening around us, or paralysed by the enormity of the changes we know we need to make.

A 'non-listening culture'?

In this chapter we have explored a little further some of the dynamics that often make us – we who find ourselves 'privileged' in one or more of the aspects of identity that run through this book – *oblivious* to those human and other-than-human beings who are in various ways 'others' to us. But there is something broader going on as well. The philosopher of language, Gemma Corradi Fiumara, observed that across 'Western' culture (and global capitalism means that the culture of 'the West' has spread its tentacles much farther than merely Europe and North America), a 'non-listening culture' is pervasive: 'we know how to speak but have forgotten how to *listen*'. Decades before we were accustomed to talking about 'social media bubbles', Fiumara charted the way Western culture 'divides itself into separate discourses, which are free from the desire or obligation to listen to others', and where powerful discourses seek to expand their territory by silencing others and defining what counts as 'truth'.[21]

It also seems often to be the case that those powerful discourses, and their speakers, exert a gravitational pull on all of us that is hard to resist.

---

19 Glenn Albrecht, *Earth Emotions: New Words for a New World* (Ithaca: Cornell University Press, 2019), pp. 75, 199–201.

20 Robert J. Brulle and Kari Marie Norgaard, 'Avoiding cultural trauma: climate change and social inertia', *Environmental Politics*, 2019, https://pages.uoregon.edu/norgaard/pdf/Avoiding-Cultural-Trauma-Brulle-Norgaard-2019.pdf, accessed 8 May 2020.

21 Gemma Corradi Fiumara, *The Other Side of Language: A Philosophy of Listening* (Abingdon: Routledge, 1990), quoted in Rachel Muers, *Keeping God's Silence: Towards a Theological Ethics of Communication* (Oxford: Blackwell, 2004), pp. 53–6.

As liberation theologian Joerg Rieger observes of his North American context:

> difference has often been used by the 1 percent to divide and conquer the 99 percent. Differences of race, ethnicity, and gender have been used for the benefit of the system. When white land-owners in seventeenth-century Virginia used the category of race to pit poor white people against black people, the poor white people gained some small privileges over their black peers. At the same time, they lost something much more essential – namely, their deep solidarity with black people, which would have put them in a much stronger position ... racism and sexism benefit the masters and the employers more than they benefit the workers.[22]

If poverty, as Alastair McIntosh has argued, comes from a 'deficit of empathy' among the rich, then that empathy deficit seems to be something that often 'trickles down' and 'trickles out'. Why do we so often seem to be more interested in those who have *more* power and privilege than ourselves, than those who have *less*? Why do we so often seem more empathetic with, shed more tears for, the former than the latter?

This obliviousness is embedded deep in our psyches – or in the psyches, at least, of those of us who have been formed by Western culture. Whether we are white, middle-class and male, or none of those things, we live and breathe this non-listening culture. If we are white, middle-class or male, or all of those things, it is likely that there are aspects of this culture that have been, for at least some of our lives, invisible to us. Simply as adults, and as humans in a more-than-human world, there may still be areas of life to which we remain oblivious, if we have not yet learned to be attentive to the presence and voices of children, and to the cry of the earth itself.

---

22 Joerg Rieger, 'Instigating Class Struggle? The Study of Class in Religion and Theology and Some Implications for Gender, Race, and Ethnicity', in Joerg Rieger (ed.), *Religion, Theology and Class: Fresh Engagements after Long Silence* (New York: Palgrave Macmillan, 2013), p. 201.

Further reading

On class:

- Lynsey Hanley, *Respectable: Crossing the Class Divide* (Harmondsworth: Penguin, 2016)
- Darren McGarvey, *Poverty Safari: Understanding the Anger of Britain's Underclass* (London: Picador, 2019)
- Lisa McKenzie, *Getting By: Estates, Class and Culture in Austerity Britain* (Bristol: Policy Press, 2015)
- Joerg Rieger (ed.), *Religion, Theology and Class: Fresh Engagements after Long Silence* (New York: Palgrave Macmillan, 2013)
- Imogen Tyler, *Stigma: The Machinery of Inequality* (London: Zed, 2020)

On race:

- Akala, *Natives: Race and Class in the Ruins of Empire* (London: Two Roads, 2018)
- Robin DiAngelo, *White Fragility: Why It's so Hard for White People to Talk About Racism* (Boston, MA: Beacon, 2018)
- Reni Eddo-Lodge, *Why I'm No Longer Talking to White People about Race* (London: Bloomsbury, 2017)
- Afua Hirsch, *Brit(ish): On Race, Identity and Belonging* (London: Vintage, 2018)

On gender:

- Laura Bates, *Everyday Sexism* (London: Simon and Schuster, 2014)
- Caroline Criado-Perez, *Invisible Women: Exposing Data Bias in a World Designed for Men* (London: Vintage, 2019)
- Audre Lorde, *Sister Outsider* (Freedom: Crossing, 1984)
- Lola Olufemi, *Feminism, Interrupted: Disrupting Power* (London: Pluto, 2020)

On children:

- Libby Brooks, *The Story of Childhood: Growing up in Modern Britain* (London: Bloomsbury, 2006)
- Chloe Combi, *Generation Z: Their Voices, Their Lives* (London: Hutchinson, 2015)

- Erik H. Erikson, *Childhood and Society* (New York: Norton, 1993 [1950])

On climate change:

- Glenn Albrecht, *Earth Emotions: New Words for a New World* (Ithaca, NY: Cornell University Press, 2019)
- Naomi Klein, *This Changes Everything* (Harmondsworth: Penguin, 2015)
- George Marshall, *Don't Even Think About It: Why Our Brains are Wired to Ignore Climate Change* (New York: Bloomsbury Publishing, 2014)

On obliviousness and non-listening culture:

- Mary McClintock Fulkerson, *Places of Redemption: Theology for a Worldly Church* (Oxford: Oxford University Press, 2007)
- Rachel Muers, *Keeping God's Silence: Towards a Theological Ethics of Communication* (Oxford: Blackwell, 2004)

Questions for reflection/discussion

- If you did the exercise at the start of this chapter, how did you feel about your score, and why?
- Which of the areas explored in this chapter have had a significant impact on your life, how, and why? What about the lives of your neighbours? The shared life of your community?
- Are there any areas in this chapter which surprised you, or which you weren't aware of before? How will that awareness change your response?

4

The Church's Privilege Problem

What about the Christian Church, then? The Spirit-filled community of followers of Jesus? How do we, collectively, fare on the kinds of 'obliviousness', the 'power-related-willingness-not-to-see', that we explored in the previous chapter?

There are at least three possible answers to this question, and they are probably all, to some extent, true.

First, it might be the case (and it would need to be accompanied by concrete evidence!) that the Church does *better* than the wider world. With the gifts of the Spirit, the wisdom of the Scriptures, the Jesus-shaped habits of our church communities, it could be argued, our eyes are open to people and parts of the world that are generally overlooked, and to relationships and dynamics that are harmful, and our behaviour is so *formed* and *transformed* by our participation in the way of Jesus that we resist and reject the destructiveness of structural privilege at every turn.

A second possible answer would acknowledge that as Christians we're never neatly sealed off from 'the world' beyond the boundaries of the church – that our ways of seeing (and not seeing), our ways of behaving and relating, are as much formed by the life of the world as they are by the life of the church. There is a two-way flow as we move back and forth between 'church space' and 'world space' (something we'll return to as this book unfolds). We might well be involved in changing the world for the better – at least a little bit – as followers of Jesus, but being Christian does not exempt or immunize us from obliviousness either. If our identities in wider society are enmeshed in forms of structural privilege, then those privileges will distort the ways we seek to live as Christians.

A third, uncomfortable, possibility is that we Christians are, in some ways at least, *more* oblivious than the wider world: that there are aspects of our DNA as Christian communities – what we believe, how we behave and order our collective life – that exacerbate certain structural injustices and uphold certain privileges in ways that our wider society is in fact more conscious of, and attempting to deal with, however imperfectly.

It is this third possibility, profoundly unsettling as it might be, that we are wanting to focus on in this book. There are insidious theologies, deeply embedded in the histories and present realities of our church communities, that contribute to our ongoing obliviousness, to our denial of the contribution of huge parts of God-created reality.

When we say 'our' here, we mean particularly those of us who are both Christians and socially, structurally privileged – in terms of race, class, gender, age and being humans shaped by the 'Western' culture of global capitalism. That 'we' is, it should hardly need saying, a *minority* of Christians worldwide – the majority of whom are in the global South, black, female, and financially among the poorest in the world. Even in England, even in the Church of England, that 'we' includes significantly less than everyone. But in the context that we – Al and Ruth – are writing, in England, within the Church of England, there is nevertheless a *dominant culture and worldview*, shaped over many years by the make-up of the *majority* of its *membership* and the majority of its *leadership*, that we can justifiably claim is in 'our DNA' as a denomination. That culture and worldview is also, we would modestly suggest, recognizable in other denominations, in other parts of the world – not least because of the intertwining of our histories of mission and colonization.

In the chapters that follow, we will tease out one specific aspect of our collective DNA – the way we connect together our understandings of mission, church and Jesus – that we believe is profoundly significant in entrenching and reinforcing multiple forms of obliviousness: in terms of race, class, gender and age, climate change denial and our cultural inability to listen. If this book could be twice, or ten times, as long, we would carefully document the ways in which each of these areas is corrosively present in the life of the Church, in its explicit and implicit theologies and its lived realities. In some of these areas (such as race and gender), many others, over many years, have already documented, testified and presented critical challenges to the Church much more comprehensively and powerfully than we could ever possibly do. In some of the other areas (class and age, especially), there are still huge gaps crying out for attention, research and critical reflection. While in the last few years there has been an explosion in eco-theology – theological reflection on the more-than-human world – that area, like all the others, is very much a work-in-progress: as long as our collective obliviousness remains entrenched, there will still be work to be done in unearthing, testifying, challenging and changing the way things are.

Here, then, we offer no more than snapshots of the fault-lines that run through the Church, and a few pointers to some of those who have explored them more fully. You might want to investigate some of these resources alongside reading the rest of this book, or to commit time to working through them after you've finished reading this.

Race

We have already (at the end of Chapter 2) touched on the entanglement of Christian mission with colonialism – and the Church of England with the British empire in particular. Digging deeper, Willie James Jennings traces the invention of 'race' itself to the European missionary-imperialist enterprise, defining 'foreign' lands as 'heathen' and darker-skinned bodies as inferior while invading them, enslaving them and converting them.[1] But few white members of the Church would have even a passing awareness, let alone a penitent acknowledgement of these entanglements. One reason for this is a collective unwillingness to address this history. Another inescapable reason is the pervasive racialized segregation of many of our churches themselves.

In the mid twentieth century, as the Windrush generation of British imperial subjects responded to the invitation to come to the 'motherland' to work, many Caribbean Christians received a hostile response when first venturing into English churches: 'I would ask you not to come back because the parishioners don't like it, and we wouldn't want to lose them.'[2] Over the years since, and even into the recent era of the UK government's explicit 'hostile environment' immigration policy, what Caribbean-British United Reformed Church theologian Michael Jagessar names as the 'festering wounds' of racism in the so-called 'mainstream' British denominations have gone largely unaddressed.

Whiteness has continued insidiously to define who is part of 'us' (and who is always assumed to be 'foreign'), who is welcomed (or grudgingly accommodated) and on what terms, who leads, and whose voices are heard.[3] 'White flight' has happened in churches – as some have become more visibly multi-ethnic – as well as in the demographics of some urban neighbourhoods. People of colour in white-majority churches have been asked, again and again, 'where are you *really* from?', experienced patronizing comments over simple tasks like reading in church, and had their gifts, talents and vocations overlooked or blocked, repeatedly. White-dominated church leadership at both local and national levels has

---

1 Willie James Jennings, *The Christian Imagination: Theology and the Origins of Race* (New Haven, CT: Yale University Press, 2010).

2 Quoted in Michael Jagessar and Anthony Reddie (eds), *Black Theology in Britain: A Reader* (London: Equinox, 2007), p. 50.

3 See for example Sanjee Perera, 'Pandemic and Pestilence: When We Almost Notice that Black Lives Matter Less', *William Temple Foundation blog*, 13 May 2020, https://williamtemplefoundation.org.uk/blog-pandemic-and-pestilence/, accessed 12 June 2020.

often been slow, hesitant or resistant in its responses to challenge. 'We all have stories,' Jagessar insists, 'our problem is that we lack listeners.'[4]

Class

Like race, class is a factor that can be traced through the history of Christian denominations in Britain, and continues to be profoundly significant in shaping 'church culture'. The Church of England in particular, as the 'Established Church', has been historically intertwined with the hierarchy of society, from providing reserved pews (at the front, of course) for the lord of the manor and his family, to its ongoing entanglement at a national level with the monarchy and parliament. While the parochial system ensures, at least on paper, that every neighbourhood in the country falls within the boundaries of a Church of England parish, and that every Church of England parish has some kind of worshipping community (and in most cases, still, a church building), both the economics and the culture of the Church of England are heavily weighted towards the affluent.

The most resource-rich dioceses are in the wealthiest parts of the country, and the average spend on ministry in urban estate parishes, for example, has in recent years been close to half what is spent on average nationally. Changing the economics can be done, potentially, in a moment of collective decision-making. Changing the culture is a harder task. As Revd Lynne Cullens, currently chair of the National Estate Churches Network, puts it, 'the Church's leadership, and the Church in general, is unhealthily – and, I would say, sinfully – dominated by middle-class culture', while the working class forms between 30 and 50 per cent of the UK population. Rather than changing the structures to better value the gifts and experience of working-class Christians, the Church of England tends to prefer, at best, 'middle-class leaders with a "heart for the poor"'. 'At what point do the working classes get to speak for themselves?' Lynne Cullens asks.[5]

4 'Book Review: Mukti Barton, *Rejection, Resistance and Resurrection: Speaking Out on Racism in the Church*', *Black Theology: An International Journal* 4:2 (2006), p. 233.

5 Lynne Cullens, 'A middle-class culture dominates the Church', *Church Times*, 1 March 2019, www.churchtimes.co.uk/articles/2019/1-march/comment/opinion/a-middle-class-culture-dominates-the-church, accessed 8 May 2020.

Gender

The Church's failings in the area of gender are in some way more obvious than those relating to race and class, and in other ways every bit as subtle and insidious. The 'debate' around women's ordination as bishops, priests and deacons looms large in our recent history, and even the opening of many lay ministries to women is well within our collective institutional memory. The conclusion of the official processes to admit women to all orders of ministry has not been accompanied by an end of the theologies which called women's vocations into question in the first place. Indeed, that such theologies must be allowed to exist and to flourish within the Church of England has been enshrined in the very legislation which enables women to be ordained, first as deacons and priests, and then as bishops.[6]

The extent to which patriarchal understandings of ministry, of the Church, and of God remain ingrained is evident in a whole range of contexts – from an ordained woman being referred to as a 'woman priest' while her male colleague is simply a 'priest', to concerns about the 'feminization' of the Church, with the implicit suggestion that a 'feminized' Church, and by extension the feminine in general, is in some way inferior or diminished. The Church very often speaks in its liturgy, its preaching, its Bible study and catechesis, as if God were male. The Church very often embodies in its structures, culture and behaviour Mary Daly's assertion that 'if God is male, then the male is God'.[7]

The stark disparities in how male and female clergy are deployed – with men still overwhelmingly dominating 'senior' roles, while women do the majority of unpaid ministry – are just one way in which the Church reflects not only the patriarchal bias of the society in which it exists, but also the implicit and explicit sexism of an inherited theological tradition which has until very recently been written almost exclusively by and for men. The Church's understanding of itself and the society in which it operates in male dominated, patriarchal terms has often distorted – and continues to distort – our perception both of God's action in the world, and our place within it.

---

6 As part of the legislation enabling women to become bishops in the Church of England, the 'Five Guiding Principles' were introduced, with the stated intention of 'mutual flourishing' for all, including those who reject the validity of women's ordination, within the Church. They can be found here: www.churchofengland.org/sites/default/files/2017-10/the_five_guiding_principles.pdf.

7 Mary Daly, *Beyond God the Father* (Boston, MA: Beacon Press, 1973).

Children

We have seen already the extent to which we live in an adult-centric society. The Church has been as guilty of reflecting and perpetuating this as any institution. Where children and young people are present in church (and in an alarming proportion of churches they are not) they are marginalized in multiple ways. Lynn Alexander identifies a number of ways in which the Church needs to repent of our mistreatment of children:[8] from the most shocking and obvious cases of abuse, to our collective failure to value children as full members of the body of Christ, to all the various ways in which the Church has objectified and instrumentalized children as a means of 'drawing in' adults and/or securing the future of the Church.

It is shocking that we are still having to make a case for children's full inclusion in the worshipping life of the Christian community. The Church is, and always has been, an intergenerational community because God is, and always has been, calling people of all ages. Yet this is not widely reflected in the way our churches work and worship which is, in the vast majority of cases, as adult-centred as the rest of society.

It is a worthwhile experiment to try to imagine a church (or, indeed, any community) which is truly child-centred – in which everything is planned first and foremost with children's needs in mind, and adults are seen as an 'add-on' whose needs must be, more or less willingly, accommodated, but only in so far as they don't infringe too much on the children. You may find it difficult or uncomfortable to imagine what that would be like. That discomfort, as we allow our usual adult way of thinking to be interrupted, should point us towards the discomfort experienced by children in an adult-centred church. It should also help us to open up our imaginations to the possibility of a different way of being.

Other-than-human creatures

At the end of Chapter 2, we noted the historic entanglements between Christian mission, empire and ecological violence, through which bringing salvation to the 'heathen' went hand in hand with extracting commodities and resources from 'newly discovered' places across the planet. But there was a theology undergirding this colonialist plunder of the other-than-human world. It was another aspect of that patriarchal, dualist, hierarchical theology that placed 'Father God' over 'Mother Nature', and

---

8 Lynn Alexander, *Children, Families and God: Drawing the Generations Together to Change the World* (Evangelista Media, 2012).

emphasized the 'subjugation' and 'dominion' it read in the divine command to human beings in Genesis 1.28. It understood the earth and all its creatures (animals, plants and other kinds of organic and non-organic matter) as created entirely for human benefit: for us, 'the crown of all creation' (as a Church of England eucharistic prayer still puts it, drawing on Psalm 8), to use as we see fit.

But what it missed, that anthropocentric (human-centred) theology, was another way of imagining the relationship between humanity and the earth, also present in the pages of the Bible. It missed the testimony of Job (chapters 38–41), where 'the natural world in all its wildness is presented alongside humanity, who remains humbled before its savagery and ambiguity', and where 'God's authority reigns to support the needs of wildlife, rather than just that of human beings'. And it missed the prophetic declarations that all creation praises God (for example Isaiah 42.10; Psalms 19.1–4; 69.34; 96.11–12; 98.7–8; 103.22; 150.6) and that, when laid waste by human destruction, the desolate land cries out to God (Jeremiah 12.11) and responds to God's call to be an instrument of God's judgement (12.9).[9] Akin with other indigenous worldviews, this is the opposite of the colonialist theology of a world which 'sits silently, passively, waiting to give itself up and give up what lies within it'. Instead, it presents a vision of life which 'recognizes the world as never silent, never passive, but always already actuality, speaking in and through creatures, including [but by no means only] the human creature'.[10] Choosing between these two opposing worldviews, and their Christian theological versions, is not just a matter of past history: it remains a matter of present urgency, not just for how we imagine the world, but for how we imagine our neighbours – human and other-than-human – within it, and for how we imagine the Church and its mission.

Further reading

Race:

- Mukti Barton, *Rejection, Resistance and Resurrection: Speaking out on racism in the church* (London: Darton, Longman and Todd, 2005)
- A. D. A. France-Williams, *Ghost Ship: Institutional Racism and the Church of England* (London: SCM Press, 2020)

---

9 Celia Deane-Drummond, *A Primer in Ecotheology* (Eugene, OR: Cascade Books, 2017), pp. 25, 27–33.

10 Willie James Jennings, 'Reframing the World: Toward an Actual Christian Doctrine of Creation', *International Journal of Systematic Theology* 21:4, October 2019, pp. 3, 97.

- Katie Walker Grimes, *Christ Divided: Antiblackness as Corporate Vice* (Minneapolis, MN: Fortress, 2017)
- Michael N. Jagessar and Anthony G. Reddie (eds), *Black Theology in Britain: A Reader* (London: Equinox, 2007)
- Willie James Jennings, *The Christian Imagination: Theology and the Origins of Race* (New Haven, CT: Yale University Press, 2010)
- Ben Lindsay, *We Need to Talk about Race: Understanding the Black Experience in White Majority Churches* (London: SPCK, 2019)
- Anthony G. Reddie, *Is God Colour-Blind? Insights from Black Theology for Christian Ministry* (London: SPCK, 2009)

Class:

- Darren Edwards, *Chav Christianity: Exploring what it looks like to be a working-class Christian* (New Generation, 2013)
- Joerg Rieger (ed.), *Religion, Theology and Class: Fresh Engagements after Long Silence* (New York: Palgrave Macmillan, 2013)
- Chris Shannahan, *Voices from the Borderland: Re-imagining Cross-cultural Urban Theology in the Twenty-first Century* (London: Equinox 2010)

Gender:

- Monica A. Coleman, *Making A Way Out Of No Way: A Womanist Theology* (Minneapolis, MN: Fortress, 2008)
- Fran Porter, *Women and Men After Christendom: The Disordering of Gender Relationships* (London: Paternoster, 2015)
- Gail Ramshaw, *God Beyond Gender: Feminist Christian God-Language* (Minneapolis, MN: Fortress, 1995)
- Nicola Slee, *Faith and Feminism: An Introduction to Christian Feminist Theology* (London: Darton, Longman and Todd, 2003)
- Natalie Watson, *Introducing Feminist Ecclesiology* (Sheffield: Sheffield Academic Press, 2002)

Children:

- Kate Adams, Brendan Hyde and Richard Woolley (eds), *The Spiritual Dimension of Childhood* (London: Jessica Kingsley, 2008)
- Lynn Alexander, *Children, Families and God: Drawing the Generations Together to Change the World* (Evangelista Media, 2012)
- Jerome W. Berryman, *Children and the Theologians: Clearing the Way for Grace* (London: Morehouse, 2010)

- Bonnie J. Miller-McLemore, *Let the Children Come: Reimagining Childhood from a Christian Perspective* (San Francisco, CA: Jossey-Bass, 2003)
- Ann Richards and Peter Privett, *Through the Eyes of a Child: New Insights in Theology from a Child's Perspective* (London: Church House Publishing, 2018)

Other-than-human creatures:

- Fred Bahnson and Norman Wirzba, *Making Peace with the Land: God's Call to Reconcile with Creation* (Downers Grove, IL: IVP, 2012)
- Celia Deane-Drummond, *A Primer in Ecotheology: Theology for a Fragile Earth* (Eugene, OR: Cascade, 2017)
- Jeremy Williams (ed.), *Time to Act: A resource book by the Christians in Extinction Rebellion* (London: SPCK, 2020)
- Randy S. Woodley, *Shalom and the Community of Creation: An Indigenous Vision* (Grand Rapids, MI: Eerdmans, 2012)

Questions for reflection/discussion

For each of the dimensions discussed in this chapter (race, class, gender, children, other-than-human creatures), think about your church (if you belong to one), or any faith traditions or communities with which you identify:

- Is this topic discussed in your church? If so, how and by whom?
- How do you feel about the way your church or faith tradition approaches this topic?
- Can you identify any action your church has taken, or change it has made, in relation to this topic?

5

A Tale of Two Economies

Let's talk about *economies*. But broader than the usual meaning of that word. Let's think not just about money, and how it circulates, where it accumulates, how it's invested, and so on. Let's think about an economy as any system in which things – all sorts of things – move and are exchanged. Let's think about economies as systems *in which we participate*, with our bodies and our imaginations. Let's think about economies as systems which *shape us*, and shape:

- what we *value*
- what we *desire*
- what we *worry over*
- what we *celebrate* and delight in
- what we do with our *bodies*
- how we see and treat other *people* (and, indeed, other non-human creatures).

It might be helpful to know that the word economy comes from the Greek words *oikos* (home, household, habitat) and *nomos* (law, rule, ordering). Put like that, it's hopefully becoming clearer that all of us participate in all kinds of different economies, all the time – and also that some economies have a more profoundly formative, shaping effect on us than others.

Here, let's think in particular about two different kinds of economy that are powerfully shaping the Christian Church – and more specifically, the Church in England – in the early twenty-first century. Both of us know the Church of England better than any other denomination, and there may well be particular reasons why the Church of England is especially entangled in the economies we describe here. We'll touch on some of those reasons as we go. But if you're more familiar with another Christian denomination, we have a hunch you will still recognize at least some of what we're about to describe.

Economy #1: 'counting in'

Figure 3: Economy #1

In the first economy, what is most valued is what can be most easily *counted*: numbers of people who attend church, and money. In this economy, 'keeping accounts' and 'keeping a count' are vital practices. At the level of the local (parish) church, substantial amounts of money come in from a 'central' fund (often called 'the diocese'), mostly in the form of some kind of paid ('stipendiary') ministry – a vicar, or similar. In this economy, that 'investment' is understood primarily as a resource to equip and empower church members to *go out* from church into the places of their daily life, and to *bring in* new people, to add to their number – those who, in one way or another, 'come to church'. Because money and church attendance numbers are most valued in this economy, the financial investment from the 'centre' is always looking for a 'return'. 'Value for money' equates to increased church attendance and, ideally, an increase in the money paid into the centre from the local church.

But look at what this does to our imaginations. Our non-Christian neighbours are valued primarily in their capacity as 'potential Christians' – even, most crudely, as potential sources of income. If they do end up 'coming to church', their value in this economy (indeed, the value of *any* church member in this economy) is threefold: as a number on attendance counts, as a financial contribution, and as a potential agent to go out and bring more people 'back to church'. Those who fail on any of those three counts are, in this economy, less valuable parts of the system – irregular attendees, deficient givers, or ineffective evangelists. A parallel image might be that of a mining company, focused on the extraction of valuable resources from a piece of land, with an eye for the biggest possible return on their investment.

The Scottish theologian John Drane describes the powerful influence of this kind of economy as the 'McDonaldization' of the Church: treating a complex web of human relationships (and relationships with God!) as if they are a 'rational system' (like a 'machine'), and treating what that system produces as a 'commodity' to be bought and sold.[1]

Drawing on sociologist George Ritzer's analysis of the 'McDonaldization of Society', Drane highlights some of the ways in which the contemporary Church is caught up in McDonaldization's four key characteristics: efficiency, calculability, predictability and control.

Efficiency

Efficiency, the drive to push through your system as many people as possible, as quickly as possible, Drane sees particularly in 'pre-packaged church', the 'spiritual equivalent of fast food', where 'somebody else does the thinking for you, predigests it, and serves it up in an efficient manner' – in contrast to the home-prepared meal that takes time and effort to prepare, a collective involvement in the cooking, a generous time to enjoy eating together, and often a fair amount of mess!

Calculability

Calculability works on the assumption that 'more' equates to 'better'. While numbers 'do have a place in taking the spiritual temperature of our congregations', says Drane, they 'often have little to do with what is *really* happening'. How much of what is called 'church growth', he asks, is about people simply moving from other churches, consumers making choices in a competitive market-place? And what depth and breadth of relationship, encounter, even spiritual community is missed when the only things that are counted are attendance at worship and money in the collection plate? 'An over-emphasis on what is quantifiable', Drane

---

1 John Drane, *The McDonaldization of the Church: Spirituality, Creativity and the Future of the Church* (London: Darton, Longman and Todd, 2000), pp. 28–48.

argues, 'will generally hinder if not undermine personal and spiritual growth'.

Predictability

Predictability, in a system, assumes that if we know what we put *in* to the system, then we also know what will come *out* at the other end. If we do church growth programme *A*, we will get *B*% numerical growth in our congregation. If we do *that* discipleship course, we will produce disciples whose lives look like *this*. The church down the road did *X*, and it got impressive results, so we should do it too. And yet, Drane reminds us, 'it is easy to become so enamoured with what God has done somewhere else that we fail to discern what God might actually do in this place and at this time ... Is it possible', he asks, 'to have a world view – or a church structure – dominated by predictability without at the same time denying, or at least seriously jeopardizing, belief in a biblical God?'

Control

For Drane, each of these first three characteristics of McDonaldization ultimately comes down to the question of power and control – and the tendency of institutions (the Church being just one among many) to *accumulate*, rather than *disperse*, such control. In particular here, he cites examples – from big evangelistic events, to church 'small group' structures, to the encouragement of lay ministries – where forms of church life that could be profoundly enabling of the flourishing of diverse gifts, and relationships of 'mutual support, encouragement and healing', can all too often end up being narrowly controlling. The rich unpredictability of genuine diversity – the best imaginable 'bring and share' feast where who-knows-what tasty surprises are brought to the table – is replaced instead with 'a McDonaldized kind of difference – in much the same way as the market-place is increasingly turning ethnic foods into yet more rationalized restaurant chains'.[2]

Now, of course, no one in any church would dream of advocating an economy so explicitly, and simplistically, focused on 'counting in' as

---

2 As Azariah France-Williams argues in relation to the institutional racism in the Church of England, despite the Church's rhetoric of wanting 'strong communities or empowered congregations', its anxious push towards numerical growth means it often seems more interested in the most efficient ways to produce 'clones' (France-Williams, *Ghost Ship*, pp. 12, 126).

we've just presented it here. But anyone who has had anything to do with the Christian Church in any form will surely recognize aspects of this description. And when the Church is suffering from huge institutional insecurity – when the numbers and the money are both heading downwards in more-or-less dramatic ways, as they are in the so-called 'mainstream' denominations of the UK – then it's quite possible that this economy begins to dominate the ways we think, and interact, and make decisions, even when we're claiming to be driven by quite different priorities.

Economy #2: 'giving out'

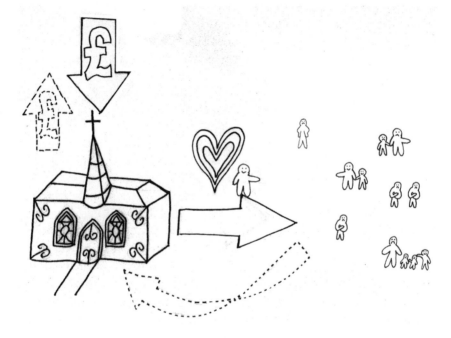

Figure 4: Economy #2

A second kind of economy shaping church life looks almost the polar opposite of the first. In this economy, what is valued most is what happens *beyond* the walls of the church: the growth of God's kingdom, it's often called (we prefer 'kin-dom', with its rejection of the patriarchal term 'king', and its affirmation of the interconnectedness, kinship, between all God's creatures). There's a flow, an 'outpouring', from church into the wider world, and while Christians will place the emphasis differently, that 'outpouring' is commonly expressed either in 'service' (a self-giving love for others, meeting their practical needs, or campaigning for their fairer, more just treatment by wider society), or 'proclamation' (communicating the good news of Jesus in ways that meet spiritual needs, bringing hope in situations of hopelessness) – or both. There's still a significant 'investment' here – in money, time and energy – but this is giving without expecting any kind of direct 'return', financial, numerical or otherwise.

Both ethically and spiritually, this would seem to be a dramatic improvement on a life shaped by the first economy. In this second economy, the significant context is much less the declining resources and power of the church, and much more the entrenched and deepening inequality and divisions in the society around us. Here, the church is not governed by self-interest and anxiety about its own survival, but instead gives freely of what it has been given by God, in God-commanded love for our neighbours. In the words of Sri Lankan Anglican bishop Duleep de Chickera, 'we do not live for ourselves, and all our energy, all our gifts are directed to abundant life for the other'.[3]

Three temptations to 'heroic' power

The trouble is, this second economy can also, all too easily, distort the way we see, and treat, both our neighbours, and ourselves. There is huge *power* in this kind of 'self-giving', and that power can, at worst, be both seductive and destructive.

In his stunning book *The Christlike God*, John V. Taylor (another Anglican bishop, and General Secretary of the Church Mission Society for ten years) reads the spiritual struggle Jesus faces in the desert (as told in Matthew 4.1–11 and Luke 4.1–13) as a wrestling with temptations to three different, and heroic, kinds of power.[4] We will explore each, in turn, in a moment. But we should first pause to notice – because it is easy to rush on and overlook – that each of the temptations begins with a questioning of Jesus' identity.

Remember the context here: Jesus is led 'by the Spirit' into the wilderness immediately after he has been baptized by John – immediately after he has seen the heavens torn apart and the Spirit descending on him like a dove, and heard a voice from heaven announcing 'this is my Son, the Beloved, with whom I am well pleased' (Matthew 3.17). So immediately after Jesus has heard God call him 'Beloved Son', the tempter in the desert

3 Sermon given by Rt Revd Duleep de Chickera, Bishop of Colombo, 20 July 2008, https://episcopalchurch.org/files/attached-files/duleepdechickera_sermon_072008.pdf, accessed 5 March 2020.

4 John V. Taylor, *The Christlike God* (London: SCM Press, 1992), pp. 260–4.

tests how strong that sense of identity really is: '*if* you are the Son of God...' why not do something to prove it, to make sure...? If we, as the church of Jesus, are going through something of an identity crisis ourselves, anxious about our future survival and our current status in society – signs on the surface, perhaps, of deeper insecurities about our identity in God's eyes – we should be alert to Jesus' temptations as dangers for us too.

The power of the provider

The first temptation, then, is to *the power of the provider*. 'Turn stones into bread,' suggests the tempter. Maybe not for Jesus to feed himself, but to feed others. As John Taylor reminds us, feeding hungry people with bread is exactly what Jesus *does* do, a number of times in the gospel narrative. 'It is the power of every responsible mother and father', he notes. 'But this can all too easily slide into, "They who provide know what's best for you."' Feeding people who are hungry is good, necessary, vital work. But the power of providing can become addictive for the 'feel-good' effect it leaves behind in us, and we end up, perversely, *needing* hungry people to make it possible for us to keep on being the provider. And look what it's done to our relationship with our neighbours: if we are stuck in the 'provider' role, then at the same time we've fixed them into the role of 'hungry', 'needy', 'lacking'. They come to us (or we see them, as we come to them) as empty hands – or empty minds, or empty lives – waiting to be filled with what we have to give them. We, on the other hand, enter the interaction acknowledging no needs of our own, no desires or hungers to be fulfilled (or none we'll admit to, anyway!), nothing to learn, nothing to receive.

The power of the performer

In Matthew's version, *the power of the performer* comes next: 'throw yourself off the temple, and the angels will catch you'. The best performances are *persuasive*: 'if only people have the chance to see you in action, then they'll believe', goes the logic. If only we can make this worship service more attractive, if only we can communicate our message more clearly, if only people can see the good things we're doing in the community ... We live in a society where 'demonstrating impact', 'showing how hard you've been working', is expected of us, whether we're a chief executive of an organization or we're reporting in to the Job Centre. And the church is far from immune: if it's not celebrating a positive increase in our attendance figures for worship, it'll be telling the

world how many food banks, toddler groups and debt advice centres we're running. We can tell ourselves that if our light shines brightly, people will 'see [our] good works and give glory to [our] Father in heaven' (Matthew 5.16), but the truth is often more complex: we'd quite like a bit of that glory for ourselves, especially if it can help keep the show on the road for another month or two. But again, look what this temptation does to our relationship with our neighbours: if we are the performer, then they are placed firmly in the 'audience' – passive recipients of our stage-show, 'punters' to be impressed and persuaded. No hint that we might, in turn, be interested in what they're saying or doing – let alone that we might allow it to have its own impact on *us*.

The power of the possessor

So, finally we have *the power of the possessor*: 'all this shall be yours'. The deal offered by the tempter seems to hinge on Jesus bowing down and worshipping *him*, rather than worshipping God, and possession of the world being the reward – but it's not as simple as 'cause and effect'. To see the world and all its creatures as something to possess, to own, to control is surely, *in itself*, to worship a form of power that is what we should call 'demonic'. We are, many of us at least, only just awakening to the destruction that has been wrought on our planet and its ecosystems, by just such an attitude among the more

powerful human beings among us. And the history of environmental destruction is itself entangled with a whole host of other equally demonic forms of possessive power: from capitalism's accumulation of wealth and exploitation of cheap labour, to colonialism and empire's violent capture of land and racist enslavement of black bodies.

On a much more mundane level, we've already seen John Drane highlighting the ways in which the 'McDonaldization' of our church structures – seeking 'efficiency', 'calculability' and 'predictability' – inevitably leads to accumulations of power and control in the hands of some over others. And it probably isn't hard to think of some dispute in church life – whether tediously long-running or an explosive moment – that has focused on 'territory' (the kitchen, the worship space, a particular cupboard, a role on a committee, you name it!) and who controls it. Looking beyond internal church politics, even churches profoundly committed to being 'welcoming' and 'inclusive' can often end up, in practice, offering such inclusion *on their own terms* – 'you're welcome here, but here's how we expect you to behave' – terms often unconsciously rooted in particular cultural, racialized or class 'norms'. The Church of England's attachment to its position as the 'established' church, with the associated trappings of power, privilege and influence – the expectation that people will listen when we speak, or that we have a guaranteed seat at the tables where decisions are made – is just another example of the temptation to the power of the possessor that afflicts many of us, collectively as well as individually.

Where have we got to?

It's time to look back on the journey so far. In Chapter 2, we highlighted the roots of the pro-Brexit vote not just in the inequalities of poverty, and in a sense of being 'left behind' or 'left out' by economic, cultural and political changes, but also in what Paul Gilroy has identified as a 'post-imperial melancholia': a loss of the national prestige that went with the end of the British empire; a loss that has been, as yet, barely acknowledged, let alone mourned within British society. But we also sketched out five ways in which the British empire was built on, and in turn built, exploitative, destructive fault lines both abroad and 'at home' – in terms of race, class, gender, ecological violence and the Christian/non-Christian divide – leaving a toxic legacy in our world today.

In Chapters 3 and 4, we teased out the impact of the first four of these fault lines (with the additional dimension of the marginalization of children) within our contemporary society, and within the Christian Church. On one side of these divisions, we explored the privilege and power that some of us benefit from, often unconsciously. But we also highlighted the ways in which these divisions produce forms of obliviousness – a 'power-related willingness-not-to-see' – that renders many humans and other creatures in our world unseen, unheard, devalued, pushed to the edges.

In this chapter, we have sketched out the two 'economies of mission' that, we suggest, dominate the thinking, talking, decision-making and resourcing of the Church of England, of which we are both a part, and quite possibly other denominations in other contexts too. What we've suggested here is that these dominant economies both set up and reinforce power-laden divisions between 'Christian' and 'non-Christian', and between 'centre' and 'edges', that mimic the power dynamics of empire and colonialism. These economies, moreover, further entrench the fault lines and obliviousnesses that haunt not only the Church's *outward*-looking relationships with its neighbours, but also the Church's *internal* economy of relationships. That is, they reinforce the ways in which Christians with multiple forms of power and privilege – who are defined as and define what is 'normal', and at the 'centre' – relate to other Christians: Christians who are 'othered' and pushed to the edges of both wider society and the Church. This seems to be true not just when we're caught up in the business of 'counting in' (the first economy), but also when we're engaged in the apparently 'selfless' labour of 'giving out' (the second economy).

Further reading

- Al Barrett, *Interrupting the Church's Flow: A radically receptive political theology in the urban margins* (London: SCM Press, 2020)
- Steve Corbett and Brian Finkkert, *When Helping Hurts: How to Alleviate Poverty without Hurting the Poor and Yourself* (Chicago, IL: Moody Publishers, 2014)
- John Drane, *The McDonaldization of the Church: Spirituality, Creativity and the Future of the Church* (London: Darton, Longman and Todd, 2000)
- Marion Grau, *Rethinking Mission in the Postcolony: Salvation, Society and Subversion* (London: T&T Clark, 2011)
- Ann Morisy, *Journeying Out: A New Approach to Christian Mission* (London: Morehouse, 2004)
- Stefan Paas, *Pilgrims and Priests: Christian Mission in a Post-Christian Society* (London: SCM Press, 2019)
- John V. Taylor, *The Christlike God* (London: SCM Press, 1992)

Questions for reflection/discussion

- What elements of the two 'economies' described in this chapter do you recognize from your own experience of church?
- Which of these temptations to 'heroic' power do you recognize as most seductive for you personally? And for the church(es) or organization(s) to which you belong?
- How do these temptations show themselves in practice? What strategies do/could you use to resist them?

6

Getting on the Wrong Side of Jesus

In this chapter, we'll continue thinking about the second economy we began to describe in the previous sections: the economy of 'giving out'. Having already outlined some of its dangers, we'll think more here about two things that keep us operating in 'giving out' mode – two things whose gravitational pulls are so strong they are very hard to escape. One is our understanding of what worship does to us. The other focuses on where we imagine Jesus to be present in the world.

Worship: 'filling us up' to 'give out'?

What do we think happens when we 'go to church'? If it's something *transformative*, what is it in us that is changed? If it's *formative* (and in many different church-related contexts we're talking a lot about 'formation'), in what ways is our participation in worship 'forming' us?

Whether you're from a sacramental tradition (with a regular sharing around the eucharistic, or communion, table) or one that is more focused on hearing and responding to the word of God, most acts of worship, at their simplest, have a four-fold structure: they begin by *gathering* people together; the *word* is read, spoken, preached and heard; we *respond* in some way to what we've heard; and the service concludes by *sending* us out into the world, to live our lives until we gather together again. In the Christian traditions that have been most formative for both of us, the *response* stage will often culminate in sharing in the Eucharist together – and the combination of *word* and *table* can often serve to reinforce some of the dynamics of formation that we're exploring here. So, for the moment, let's give some closer attention to that version of the 'worship cycle': Gathering – Word – Table – Sending – World.

One of the questions we might ask of this cycle – a question that runs right through this book – is, 'who is giving what, to whom?' In most Christian traditions, when it comes to the *word* stage of the circle, one person will read from the Bible, and everyone else will listen. Often, one person will then 'preach' (in some traditions, this will be someone who

74

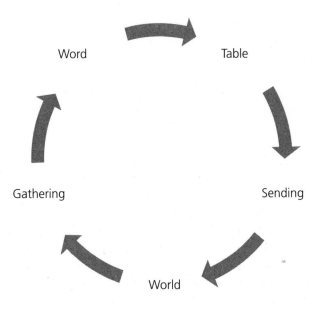

Figure 5: The 'cycle' of worship

is specially authorized to do so) – again, with everyone else listening. In traditions that gather around a eucharistic *table*, the person distributing the bread and wine of communion will often, again, be specially authorized to do so, and most other members of the congregation will be on the receiving end. The experience of worship, for the vast majority of those who are present, can be largely one of *coming to receive* – to hear God's word for us, to be fed around God's table.

At least since the 1990s, many Christian traditions have been much more attentive to the final phase of worship – *sending* people out into the *world* – as a critical aspect of 'what worship *does*'. The 'Decade of Evangelism' in the Church of England and a number of other denominations gave a new emphasis to the role of Christians not only as *worshippers* but as *evangelists*: as those who go out from worship to share the good news of Jesus in the world. This meant that worship began to be seen much more definitively as the place where Christians were *equipped* and *energized* for that task: we *hear* God's word in worship, to go and *proclaim* it in the world; we are *fed* around God's table in worship, to go out and *feed* others in the world. How often have we heard worship talked about as a spiritual 'filling-up' or 'refuelling' – after what presumably has been a 'draining' week out in the world? One of the Church of England's post-communion prayers in *Common Worship* expresses it more poetically:

May we who share Christ's body live his risen life;
we who drink his cup bring life to others;
we whom the Spirit lights give light to the world.[1]

Here, then, is the second economy, the 'giving out' economy, in a nut-shell: in worship the church *receives* from God, to *give out* to the world.

Where is Jesus?

If the trajectory of our worship is one significant factor that moulds our imaginations into the shape of the 'giving out' economy, then we want to suggest that an equally powerful factor is where we expect to experience the presence of Jesus in the world. For many of us Christians, 'the incarnation' was not just the presence of God in the first-century human being Jesus of Nazareth: we also want to talk about some kind of 'incarnational' approach to the world we live in today, through which we seek to recognize, or even embody, something of the character, or pattern, of the life of Jesus. While many of us are passionately committed to such an 'incarnational' approach, we can often be rather less than precise about what we mean by it – and, in the process, risk dangerously distorting our relationships with our neighbours.

What would Jesus do?

When both of us were growing up, many of our Christian friends would wear brightly coloured wristbands printed with the letters 'WWJD?' – What Would Jesus Do? The wristbands were meant to remind their wearers that, in every decision they made, in every word they spoke, in everything they did, they should ask themselves if they were being 'Christlike'. Were they reflecting the character of Jesus in the way they acted and spoke – in the ways they treated others?

It's not a bad question. The colourful wristbands are drawing on a much more ancient Christian tradition of *imitatio Christi* – the imitation of Christ.[2] And if 'WWJD?' tends to be more common at the 'evangelical' end of the spectrum of church tradition, then the more 'catholic' end has an equivalent: the understanding that Christians are to be 'the body of

1 *Common Worship: Services and Prayers for the Church of England* (London: Church House Publishing, 2000), p. 182.

2 The phrase is particularly associated with Thomas à Kempis, who wrote the classic devotional book *The Imitation of Christ* in the fifteenth century.

Christ' in the world. In the words attributed (possibly incorrectly) to St Teresa of Avila:

> Christ has no body now but yours.
> No hands, no feet on earth but yours.
> Yours are the eyes with which he looks
> with compassion on this world,
> yours are the feet with which he walks
> to do good,
> yours are the hands,
> with which he blesses all the world.

Notice how both of these traditions locate Jesus *in* the person, the actions, the body of the Christian. 'Following Jesus' (that's what the word *disciple* implies) here means, in some sense, putting ourselves in Jesus' place – even, we might sometimes dare to suggest, '*being* Jesus' to those we meet.

'I was hungry ...'

There's a second approach, almost the opposite of the first, but often deployed by the same people, in almost the same breath, for almost the same purpose (and we'll own up, we've done it ourselves often enough!). Where the first approach locates Jesus *in the Christian*, in relationship to their neighbour, the second approach locates Jesus *in the neighbour*, and grounds itself in one of the famous parables of judgement near the end of Matthew's Gospel:

> 'Then the king will say to those at his right hand, "Come, you that are blessed by my Father, inherit the kingdom prepared for you from the foundation of the world; for I was hungry and you gave me food, I was thirsty and you gave me something to drink, I was a stranger and you welcomed me, I was naked and you gave me clothing, I was sick and you took care of me, I was in prison and you visited me." Then the righteous will answer him, "Lord, when was it that we saw you hungry and gave you food, or thirsty and gave you something to drink? And when was it that we saw you a stranger and welcomed you, or naked and gave you clothing? And when was it that we saw you sick or in prison and visited you?" And the king will answer them, "Truly I tell you, just as you did it to one of the least of these who are members of my family, you did it to me."' (Matthew 25.34–40)

Taking Jesus at his word – and identifying him with 'the king' – in this parable, this second approach treats every hungry person, every thirsty person, every stranger, every person in need of clothes, every imprisoned person *as Jesus*. Whenever we feed the hungry, give a drink to the thirsty, welcome the stranger, clothe the naked, visit the prisoner, we are *serving Jesus* as directly, literally, physically as is possible to do in this world. Again, this is not a new idea, a novel interpretation of this ancient text. The Rule of St Benedict, the sixth-century foundation for many monastic communities across the world, commands the monk: 'All guests who present themselves are to be welcomed as Christ for he himself will say: "I was a stranger and you welcomed me."'[3]

But notice, now, what both this and the first approach do to the relationship between the Christian and their neighbour. In the first, the focus is on the Christian's 'Christlike' action, with the neighbour on the receiving end; in the second, the focus is on Jesus' presence in the neighbour, but the latter seen exclusively as a needy recipient of the Christian's compassionate activity. In both cases, the Christian is in the active role, taking the initiative, giving, serving; and the neighbour is in a passive role, on the receiving end, 'in need' (see the axis below).

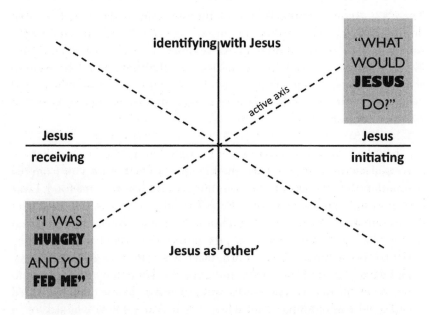

Figure 6: Where is Jesus? (active axis)

---

3 From the *Rule of Saint Benedict*, chapter 53. Versions of the *Rule* can be found in print and online – see www.osb.org.

Identifying with the divine

There are other possible ways of locating Jesus in our relationships with our neighbours – and we will explore two of them shortly. But if these first two happen to be the most common, the most dominant, in the ways we imagine and live out our Christian discipleship in the world, then we have a problem. Our relationships with others will tend to be lopsided. We will tend to gravitate towards activity, 'doing for' others, taking the initiative, speaking more than listening, placing ourselves 'centre-stage', imagining it ultimately all comes down to us.

Jennifer Harvey is a 'critical white theologian' from the USA. It's a relatively new sub-discipline of theology, that begins from a critical examination of the ways in which 'whiteness' distorts and disfigures the attitudes, behaviours and relationships of those who, by the colour of their skin and the embedded structures of our society, are racialized as 'white'. It just so happens, Harvey observes, that placing ourselves in the centre of our stories, 'doing for' others and 'working on behalf' of others in ways that are paternalistic, are just the kinds of patterns of behaviour that white people have already been 'trained' in, through their invisible schooling in whiteness. And it just so happens, Harvey goes on, that such 'broken ways of being' towards which white people are already prone, 'are likely to be triggered, maybe even amplified', by identifying with a 'social justice Jesus who is the central power-agent in his saga', the 'superhero standing up to evil forces around him and attempting to inveigh on behalf of suffering others'. 'Simply put,' she concludes: 'identifying with the divine is about the last thing that a white person whose life is embedded in white-supremacist structures should be doing.'[4]

When I (Al) first read these words, they hit me between the eyes like a small, smooth stone from David's slingshot. That was it! Of course, I'd never consciously wandered around imagining I was actually God, but I realized in that moment that for so much of my life as a Christian I had been putting myself in 'the Jesus place' in Gospel stories, and in day-to-day encounters, and more specifically, in the place of a busy, active Jesus (exemplified, perhaps, in the larger part of Mark's Gospel) who seems to be constantly rushing around, teaching, healing, hosting, feeding, turning over tables, and so on. And what Jennifer Harvey's words brought home to me most intensely was that not only was this way of being profoundly unhealthy for me, it was also profoundly unhelpful for those I

---

4 Jennifer Harvey, 'What Would Zacchaeus Do? The Case for Disidentifying with Jesus', in George Yancy (ed.), *Christology and Whiteness: What Would Jesus Do?* (New York: Routledge, 2012), pp. 94–5.

was interacting with. It only served to reinforce, perpetuate, deepen, the power imbalances that were often already between us, with me being the multiply privileged white, middle-class, straight, able-bodied male ordained minister that I inescapably am.

And I realized, the more this difficult truth sank in, that although Harvey's words are first and foremost about whiteness, they could also be translated meaningfully into some of the other dimensions of power and privilege we've been considering: identifying with the divine is about the last thing that ...

- a *white person* whose life is embedded in *white supremacist* structures ...
- a *man* whose life is embedded in *patriarchal* structures ...
- a *middle-class person* whose life is embedded in *unjust economic (i.e. 'class-ridden')* structures ...
- an *adult* whose life is embedded in *child-marginalizing* structures ...
- a *human being* whose life is embedded in *ecocidal ('world-destroying')* structures ...[5]

... should be doing.

Of course, the danger of 'identifying with the divine' does depend, critically, on how we understand 'the divine' to operate, and relate to us. We will return to this question in Part 3, especially at the beginning of Chapter 15. But for the moment, we want to make just one observation. Even if, as Sam Wells has repeatedly argued, those of us who benefit from structural privilege rightly shift our focus from 'doing for' to *'being with'*,[6] we should just note how tempting it can be to hold on to an identification with the divine, placing ourselves in Jesus' shoes in more subtly 'heroic' ways: we decide to 'be with' others because that is how Jesus is with his others, that is how *God* is with us. It can too easily gloss over those multiple structural injustices in which we're entangled that might

---

5 This last suggestion might need a little further clarification. Of course, the meaning of Jesus' incarnation is precisely God's becoming human, God's identification with us human beings. But in Jesus, God also identified Godself *against* abusive, exploitative forms of human power. Imagining ourselves as exercising God's 'dominion' as we abuse and exploit the more-than-human world has been, as we saw in Chapter 4, one of the recurring failings of much Christian theology, especially where that theology has been entangled with a dualistic, patriarchal and colonialist worldview. Harvey's path of 'dis-identification with the divine' is a challenge too, then, for those of us human beings still caught up in such ways, and wider social and economic structures, of living in the world. We need to find radically different ways of configuring the relationship between ourselves, our human and other-than-human creature-kin, and God.

6 See for example Samuel Wells, *A Nazareth Manifesto: Being with God* (Chichester: Wiley Blackwell, 2015), and *Incarnational Mission: Being with the World* (Norwich: Canterbury Press, 2018).

well mean, for our 'othered' neighbours (and many of our Christian siblings within the Church too), that us attempting to 'be with' them 'incarnationally' – 'as God' – is, as Jennifer Harvey puts it, about the last thing that they want or need from us. It might also – to get ahead of ourselves a little – be a subtle attempt to predetermine how our 'othered' neighbours (and Christian siblings) engage with *us*, ruling out – however consciously or unconsciously – forms of agency and ways of engagement that might be more proactive, more disruptive, than 'being with' implies. Our 'being with' our neighbours, we're suggesting in this book, needs to make space also for our 'being interrupted' by them, and for all kinds of divinely inspired and divinely energized ways of 'being' and 'doing' beyond the spaces that we inhabit, let alone understand or control.

Questions for reflection/discussion

- If you recognize one or more dimensions of structural privilege in your identity, where in your life have you been tempted to put yourself in 'the Jesus place' or 'identify with the divine'?
- Have you been a member of a church or organization that collectively, in its words and/or actions, has put itself in 'the Jesus place' or 'identified with the divine'?
- Where else in your experience of church (or beyond) have you seen this dynamic in action?

What would Zacchaeus do?

We've now reached the point of no return – at least in our journey through this book! In our experience, once you've *seen* the privilege that was previously invisible – once the penny has dropped – it's impossible to 'unsee' it. The world looks different, and irreversibly so. And although it might be tempting to imagine that this new insight is, itself, a kind of 'privileged wisdom', what you're now able to see is, in fact, part of the reality that many of your human kin have lived and breathed every moment of their lives.

But what, now, can we *do*? There is a real possibility that the 'small, smooth stone' of realization might do to us something similar to what David's stone did to Goliath: bring us to the floor and paralyse us from any further action. That paralysis might be an effect of *guilt*: realizing our own involvement – through what we have *done*, wittingly or unwittingly, and though the ways in which we have *failed* to act or speak out – in histories and structures of injustice. And for some of us, guilt might slip into *shame*: a sense that there is something not just about our *actions*, but about *who we are*, our very sense of our self, that isn't right or good. Both guilt and shame can become a pit that we feel unable to get out of.

Which is where Zacchaeus comes in.

He entered Jericho and was passing through it. A man was there named Zacchaeus; he was a chief tax collector and was rich. He was trying to see who Jesus was, but on account of the crowd he could not, because he was short in stature. So he ran ahead and climbed a sycamore tree to see him, because he was going to pass that way. When Jesus came to the place, he looked up and said to him, 'Zacchaeus, hurry and come down; for I must stay at your house today.' So he hurried down and was happy to welcome him. All who saw it began to grumble and said, 'He has gone to be the guest of one who is a sinner.' Zacchaeus stood there and said to the Lord, 'Look, half of my possessions, Lord, I will give to the poor; and if I have defrauded anyone of anything, I will pay back four times as much.' Then Jesus said to him, 'Today salvation has come to this house, because he too is a son of Abraham. For the Son of Man came to seek out and to save the lost.' (Luke 19.1–10)

Jennifer Harvey suggests to those of us who are racialized as white in societies entangled in white supremacism, that rather than identifying ourselves with Jesus and asking, 'What Would Jesus Do?', we identify instead with Zacchaeus:

> What we know about Zacchaeus is that when he encountered Jesus he did so as someone who had been utterly complicit with the powers that be. Just like white people in [white supremacist societies], he had forsaken brotherhood and sisterhood, and been seduced into allegiance with death-dealing power structures. He had been massively and unjustly enriched by way of this allegiance. Despite sharing a religious-ethnic heritage with Jesus, he was Jesus' structural enemy.[7]

When Jesus encountered Zacchaeus, however, Zacchaeus didn't hang on defensively to the allegiances that had given him privilege and power up until that point. He chose the path of 'radical conversion', switched his loyalties – committed 'treason', even. He also disrupts and reverses the flow of money that had enriched him: from extracting money from others with ruthless consistency, he now gives it away freely – making reparations to the victims of his exploitation, but also freeing himself from money's stranglehold:

> Evidence of this conversion was not his mere verbal declaration of belief in Jesus' divine mission or social vision. Nor was it a declaration that he would become Jesus' disciple. Rather, the evidence of Zacchaeus' conversion came when he determined to give half of his wealth to the poor and to repay anyone whom he had defrauded with four times what he had taken.[8]

It was to Zacchaeus' response of both repentance and reparation that Jesus affirmed that 'salvation has come to this house'. White people committed to justice, Jennifer Harvey suggests, can discover in Zacchaeus a model for figuring out ways to become conscious of our whiteness and the privilege and power that comes with it, and to 'go back through our whiteness and become traitors to it', so that we are freed to find a new loyalty to our shared humanity.[9]

---

7 Harvey, 'What Would Zacchaeus Do?', p. 98.
8 Harvey, 'What Would Zacchaeus Do?', p. 98.
9 Harvey, 'What Would Zacchaeus Do?', p. 99.

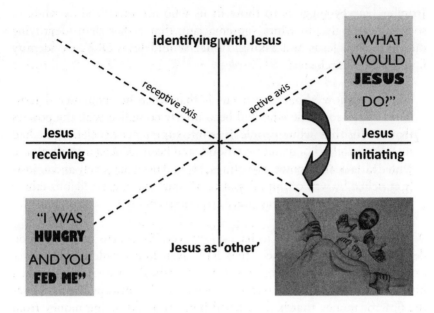

Figure 7: 'What would Zacchaeus do?' (dis-identifying with Jesus)

Dis-identifying with Jesus, or identifying differently?

Whether it is in the race privilege of our whiteness, the gender privilege of our maleness or the economic privilege of our middle-classness; whether it is in our age-related power as adults, or our capacity for unthinking ecological destruction as human beings, Jennifer Harvey's challenge is for us to let go of our addictions to being first to speak or act, central to the story, the heroic providers, performers and possessors. She challenges those of us with any kind of structural power or privilege to dis-identify with a Jesus who might reinforce any of those forms of power, and points us to Zacchaeus as a model of disentangling himself from the exploitative structures that gave him wealth, security and status.

We will return to Jennifer Harvey's challenge in Part 3. But before we do, we need to reposition ourselves a little – come out of Zacchaeus' tree, perhaps, and mingle with the crowd – and ask, of our images of Jesus in general, and of Mark's Gospel in particular, is Harvey's 'social justice Jesus' the only Jesus on offer? Is Jesus really, always, 'the central power agent in his saga', always taking the initiative, always 'giving out' for the good, and the transformation, of others? *What if Jesus himself is interrupted, disrupted, changed, by (at least some of) his encounters with those around him?* That will be our key question in Part 2.

Further reading

- Jennifer Harvey's 'What Would Zacchaeus Do?', and other chapters in George Yancy (ed.), *Christology and Whiteness: What Would Jesus Do?* (New York: Routledge, 2012)

Questions for reflection/discussion

- How do you feel about the character of Zacchaeus – how easy or difficult do you find it to identify with him, and why?
- Can you think of any examples of when you have heard somebody identify themselves with Jesus? What did you find helpful or unhelpful about that, and why?

PART 2

Being Interrupted

Interruptions in Mark's Gospel: Finding Our Way In

The next five chapters pay close attention to five stories in Mark's Gospel. Each of them is an encounter between Jesus and someone – or some-thing – else: three are encounters with different women, one is with some children, and one is with a tree! All of them, in different ways, *interrupt* and *disrupt* Jesus' activity, his direction of travel, his agenda. In most of the encounters – but not quite all of them – we see Jesus receiving those interruptions in ways that *change* him.

We are aware that we read three of these stories differently. As we explored in Chapter 1, each of our identities is more complex than simply 'a man' or 'a woman', and with any character in any story we will find some experiences we have in common, and many ways in which we are very different. But in the three encounters between the man Jesus and a woman, our own gender means that we naturally tend to gravitate towards identifying with one character or the other: Al with the man Jesus, Ruth with the female character in each story. And the power-rela-tionships negotiated between Jesus and his female 'others' has a lot to do with gender, in each of these stories, even if other factors are also at play. We have therefore chosen to offer our different readings of these encoun-ters, one after another: Al (with Jesus) on 'being interrupted', Ruth (with the woman) on 'interrupting'.

As we have teased out throughout the first part of this book, however, the male-female gender binary is not the only form of privilege and hier-archy that our societies, our cultures and our churches press upon us. So, more dangerously, we might also read these stories through one of these other lenses: as *whiteness* interrupted by a person of colour; as middle-classness interrupted by a person from a working-class background; and, as Chapters 10 and 11 testify more directly, as adults interrupted by children, and humans interrupted by other-than-human creatures.

In each of the short chapters that follows, we offer an image (drawn by the priest and artist, Ally Barrett), the biblical text (from the New Revised Standard Version), and – before our reflections – some 'wondering' questions. These wonderings are rooted in the tradition of Godly Play, an approach to the Christian faith that places a high priority on open, questioning exploration of our treasure-trove of stories. Godly Play practitioners may recognize that these are not necessarily wondering questions in the traditional Godly Play form – they may be more focused towards drawing our attention towards particular themes or ideas, and they will necessarily be shaped by their location as part of this book – but the intention is the same as with Godly Play wondering: to create an open space in which there are no 'right' answers, but an invitation to go deeper and allow ourselves to be formed and shaped by the God we encounter through Scripture.

Last, before we enter the world of Mark's Gospel, we offer four possible 'ways in' to engaging with the biblical text, either in a group context or on your own. Some of them may be familiar to you, and some may be novel and even a bit strange. But each of them approaches the biblical text as a living thing to be encountered, rather than merely a document to be analysed. If you find one or more of these helpful, then we encourage you to use them. If you have your own preferred ways of encountering the text, then why not dive in right now, to Chapter 7!

'Re-membering' the story

This is a deceptively simple way of engaging with Scripture without using written Bibles, developed by Janet Lees, a speech therapist and minister in the United Reformed Church.[1] Everyone can get involved – young and old, and of all abilities – and it can both fire imaginations and bring out a multitude of different perspectives and experiences.

At its simplest, it involves getting the whole group to try and *remember* the Bible story between them, to piece it together – 're-member' it – from their different memories of it. As Lees herself says: 'try not to worry that people will remember the wrong thing, or get it wrong in some other way. It is true that sometimes details get mixed up or missed out in the remembering ... One person's version of a remembered text is likely to be different to another's, but that does not make it wrong ... It is possible that on occasions an important bit gets forgotten. Of course, that begs the question of how an important bit is defined.' She suggests several approaches the facilitator might take:

• wait for a while, as silence is not a waste of time;

---

1 Janet Lees, *Word of Mouth: Using the remembered Bible for building community* (Glasgow: Wild Goose Publications, 2007).

- prompt the group gently, as in a big group there is often someone who remembers, even if only sketchily;
- leave it out this time, as it may get remembered another day.

The key to facilitating this method is offering *clues* to help the group remember the story. Lees suggests various ways of doing that:

- on a flip-chart, offer headings for the main sections of the story, and invite the group to fill in the gaps;
- present the story as a series of half-finished sentences, and invite the group to finish off each sentence in turn;
- offer some toys, cut-outs, puppets or other props to represent the characters in the story, and invite some members of the group to move them around, as directed by other group members;
- the facilitator acts out the story, 'charades' style, inviting people to shout out what they think is going on as you go.

Lees' final suggestion is what she calls the 'go for it method': offer a familiar title or name often given to the story, name the central characters, or tell people where the story took place, and see what emerges from there. In this book, we offer an image intended to evoke a remembering of each story – you might want simply to start the group off with the image.

In 're-membering' the story together, some prompting questions might help:

- who features in the story?
- where does it happen?
- how did it begin?
- what happened?
- who said what?
- how did it end?

Reading the verbs first

A different method requires a much closer attention to the written text – closer attention than we often pay when we think we're 'reading' it. Anna Carter Florence teaches trainee ministers to preach, but what she's *really* interested in, she says, is helping groups of people encounter Scripture together as a community. 'The biblical text is a wild thing, and it takes us to where the wild things are. When we read Scripture in community, we have no idea what will happen or where it will take us, except that whatever it is won't look like anything we know – it is the wild and free vision of God's reign, breaking its way in.'[2]

The echoes of Maurice Sendak's classic children's book, *Where the Wild Things Are* is deliberate: 'We need to put on our wolf suits, like young Max in the story, and sail away... Which is really another way of saying we need a reading space where we can make mischief of one sort or another (as Sendak puts it) ... with the biblical text.' At the heart of Florence's approach is to notice, explore, play with *what happens* in the text, and that means 'reading the verbs'. Often, when we read Scripture, we get fixated on the 'nouns' – the *things*, the *names*, the *places* – which are so often, Florence suggests, 'just so distractingly *not* of our world'. They're so often strange to us, and that strangeness distances us from the text.

But the verbs, on the other hand, are much more familiar. Verbs, as you may remember from school, are the 'doing words'. 'We all have verbs – the same ones, actually. You and I share verbs with Adam and Eve, Abraham and Sarah, Moses and Miriam, Ruth and Naomi. We share verbs with Mary and Joseph, Peter, James and John, Martha, Lydia and Paul. We even share verbs with Jesus. You may not know what a Samaritan is, but you definitely know his verbs (came near, saw, was moved with pity, poured oil, bandaged, put on his own animal, brought, took care of, took out two denarii, gave, came back, repaid, showed mercy) ...'

To help us read the verbs of a Bible story, Florence offers us some questions:

- Who gets what verbs?
- What's the order of those verbs?
- What do the verb tense and mood tell you? (When did something happen and how long has it been going on? Where are the 'imperative' commands, the 'interrogative' questions, the 'if ... then ...' conditionals, and the 'indicative' statements of fact? And so on ...)
- What do the verbs stir or evoke in you? What do you remember about them from the times you or others have played them?
- Are these verbs associated with certain groups or people? Are they used to stereotype or make broad generalizations?
- If you run the verbs through your biblical echo chamber, what do you hear?

---

2 Anna Carter Florence, *Rehearsing Scripture: Discovering God's Word in Community* (Grand Rapids, MI: Eerdmans, 2018), p. 7.

- If God is a character in this verse, how are God's verbs different from the others?
- Do any of the verbs surprise you? Why? What were you expecting?
- Did you spot any adjectives?
- And what about those nouns?

Sculpting the encounters

A third method draws on the work of Augusto Boal, the Brazilian theatre-maker, theorist and activist who developed the 'Theatre of the Oppressed'. Boal's work is all about exposing *power* at work, in our relationships and interactions, in the structures that 'place' us within our societies, our world. He was interested in turning 'spectators', watching the action from the edges, into 'spect*actors*' – joining in the action and playing their part in making change.[3] The suggestions here are Al's rather than Boal's, but profoundly inspired by his approach.

In each of the stories of Chapters 7 to 11 (including Jesus and the fig tree in Chapter 11, but maybe not including the parable of the mustard seed!), there is an *encounter* between Jesus and someone else. In many of the stories there are other people too, looking on at this encounter and engaging with it in different ways. This method works best if members of the group are willing to inhabit the roles of:

- Jesus
- The person (or people) in direct encounter with Jesus
- Any onlookers.

In each encounter, for each of these characters, begin by doing the 'I am ...' exercise from the beginning of Chapter 1. What words would they use to describe themselves? What words does the biblical text give us, and what other words might we imaginatively add?

As a second stage, together identify within the story a few key moments of interaction (we've suggested some of them by inserting [*] within the texts below). Within the group, read the story out loud, and when you get to one of those key moments, pause. In the pause, invite those inhabiting the story's main roles to form a *tableau* – a static scene, showing the characters interacting with each other.

---

3 Augusto Boal, *Games for Actors and Non-Actors*, 2nd edition (London: Routledge, 2002).

A third stage, at each pause, would be to invite the 'actors', and those other members of the group who are watching, to speak. Open questions that people might want to respond to include:

- What are you *feeling/thinking* right now (in role, or as yourself)?
- What do you *notice* about the scene?
- Which of the character's 'I am …' statements is at play in this moment?
- What *questions* do you want to ask?
- What do you want to *change* about this scene?

A fourth stage, again at each moment of pause in the story, would invite members of the 'audience' to come forward and 'sculpt' the scene – to reshape the actors' positions, gestures, even facial expressions – either to better reflect how they imagine the encounter in the text, or to provocatively retell the encounter: 'what if …?'[4]

Lectio divina

These two Latin words simply mean 'divine reading', and name an ancient method of reading the Bible, practised for generations by many monastic orders. The exact shape of *lectio divina* varies, but here we'll outline a simple form that we have often used in our church community in Hodge Hill:

- Begin with a time of silence and stillness, getting ready to encounter God through reading and prayer.
- Someone reads the passage out loud, followed by a time of silent reflection.
- The passage is read a second time, followed by this invitation: 'Is there a word or phrase that particularly stands out for you?'
- Anyone who wants to, can speak that word or phrase out loud, or quietly to themselves.
- The passage is then read a third time, followed by this invitation: 'What do you find yourself noticing, or wondering, in this passage?'
- Again, anyone who wants to, can say something out loud, or quietly to themselves.

---

4 There is something profoundly vulnerable about the role of being 'sculpted' by others. See the section in Chapter 15 on 'being sculpted' for some reflections on power and safeguarding in relation to this.

- The passage is then read a fourth time, followed by this invitation: 'What do you sense God is saying to you through this passage, today? What prayer do you sense forming inside you?'
- There is an opportunity for people to share what they are hearing, or what they want to offer to God in prayer.
- The time of reflection finishes with stillness and silence, as we hold ourselves and all we have heard and shared, within God's love.

Whether you choose to play with one of the methods suggested above, or engage with the story a different way entirely, we invite you to spend some time with each biblical story itself first, before re-engaging a second time, prompted by the questions and reflections we offer here.

Further reading

- Augusto Boal, *Games for Actors and Non-Actors*, 2nd edition (London: Routledge, 2002)
- Anna Carter Florence, *Rehearsing Scripture: Discovering God's Word in Community* (Grand Rapids, MI: Eerdmans, 2018)
- Janet Lees, *Word of Mouth: Using the remembered Bible for building community* (Glasgow: Wild Goose Publications, 2007)

7

On the Road

And a large crowd followed him and pressed in on him. Now there was a woman who had been suffering from haemorrhages for twelve years. She had endured much under many physicians, and had spent all that she had; and she was no better, but rather grew worse. She had heard about Jesus, and came up behind him in the crowd and touched his cloak, for she said, 'If I but touch his clothes, I will be made well.' [*] Immediately her haemorrhage stopped; and she felt in her body that she was healed of her disease. Immediately aware that power had gone forth from him, Jesus turned about in the crowd and said, 'Who touched my clothes?' And his disciples said to him, 'You see the crowd pressing in on you; how can you say, "Who touched me?"' He looked all around to see who had done it. [*] But the woman, knowing what had happened to her, came in fear and trembling, fell down before him, and told him the whole truth. [*] He said to her, 'Daughter, your faith has made you well; go in peace, and be healed of your disease.' (Mark 5.24b–34)

Wonderings

- I wonder what it felt like to be moving along in that crowd; for Jesus; for the disciples; for the woman?
- I wonder what happened when the woman touched Jesus' cloak; for the woman; for Jesus?
- I wonder what had to happen for the woman and Jesus to come face to face?
- I wonder what 'the whole truth' was, that the woman told Jesus?
- I wonder what difference the encounter made; to the woman; to Jesus; to the onlookers?

Following through the story

Jesus is on the move. One of the leaders of the synagogue, Jairus, is bringing Jesus to his house so that Jesus can heal his dying daughter. There's a sense of urgency. They are in a hurry.

And a large crowd is moving with them, pressing in on them.

And in the crowd is a woman. A woman who has been bleeding, badly, for 12 years. Her flow of blood hasn't stopped, but her flow of money has – the doctors have bled her dry, financially at least.

But she has heard about Jesus. A rumour on the grapevine. And she finds him, in the crowd, comes up behind him and touches him.

And two things happen. Immediately.Immediately her bleeding stops. She knows it. She knows in her body that healing has come.

And immediately, Jesus is aware that power has flowed out of him. But he does not know why, or how. But it stops him in his tracks. It interrupts his flow, his purpose, his haste. It turns him round.

'Who touched me?' he asks, and those around him point out that, in a jostling crowd, this is an odd question to ask. But in the midst of the mass of people, Jesus knows, at least, that there is a 'someone': someone whose touch has brought him to a standstill.

The woman was behind him. Now, as he has turned, she is in front of him. As she falls down at his feet, might we imagine that Jesus kneels down too, so that they are face to face, eye to eye? Only then can they have a conversation.

What a conversation! She, in fear and trembling, tells him the whole truth. The word for truth (Greek *alétheia*), is theologically heavy: truth is usually Jesus' domain! And yet here, *she* presents the whole of it to *him*. And in return, this stranger, this unnamed, unknown woman, the Son of God names 'Daughter'. Kin. Part of the family – part of *God's* family.

Then he sends her on her way with the knowledge of her healing. Healing that she has already known – in her body – before he was even aware of what happened.

Being interrupted

In the fifth chapter of Mark's Gospel, this unnamed woman disappears – goes on her way – as quickly and as unobtrusively as she first appeared in the midst of the crowd. Her encounter with Jesus could almost be incidental to Mark's bigger narrative – the accidental cause behind the much more dramatic moment that is to come: Jesus raising Jairus' daughter from death. *This* woman is merely the brief delay that makes *that* story 'work'.

But there is something much more significant going on here. In much of Mark's Gospel, Jesus is on the move, often with a clear sense of purpose and direction. For most of Mark's narrative (at least up to chapter 14), it is mostly *Jesus* who is active, who takes the initiative, who appears to be in charge of events – and others who respond to him, and follow in his wake. But here, in this passage – in passing, we might say – that sense of purpose and direction, initiative and drive, is interrupted, disrupted, brought to a (temporary) halt.

The initiative here belongs entirely to the woman. From first hearing about him from afar, she slowly but surely closes the gap between them and, touching him, triggers a flow of power from Jesus that is beyond Jesus' control, intention or even awareness. She is healed before Jesus is even conscious of her presence. When, finally, he says 'your faith has made you well', he is simply naming what has already happened – responding to 'the whole truth' that *she* has told *him*. Her 'faith' has been in her movement, her approach, her touching, her telling – her 'act of entrustment',[1] bridging the gap between herself and Jesus, reconfiguring their relationship in a way that Jesus only gradually comes to understand. Many commentators on this passage make much of the fact that the woman, by her bleeding, would have been ritually unclean within usual Jewish understandings of purity – and by touching Jesus, would have made him ritually unclean too. But neither the narrator, nor any character in the story, seems remotely interested in this – other than to

---

1 The phrase is Graham Ward's (*Christ and Culture*, p. 63). Ward's reflections on this passage are behind much of the direction of this section, but read through a critical feminist lens, especially with Sigridur Gudmarsdottir, 'Touch, Flux, Relation: Feminist Critique of Graham Ward's "The Schizoid Christ"', in Lisa Isherwood and M. Zlomislic (eds), *The Poverty of Radical Orthodoxy* (Eugene, OR: Wipf and Stock, 2012).

highlight and compound the initial distance between her and Jesus. What the narrator describes is a new space created by the woman's touch and her truth-telling: a space in which those things that have been in flow (her blood, her money, Jesus and the crowd) have been brought to a standstill, and that which was held in (the power in Jesus) has been made to flow; a space in which distances and divisions are bridged, parallel worlds are brought intimately together, anonymity is turned into kinship.

Interrupting

The woman in this story – not named, as women in Scripture so often are not – has frequently been seen by commentators as little more than a plot device in the Gospel narrative. Perhaps for some commentators (many of them male, many of them privileged in various other ways) taking seriously this woman's interruption of Jesus would be too much of a disruption to their own chosen hermeneutic, their own way of interpreting Scripture.

But we must take this woman seriously. She seriously disrupts not only the narrative, but also the assumptions of the reader, the disciples, the crowd and perhaps even Jesus himself. So, what is she interrupting?

As we have seen, she is interrupting the narrative. The action of the narrative up to this point is dynamic, fast-paced. I can imagine Jesus striding purposefully towards Jairus' house, with the crowd and hurrying and jostling around him. Until, suddenly and immediately, the woman brings all that to a standstill. By her action, she literally stops Jesus in his tracks.

And in that stopping, that pause which the woman creates in the narrative, all sorts of other things are interrupted, and patterns of thought and action are challenged, changed and disrupted.

The woman interrupts the flow of power. That power which had seemed to lie with Jesus, which had seemed to be able to be influenced by the powerful leaders of the synagogue, this unnamed woman now claims for herself. And Jesus allows her to do so, allows his own power to be interrupted and intercepted by her.

She also interrupts the drive to always be doing something, the compulsion towards continual busy-ness. Mark's Gospel is a particularly action-focused narrative, and here we see Jesus on his way to do something, to solve a problem, to sort things out for people. Until he is interrupted. And in this encounter, Jesus does nothing.

By bringing the narrative to a standstill, the woman challenges the idea that power is bound up in action. Here we see that stopping the action is a form of action in itself, and can be a transformative one. Perhaps it is not too much of a stretch to see parallels between this woman's interruption and the disruptive power of direct action.

Finally, and perhaps most importantly, the woman interrupts Jesus' agency. For most of the Gospel narrative, we see Jesus doing things and other people responding. Here it is the woman who acts, and Jesus who responds. She turns the expected power dynamics of the encounter on their head, and Jesus is a willing participant in the disruption which she initiates.

Questions the story asks us

- What questions might this story be asking; of you; of the churches/ communities/organizations to which you belong?
- What, for you, might *get in the way* of genuine person-to-person encounters that transform you both?

  - A clear direction and purpose, or urgent needs and demands, that produce a kind of 'tunnel vision'?
  - A jostling crowd – of people, or tasks, or concerns – in which one particular person might get lost?
  - A fear of criticism, or a lack of understanding, from others – if you were to stop and attend to this particular person, here and now?
  - Social divisions that make some people 'others' to you (e.g. race, class, gender, dis/ability, sexuality, etc.)?
  - Something else?

- What might need to change – for you personally, or in your church, community or organization – for you to be more open to being interrupted?
- How can we interrupt the continual drive to busy-ness, in our own lives and the life of our communities?
- How might God be calling us to interrupt the flow of power?

Further reading

- Frances Taylor Gench, *Back to the Well: Women's Encounters with Jesus in the Gospels* (Louisville, KY: Westminster John Knox Press, 2004)

8

At the Edges

From there he set out and went away to the region of Tyre. He entered a house and did not want anyone to know he was there. Yet he could not escape notice, but a woman whose little daughter had an unclean spirit immediately heard about him, and she came and bowed down at his feet. Now the woman was a Gentile, of Syrophoenician origin. She begged him to cast the demon out of her daughter. He said to her, 'Let the children be fed first, for it is not fair to take the children's food and throw it to the dogs.' [*] But she answered him, 'Sir, even the dogs under the table eat the children's crumbs.' [*] Then he said to her, 'For saying that, you may go – the demon has left your daughter.' So she went home, found the child lying on the bed, and the demon gone. (Mark 7.24–30)

Wonderings

- I wonder what Jesus was doing in this region, a long way from home?
- I wonder why Jesus responded to her the way that he did?
- I wonder how the woman felt about Jesus' response?
- I wonder what difference the encounter made ... to the woman; to Jesus; to any onlookers?

Following through the story

Jesus is far from home. He is 'up north', about as far away from Galilee – and indeed from the capital city Jerusalem – as he can get. And he's looking to go unnoticed, to go 'under the radar' for a while.

But word has spread, and a woman comes and finds him. Her daughter is sick, and she is desperate. She begs Jesus to cast out the demon. One word from him would do it.

Jesus, however, is unmoved. The woman, a local to the area, is a Gentile. She is not one of the children of Israel. She is not his concern right now. And he tells her as much, reminding her, in passing, that she is one of the 'dogs'.

The woman, however, is not taking No for an answer. Determined, persisting, she takes his No, his demeaning insult, and turns it around on him: 'even the dogs under the table eat the children's crumbs'.

And for saying that, Jesus responds, her daughter is healed.

Being interrupted

We are right at the edges of the world of Mark's Gospel, but at the very centre of his narrative. Of the short 15-and-a-bit chapters that make up the book of Mark, we find ourselves towards the end of chapter 7. And this is a turning point, in every sense.

And although 'in the region of Tyre' the woman is at home and Jesus is the foreigner, in Mark's story (centred on Jesus and, ultimately, Jerusalem) she is pretty much the ultimate outsider: a woman, a Syro-Phoenician, a Gentile. In crude, black-and-white terms (and that is the kind of 'flattening' through which prejudice operates), she is not one of 'the children', so she is one of 'the dogs'.

Although many commentators on this passage fall over themselves to come up with an alternative explanation, Jesus' response to her deploys a term of racist abuse. It would have been in common usage in the society in which Jesus grew up and lived and moved. He probably first heard the word used in the school playground, or its first-century equivalent. But I wonder what his mother would have said, if she'd heard it cross his lips? Had she brought him up to be better than that?

The woman, however, is unfazed. What she wants is healing for her daughter and so she takes his No (which is both a 'not for you' and also, we readers understand, a 'not *yet*'), she *accepts* it (some versions have her saying '*Yes*, Lord ...'), but with a clever twist: in Jesus' picture of food, children and dogs, the dogs *do* get fed, she reminds him – even if it's a matter of scavenging the crumbs that fall from the table. Her verbal 'judo'[1] is an example of what Sam Wells has called 'overaccepting' – a term used in improvised theatre to describe a way of 'accepting' what another actor has said or done, even if it is apparently unpromising, unhelpful or even hostile, and making something more of it in the light of a bigger picture, a larger story. Rather than 'blocking', which refuses, ignores or closes down what someone else is 'offering', overaccepting is 'an active way of receiving ... without losing the initiative'.[2] And it is through her clever use of words here, Jesus tells her – the Greek he uses (in verse 29) for 'word', *logos*, is the same word used in John's Gospel for '*the* Word – that the woman's daughter is healed.

Has the healing happened, as for the woman with the haemorrhage, independent of Jesus' conscious decision, and solely due to the woman's (faith-full) initiative and verbal dexterity? Or just as striking, has this determined woman changed Jesus' mind? Again, many commentators resist the latter interpretation, but there is good evidence for this being 'a moment of initiation', a turning-point, for Jesus.

First, we have already noted that this encounter happens at the geographical edge of Jesus' ministry. He comes here, apparently, to escape. He gets into an exchange with this woman. And then without any further ado, he turns around and heads back towards Galilee (verse 31). In spatial terms, his encounter with the Syro-Phoenician woman causes him to turn 180 degrees, back the way he came.

Second, if we follow the crumbs of bread out in either direction in Mark's narrative from this 'hinge' story, we will quickly come across a couple of stories where bread, in Jesus' hands, feeds thousands of people.

---

1 My reading of this story (including the term 'verbal judo') owes much to an article by Jim Perkinson, 'A Canaanitic Word in the *Logos* of Christ; or The Difference the Syro-Phoenician Woman Makes to Jesus', *Semeia* 75 (1996), pp. 61–85.

2 Samuel Wells, *Improvisation: The Drama of Christian Ethics* (Grand Rapids, MI: Brazos Press, 2004), pp. 131ff. Where Wells suggests that in 'provok[ing] Jesus into healing her daughter' the woman has 'imitated his practice faithfully' (p. 138), however, we are suggesting here, with Jim Perkinson, that it is *the woman* who is in fact schooling *Jesus*.

In Mark 6.30–44, Jesus feeds over 5,000 people, with 12 baskets left over. And in Mark 8.1–10, Jesus feeds about 4,000 people, with seven baskets left over. Now if the number 12 stands in, repeatedly in the Bible, for the tribes of the children of Israel, *seven* is the number of completeness, of totality, of *all creation*. There is a strong suggestion – and Mark is a cleverer storyteller than he has often been credited – that Jesus has gone from feeding a crowd of Jews, to a crowd which includes Gentiles, via his eye-opening, horizon-widening, ministry-enlarging encounter with the Gentile woman in the region of Tyre. We may be profoundly unsettled by the idea of Jesus *repenting*, but here we see in Jesus quite literally a *metanoia* (Greek for both repenting and 'turning around') – and it is the Syro-Phoenician woman's doing.

Interrupting

The Syro-Phoenician woman does not just interrupt Jesus, and disrupt his way of thinking. She also disrupts and interrupts the established power dynamics and social norms of her society. For her, a woman and a Gentile, to interrupt Jesus is a radical, brave and risky thing to do. For Jesus to allow and engage with that disruption is also radical and risky.

For Jesus, who in this encounter holds all the power and privilege, being receptive to interruption – and interruption by a woman at that – is a radical, countercultural and transformative move.

For the woman, on the other hand, it is her refusal to be passively receptive that is transformational. By interrupting and challenging Jesus, she is refusing to accept the patterns of power, privilege and oppression which should have kept her 'in her place'.

In order for this transformational moment of *metanoia* to come about, both Jesus and the woman have to refuse to accept their own, and each other's, assigned social roles.

Some commentators point to this passage as an argument for inclusion, but really there is something far more radical than that going on. In conventional models of inclusion, those with the power and privilege choose to include those without. But that is not what is going on here. Jesus is not choosing to include the woman. Rather, she is choosing to draw him into her worldview, and he is allowing himself to become – at least to some extent – receptive to that.

By becoming an interruption to the Gospel narrative, and to Jesus' way of thinking, the Syro-Phoenician woman is not only disrupting existing dynamics of power and privilege, but also offering an alternative vision.

Questions the story asks us

What questions might this story be asking of you?

- In what ways might you have been shaped, consciously or unconsciously, to resist the approaches, requests and challenges of others? Because of your gender, skin colour, nationality, class or status, dis/ability, sexuality? Or because of theirs?
- How do you tend to respond when challenged or criticized? What are the tactics you tend to deploy – consciously or unconsciously – to defend yourself from challenge or criticism?
- What might need to change – for you personally, or in your church, project or organization – for you to be more open to being challenged?

Further reading

- Amy-Jill Levine (ed.), *A Feminist Companion to Mark* (Sheffield: Sheffield Academic Press, 2001)
- Samuel Wells, *Improvisation: The Drama of Christian Ethics* (Grand Rapids, MI: Brazos, 2004)

9

At the Table

While he was at Bethany in the house of Simon the leper, as he sat at the
table, a woman came with an alabaster jar of very costly ointment of
nard, and she broke open the jar and poured the ointment on his head.
[*] But some were there who said to one another in anger, 'Why was the
ointment wasted in this way? For this ointment could have been sold
for more than three hundred denarii, and the money given to the poor.'
And they scolded her. But Jesus said, 'Let her alone; why do you trouble
her? She has performed a good service for me. [*] For you always have
the poor with you, and you can show kindness to them whenever you
wish; but you will not always have me. She has done what she could;
she has anointed my body beforehand for its burial. Truly I tell you,
wherever the good news is proclaimed in the whole world, what she has
done will be told in remembrance of her.' (Mark 14.3–9)

Wonderings

- I wonder how the meal was going before the woman entered the room?
- I wonder what the woman was thinking, as she appeared with her ointment?
- I wonder how different onlookers reacted to the woman's actions?
- I wonder what kind of eye contact Jesus and the woman made with each other throughout this encounter?
- I wonder what difference the encounter made; to Jesus; to the woman; to the onlookers?

Following through the story

Jesus is at a meal. The place is Bethany – not far from Jerusalem. The time – it is two days before Passover, not long after Jesus' disruption in the temple, and the religious leaders are looking for an opportunity to get their hands on him.

His host today is a man called Simon – a leper, an outcast. But it is an unnamed woman who interrupts the meal, breaking open a jar of expensive ointment, and pouring it over Jesus' head – anointing him, just as over the centuries Hebrew prophets had anointed a new king.

For some around the table, the action is scandalous. Wasteful. An unnecessary extravagance.

But for Jesus, it comes as a gift. A gift he receives from the woman, and defends against the critics. He knows that this anointing will go with him to his death – will surround his body in its burial. And even more – that this moment, this action, this woman, will be part of the good news that is proclaimed across the world: 'what she has done will be told in remembrance of her'.

Being interrupted

With this story, more than most in the Gospels, there is a disentangling required. There are stories like this one, similar but different, in all four Gospels.

In Luke's Gospel (7.36–50), Simon is a Pharisee and the woman – a 'sinner', we're told – anoints Jesus *feet*, first with her tears, then with her kisses, and finally with the perfume she has brought in a jar. The story contrasts her extravagant love with Simon's lack of hospitality, her forgiven-ness with his self-righteousness.

In John's Gospel (12.1–8), they are in Bethany again, but this time in the home of the sisters Mary and Martha, and their brother Lazarus, whom Jesus has just raised from the dead. Here there is no interruption from outside, but around a meal table where Jesus is pretty much 'one of the family', Mary anoints Jesus' feet and wipes them with her hair, an outpouring of gratitude for what Jesus has done for her brother. Here, the house is 'filled with the fragrance of the perfume', just as in ancient times the temple had been filled with the glory of God (2 Chronicles 5.13–14, Isaiah 6.4). At another meal, very soon after this one, Jesus himself will imitate Mary's action, lovingly washing the feet of the disciples he now calls friends, and announcing to them that God's glory has come among them (John 13.1–32).

Here in Mark's version (which Matthew's Gospel follows closely), the unnamed woman is neither friend of Jesus nor 'sinner'. She appears suddenly in the story, unintroduced, and disappears just as suddenly – a fleeting encounter that is nevertheless full of blessing, like that between Abraham and Melchizedek, the 'priest of God Most High' (Genesis 14.18–19). And her action, her anointing of Jesus' *head* (not, as in Luke and John, his feet), holds within it multiple layers of meaning: showing hospitality to an honoured guest; the embalming of a body, soon to be dead; but also a consecration, the action of prophet or priest, the outpouring of *divine* anointing for a role, a task, a purpose. Here, in this moment, this unnamed woman quite literally makes Jesus 'the anointed one' – which is what 'the Messiah', 'the Christ' actually means. Judas' decision to betray Jesus follows immediately after this story, and is quite possibly precipitated by it. The woman's action is the trigger for Jesus' journey to the cross, an anointing for that Christly way – a 'sticky' anointing, a tangible expression of love that will stay with him (even as most of his disciples desert him) all the way to the tomb.

Jesus receives the woman's anointing – he accepts, takes on, the mantle she has thrown over him. But he also defends her actions, her interruption, from those who angrily criticize her.

It is as if there are different economies at work here, swirling around this passage – and its parallel forms in other Gospels – in competition for our attention. There is the economy of the critics (represented vocally, in John's version at least, by Judas), who are experts at counting, who can calculate an exact monetary value for the jar of ointment, but who turn out to know (in Oscar Wilde's memorable phrase) 'the price of everything and the value of nothing'. There is the economy of divinely initiated community, in John's account, where the dead-raising love of Jesus for Lazarus prompts in return a celebration of gratitude among friends around a meal table, and an outpouring of thankful love from Mary – a familiar pattern for many of us, that we often call 'worship'. But Mark's version of the story summons our attention to a third economy: where the transforming gift breaks in from the outside, unannounced, uninvited, interrupting the meal and shifting the paths of the story's central actors on to a decisively new stage and direction.

Interrupting

The woman who anoints Jesus – unnamed again, but vital to the narrative as it turns towards the cross – interrupts more than a meal. She interrupts the narrative, she interrupts the disciples' understanding of who Jesus is, she interrupts their assumptions and expectations about the Messiah, about kingship and anointing.

But perhaps more significant than any of that, she interrupts the economy in which they operate – in which the disciples operate, in which the first readers and hearers of the gospel operate and in which we as receivers of this Scripture continue to operate. The disciples' view is a strikingly utilitarian one – 'the greatest good for the greatest number' – and what is more striking is that it seems at first glance like 'common sense'. So ingrained in our society is the principle of usefulness, of making the most of our resources, that we may find ourselves with a sneaking sympathy for Judas here.

The other notable feature of the economy which Judas articulates and which we easily take for granted is that it is an economy of scarcity. The disciples *need* those 500 denarii for the poor, because otherwise there might not be enough to go around. There is always the fear that what we need will run out, and from this comes the desire to conserve resources, to hold on to things in case we need them later. The disciples' concern that such a valuable resource is being wasted is again one with which many of us might have sympathy.

Again, that sympathy arises from the idea of the economy of scarcity which we so unthinkingly imbibe. In a capitalist society, the idea that resources are scarce and finite, and we are in competition for them, is so ingrained that it is almost as hard to notice as the air we breathe. But it affects us, our choices and actions, at every level, both individually and as a society. From this model flows not only a financial system which drives and sustains inequality, but also a deep-seated sense that in order for others to have more we will somehow have less, which leads to all sorts of fears and prejudices.

It is this model of scarcity and competition that the woman in this story interrupts. By lavishing her valuable ointment on Jesus – by 'wasting' it, as the disciples see it – she is pointing to an important truth. This only looks like waste in an economy of scarcity and utility. In an economy of abundance, it looks very different. And this is the type of economy which Jesus points to so often in his teaching as being characteristic of the kin-dom of God.

Judas' objection makes perfect sense in an economy which takes for granted that pouring out riches to anoint the Christ and stewarding money to serve the poor must be in competition with each other. But remove that assumption, allow for the possibility of a totally different kind of economy, both financial and relational, and his argument crumbles.

This woman, by her wordless act of love, interrupts and dismantles the assumptions which underpin so much anxiety, prejudice and fear, in our own contexts as much as in hers.

Questions the story asks us

- What questions might this story be asking of you?
- Can you think of a time when the gifts offered by an 'outsider' have transformed a situation, or an event?
- Do you find it easier, in your usual day-to-day contexts, to be the 'giver', or on the receiving end?
- In what ways might you have been shaped, consciously or unconsciously, to resist receiving the gifts that others have brought with them? Because of your gender, skin colour, nationality, class or status, dis/ability, sexuality? Or because of theirs?
- What might need to change – for you personally, or in your church, project or organization – for you to be more open to receiving such unexpected, uninvited, transformative gifts from others?

Further reading

- Rita Nakashima Brock, *Journeys by Heart: A Christology of Erotic Power* (New York: Crossroad, 1988)
- Margaret Hebblethwaite, 'The Story of Mary of Bethany', in *Six New Gospels: New Testament Women Tell Their Stories* (Boston, MA: Cowley, 1994), pp. 94–114
- Elisabeth Moltmann-Wendel, *The Women Around Jesus* (New York: Crossroad, 1987)

10

With Little Children

He sat down, called the twelve, and said to them, 'Whoever wants to be first must be last of all and servant of all.' Then he took a little child and put it among them; and taking it in his arms, he said to them, 'Whoever welcomes one such child in my name welcomes me, and whoever welcomes me welcomes not me but the one who sent me. ... If any of you put a stumbling block before one of these little ones who believe in me, it would be better for you if a great millstone were hung around your neck and you were thrown into the sea.' (Mark 9.35–37, 42)

People were bringing little children to him in order that he might touch them; and the disciples spoke sternly to them. But when Jesus saw this, he was indignant and said to them, 'Let the little children come to me; do not stop them; for it is to such as these that the kingdom of God belongs. Truly I tell you, whoever does not receive the kingdom of God as a little child will never enter it.' And he took them up in his arms, laid his hands on them, and blessed them. (Mark 10.13–16)

Wonderings

- I wonder who you identify with in this story?
- I wonder what the children thought about Jesus?
- I wonder what this story tells us about the kingdom/kin-dom of God?

Following through the story

Children are disruptive. Anyone who has lived with, or worshipped with, or spent any kind of time with children will recognize the truth of that. Children disrupt and interrupt our ordered adult world – or our dearly held adult illusions of order.

Here in chapters 9 and 10, at the heart of Mark's Gospel, the narrative is disrupted by the presence of children, and by Jesus' response to them. In contrast to the way Matthew presents the same material (18.1–6), Mark intersperses it through the narrative, the repeated disruption of the narrative reflecting the disruptive nature of Jesus' engagement with children.

Matthew, on the other hand, collects all Jesus' teaching about children neatly into one block. If we accept that Matthew is writing later than, and drawing on, Mark then perhaps Matthew displays the first manifestation of the Church's ongoing tendency to try to contain the disruptive potential of children.

Generally, in Jesus' day as in our own, children are expected to be receptive. Adults expect to be in charge, and we expect children to receive what we teach them. That expectation in itself makes it clear that we have not really taken on board Jesus' teaching about children at all. Jesus totally subverts that expectation: by word and action, he makes it clear that his disciples should be open to receive children – with all the disruption that entails – to receive from children and, through children, to receive the kin-dom.

Being interrupted

Very often, we are tempted to identify ourselves with Jesus. We want to be the ones who say 'let the little children come to me, and do not stop them'. But we don't necessarily want all that that implies. Perhaps we want a Children's-Illustrated-Bible version, where the perfectly turned-out, perfectly behaved children sit in neat admiring circles, with ourselves in the role of Jesus. Or perhaps we want the opposite – the carefully managed chaos of the 'Children's Church' promotional material, which shows just how child-friendly we are, how tolerant we are of children being children. Either way, it can easily slip into a kind of commodification of the child, seeing children as an accessory to our own faith, an add-on to 'proper', 'grown-up' church. And it's the very opposite of what Jesus is talking about. So perhaps we shouldn't be so quick to put ourselves in the role of Jesus.

What about the disciples? This is, self-evidently, the least desirable role in the scene. As so often in Mark's Gospel, the disciples are the ones who get it wrong. But if we are willing to place ourselves in their shoes, we may find that we have much to learn from that position. How are we stopping children coming to Jesus? What stumbling blocks do we put in their way? These and other questions are the beginning of repentance. The Church has much to repent of when it comes to our treatment of children. We need the example of the disciples to learn how to follow Jesus, how to recognize time and again that we have been wrong, how to be willing to change in response to our encounter with Jesus.

Jesus' discourse about children is disruptive not only in its content, but also in its form. Jesus does not just speak about the place of children in God's kin-dom. He places a child in the midst of his disciples, and he does so as the answer to their questions about power, authority and hierarchy.

There is something important to be learned here about the nature of the kin-dom. It is not an intellectual concept, but an embodied one. By placing a child in the midst, Jesus is exemplifying the disruptive potential of the 'other'. To the adult disciples, the child seems so 'other' to their discussion of power and greatness, that the child's very presence effectively challenges and reframes their discourse. If we wish to follow Jesus' call to receive the kin-dom like a child, we need to consider how we allow our own presence, our own otherness, to disrupt the status quo.

In holding up children as an example of those to whom the kin-dom belongs, Jesus challenges us to welcome, rather than fear or reject, disruption. He challenges us to become as receptive and as disruptive as a child. And he encourages us to see the child – the archetypal weaker, inferior 'other' – as our spiritual equal, from whom we have much to learn and receive, through whom we encounter the kin-dom of God.

Interrupting

How about seeing ourselves as the children, longing to reach Jesus? There is some spiritual mileage in that. But while we may be keen to appropriate the eager faith and perseverance of the children coming to Jesus, we may be less keen to take on the role of the disruptor. For Jesus, however, the two are inseparable. Jesus calls his disciples to become like 'one of these little ones'. And what do we see these little ones doing? Interrupting. If we are not willing to do likewise, perhaps we are not really willing to inhabit the role of the child after all.

For Jesus, there is a clear and inextricable link between children and the kin-dom of God and the nature of that relationship is key. The verbs used here are important: 'whoever does not *receive* the kin-dom of God as a little child will never *enter* it.' The kin-dom is something to be received, and to be entered. Contrast that with the Church's pre-occupation with 'building', 'growing', or 'bringing in' the kin-dom. The kin-dom, Jesus seems to imply here, is not something we have to, or are able to, create. The kin-dom already is. Our role is to receive and enter it. This is a radical disruption of our tendency to attach importance to our own agency and productivity.

Children are, very often, not productive. Very often their agency is limited. But they can and do receive and enter into what is offered to them. We are to do likewise. To be willing, in our post-modern, capitalist society to receive and enter into something over which we have no agency or control is disruptively countercultural. To receive it like a child – as one who has no power or authority – is even more so. Receiving the kin-dom like a child is perhaps the archetype of radical receptivity.

Questions the story asks us

- How are we stopping children coming to Jesus?
- What stumbling blocks do we put in their way?
- When have we failed to welcome a child in Jesus' name?
- When have we failed to become like a child?
- When have we been resistant to change and disruption?
- When have we been unwilling to interrupt and risk rejection?
- How can we become more receptive to what children have to offer our church/family/group/community?

Further reading

For further reading, see the recommendations in the section on Children in Chapter 4.

Act 2

Children Writing the Script

Ruth

'I've got a really good idea. It involves a dancing triceratops.'

It was an unlikely start to the process of writing a nativity play for the Crib Service. Around the table were half a dozen children, and a couple of adults. There were a number of responses I could have offered to this unexpected contribution to the writing process. I considered my options.

'OK, cool. What else have we got?' And I scribbled 'triceratops (dancing)' on the blank sheet of paper in front of me.

Suddenly the ideas were coming thick and fast:

'Doctor Who could be in it.'

'Can we do a rap?'

'The wise men should be funny. And not all men.'

'What if the triceratops is the Doctor's assistant?'

'It could be about climate change.'

'I want to be a sheep. A talking sheep.'

'I don't think the triceratops talks.'

'Maybe there's a problem and the Doctor has to sort it out.'

'With the triceratops.'

'Yeah, and they have to make it so Jesus can be born.'

'And the problem could be climate change.'

I said nothing and scribbled frantically. If the children asked 'Can we do …? Can we have …? Are we allowed …?' I said 'yes'. But mainly they didn't ask, they just stated: this is how it could be. This is what we can do.

Silently, I wondered how this wonderful, glorious, creative jumble of ideas could possibly turn into something that would be ready in time, let alone something which would convey the power of the Christmas story to our neighbours who came to church. Would this process really work?

It would. Slowly, order started to emerge. A list of scenes. Snippets of dialogue. Suggestions for costumes and props. Conflicting ideas were negotiated and agreements reached.

Occasionally an adult would offer a question:

'Who's in this scene?'

'How will the audience know what's going on?'

'What do you need to get you from that point to this one?'

And suddenly there it was: a nativity play. And not just any nativity play, but something more creative, more beautiful, more powerful than I could possibly have imagined.

Responses from the congregation who witnessed it were overwhelmingly positive, but they were not the usual responses to a children's nativity play. Nobody said, 'weren't they adorable' or 'didn't they do well'.

Instead they used words like 'stunning', 'beautiful', 'moving', 'special', 'amazing', and struggled to articulate quite what it was that had affected them so profoundly. It was all of those things, and more.

In the candlelight of the Christingles, I looked around at the triceratops, the Doctor, the daleks, the magi, the talking sheep and the holy family, and at the shining faces of our neighbours encountering the story afresh. And I knew again the power of God entering the world as a child.

11

Amid the Trees

On the following day, when they came from Bethany, he was hungry. Seeing in the distance a fig tree in leaf, he went to see whether perhaps he would find anything on it. When he came to it, he found nothing but leaves, for it was not the season for figs. He said to it, 'May no one ever eat fruit from you again.' And his disciples heard it ...

In the morning as they passed by, they saw the fig tree withered away to its roots. Then Peter remembered and said to him, 'Rabbi, look! The fig tree that you cursed has withered.' (Mark 11.12-14, 20-21)

Wonderings

- I wonder why Jesus cursed the fig tree?
- I wonder how Peter and the other disciples responded to what they had seen Jesus do?

Following through the story

Jesus has just entered Jerusalem in triumphal procession, riding on a donkey, over a carpet of leafy branches, acclaimed as 'the one who comes in the name of the Lord'. It's late in the day, but there is enough time to take a look around the temple, before retiring to Bethany with his disciples – the place where he will soon be anointed.

The next day he returns to the temple, to drive out the sellers and buyers, overturn the tables of the money-changers, and unnerve the religious leaders enough to make them want him dead.

On the way from Bethany to the temple, though, Jesus is hungry, spots a fig tree in the distance, and heads over to it. Finding no fruit on it, he curses it, and goes on his way – presumably still hungry and, by the sounds of it, a bit cross. The next morning, after the drama in the temple, they find the cursed fig tree not just fruitless, but 'withered away to its roots' – dead, with no possibility of restoration.

Refusing interruption

If we follow the general direction of travel of Mark's Gospel, the cursed fig tree has no more significance – for the reader, the writer, or indeed Jesus himself – than to be a symbolic reinforcement of Jesus' judgement on the temple and its leadership: the fruitless fig tree and its withering fate are signs of the temple's current fruitlessness, and of its impending destruction (which Jesus makes explicit at the beginning of chapter 13 – 'not one stone will be left here upon another').

But what if we were to take this little encounter seriously, in its own right? What if we were to pay as much attention to the fig tree, as a living part of God's creation, as we have done to some of Jesus' *human* 'others' in Mark's narrative? Then we might well reread this passage, from the perspective of the tree, as what feminist biblical scholar Phyllis Trible calls a 'text of terror'. It appears here as a problem for us: not easily solvable, but an awkward, uncomfortable text that perhaps reveals the limits of Jesus' receptivity.

Why was the fig tree fruitless? Because, the text tells us, 'it was not the season for figs'. That's it. Wrong time of year. The fig tree was 'in leaf', thriving, doing its thing. It just wasn't, yet, fig time. So, the curse, from a hungry Jesus, was all about *his* needs, *his* agenda, *his* timescales – not those of the fig tree, nor indeed those of the seasons of the year, and of the complex ecosystem of which both the fig tree and Jesus are a part. Jesus' behaviour here is distinctly anthropocentric (imagining that the world is here entirely for the benefit of us humans), if not even egocentric (it's all about him)! Whereas four times in Mark's Gospel we have seen Jesus open himself up to have his direction, his agenda interrupted by others, coming with their needs, their challenges and their gifts – here we see him refusing the disturbance presented by a non-human other, and responding with ecocidal violence.[1] His response to the Syro-Phoenician woman was met with her robust challenge, and his change of heart and mind. Who is there to challenge him here?

Over the last few decades, ecological science has learned much about 'the hidden life of trees', as author Peter Wohlleben puts it. We know now that trees function less as individuals, and more as nodes in complex networks, sharing information, nutrients and even anti-predator toxins with each other, via gases emitted from their leaves, and a remarkable underground system of interconnected roots and fungal threads that has been dubbed 'the wood wide web'. We also now know that dying and dead trees literally give what is left of their life so that other trees might continue to live and grow, passing on their nutrients through that underground network, as well as providing home and food for birds, small mammals and a multitude of insects.

When human beings clear away dead wood or disrupt the 'wood wide web' through tree-felling, 'forest management' or the construction of roads and buildings, we weaken the trees' vital network of communication and mutual support. A fig tree where even its roots have withered is bad news for its neighbouring trees, and many other creatures in its locality too. Read from the perspective of a more-than-human ecology, this story of Jesus cursing the fig tree is truly a 'text of terror'.

* * *

---

1 'Ecocide' is the term used to name the destruction of the natural environment, especially when deliberate.

He also said, 'With what can we compare the kingdom of God, or what parable will we use for it? It is like a mustard seed, which, when sown upon the ground, is the smallest of all the seeds on earth; yet when it is sown it grows up and becomes the greatest of all shrubs, and puts forth large branches, so that the birds of the air can make nests in its shade.' (Mark 4.30-32)

Wonderings

- I wonder where the humans are in this story, and what they might be doing?
- I wonder how the seed is sown?
- I wonder what happens while the shrub is growing?
- I wonder if the humans are happy to see the birds coming?

Following through the story

Jesus is teaching a large crowd, beside the sea. He teaches them in parables: a sower sowing seed that falls into different kinds of soil; a seed that sprouts and grows, mysteriously, even to the one who has sown it; and a tiny mustard seed, that grows into 'the greatest of all shrubs', with branches that provide homes for the birds of the air. Everything comes in parables, which those 'with ears to hear' might hear and understand, but to which others listen hard, and understand nothing.

After a day of parables, Jesus and the disciples cross the lake, and in the midst of an unexpected storm they discover that 'even the wind and the sea obey him'. And yet, for at least a moment earlier that day, we catch a glimpse of an other-than-human world running wild, obeying no human master.

Interrupting

'Mustard,' wrote Pliny the Elder in around AD 78, 'is extremely beneficial for the health. It grows entirely wild, though it is improved by being trans-planted: but on the other hand when it has once been sown it is scarcely possible to get the place free of it, as the seed when it falls germinates at once.' Not good news, then, for those who like their gardens or fields well-ordered and under control. A Californian blogger recently described it as 'the single most pestilential invasive plant in the entire county'.[2]

So why would anyone dream of sowing it? In his exploration of this passage, Jim Perkinson notes that while Matthew and Luke attribute the sowing to the deliberate act of a human agent ('a grain of mustard which someone took and sowed'), Mark's version doesn't: the mustard seed here may well be simply *sowing itself*, falling to the ground, scattered on the wind – or even helped along by one of those friendly birds. And if that's the case, then this parable points beyond the human activities of ploughing and sowing, planting and tending – human efforts to make the ecosystem work for *us* – to the wild workings of the more-than-human ecosystem itself.

But as permaculture practitioner and teacher Toby Hemenway explains, it would be too simplistic to erase human agency entirely from wild mustard's story: 'opportunistic' plants like mustard 'crave disturbance, love sunlit edges, churned-up ground, and often, poor soil'.[3] Ecosystems that are much less-disturbed by human activity tend to be much more resistant to invasions by the likes of mustard, which thrives best in 'dis-rupted ecosystems, fragmented and degraded by grazing, logging, dams, road building, pollution, and other human activity. When humans make a clearing, nature leaps in, working furiously to rebuild an intact humus and fungal layer, harvest energy, and reconstruct all the cycles and con-nections that have been severed. A thicket of fast-growing pioneer plants, packing a lot of biomass into a small space, is a very effective way to do this.'

---

2 Quoted in Jim Perkinson, *Political Spirituality in an Age of Eco-Apocalypse: Com-munication and Struggle Across Species, Cultures, and Religions* (New York: Palgrave Macmillan, 2015), p. 60.

3 'Permaculture' names 'a set of techniques and principles for designing sustainable human settlements'. See Toby Hemenway, *Gaia's Garden: A Guide to Home-Scale Permaculture*, 2nd edition (White River Junction, VT: Chelsea Green, 2009).

Mustard might be an 'invader', but its role is not 'to convert all living reality into itself'. The 'invasion' of plants like wild mustard is in fact one way in which other-than-human creatures bring healing and stability to habitats that humans have disturbed, renewing the fertility of soils that humans have farmed-out and overgrazed. Even the apparent hyperbole of Jesus' parable – suggesting that the mustard seed grows into 'the greatest of all shrubs' with 'large branches' – begins to make more sense within this ecology: eventually, the 'invaded' ecosystem finds a new equilibrium, keeping invaders like mustard in check, and tending in the long-term towards the relatively stable, immensely diverse, tree-rich habitat that ecologists call 'old-growth forest'.[4]

Questions the stories ask us

• When was the last 'fig tree' you were tempted to curse? What was going on for you? What might have been going on for them?
• Where, if you pay attention to them, are the 'opportunistic', mustard-like 'weeds' in your part of the world? What kinds of healing and renewal might they be bringing with them?
• When was the last time you were stopped in your tracks by the other-than-human world? How might you be more open to being interrupted?

Further reading

• Toby Hemenway, *Gaia's Garden: A Guide to Home-Scale Permaculture*, 2nd edition (White River Junction, VT: Chelsea Green, 2009)
• Jim Perkinson, *Political Spirituality in an Age of Eco-Apocalypse: Communication and Struggle Across Species, Cultures, and Religions* (New York: Palgrave Macmillan, 2015)
• Richard Powers, *The Overstory* (London: Vintage, 2019)
• Peter Wohlleben, *The Hidden Life of Trees: What They Feel, How They Communicate* (London: William Collins, 2017)

---

4 Perkinson, *Political Spirituality*, pp. 61–5, quoting Hemenway, *Gaia's Garden*, pp. 13–14. The term 'nature' occurs occasionally in some of the writers that we quote in this book. It tends to be used as a simple way of naming all those other-than-human parts of an ecosystem, but can be a problematic word if it allows us to imagine human beings as somehow inhabiting a sphere distinct and separate from that of 'nature': *we* are part of 'nature' too!

PART 3

Reimagining

Act 3

From a Homeless Church to a
Community Passion Play

Al

On a bitterly cold Palm Sunday afternoon in April 2013, we crucified Jesus under the concrete pillars of the M6 motorway. Although lorries rumbled up above us, there was an expectant hush among the small crowd of actors and spectators (and many were a mixture of both) that had followed the route of the Bromford Passion Play through the snow-covered streets of our estate to its conclusion in 'the wasteland' – a large patch of derelict, council-owned land in the north-east corner of the Firs and Bromford estate, abandoned for some 30 years since its short-lived tower blocks had been demolished.

Phil, playing the Roman centurion, delivered the last lines of the play:

I have watched this man enter Jerusalem. I have watched him argue with these priests. I have watched him turn the other cheek when he could have escaped. I have watched him betrayed. This man's kingdom is not from this earth, so I've been told. So, I leave this up to you. Was this man truly the Son of God? It is for each of you to decide.

As Phil dropped to his knees, and the rest of the cast froze – both theatrically and quite literally – the thick silence following his last words was almost tangible. The resonances were profoundly striking between the god-forsaken cry and silencing of the crucified Messiah, and the deep stories of many of our neighbours, individual and collective stories of being abandoned, overlooked, forgotten about, demonized, crucified.

What was also striking was that this Community Passion Play was not a church-led production, but the second performance of the newly established Bromford Theatre Group, who had a few months before done their debut Christmas panto, Aladdin. Neither Phil nor many members of the Theatre Group would call themselves Christians, and yet here they were, staging a very 'faithful' version of the defining story of the Christian faith.

Phil had written the script, five acts dictated to me as the two of us sat in my front room, Phil with his notebook, me with my laptop. The Passion Play was itself Phil's idea – a passionate suggestion of his that was voiced, out of the blue, in a meeting about something completely different, not long before Christmas.

And the Theatre Group – that was Phil's idea too. In March 2012, Phil was one of 97 people who had been nominated by neighbours as Hodge Hill's 'Unsung Heroes': ordinary people who lived or worked locally in whom could be seen an extraordinary compassion, generosity, trust, friendship or hope. 'Unsung Heroes' had been an initiative of Hodge Hill Church – the culmination of six months of mapping our neighbourhoods, spotting the 'bumping spaces' (the places where people naturally bump into each other, hang out together), and spending time in those spaces listening to people tell us their stories, their passions, their hopes and dreams for where they lived. So much of what we heard was crying out to be shared more widely, celebrated, given thanks for. And so 'Unsung Heroes' did just that: gathered together those who had been nominated, as we shared food and told the stories of their nominations, presented them with awards, and celebrated the passion, energy and commitment we had discovered, right under our noses, in our neighbourhoods. And before we finished, we asked our guests one question: 'If you could find two or three people to join you, what would you start in your neighbour-hood?' Phil had written down his idea of a theatre group. He had the vision, the passion, the knowledge and some incredible skills at recruiting neighbours to the cause. All he needed was a little bit of help accessing a small amount of money to help his idea 'take off'.

Less than four years earlier, back in the summer of 2008, congregation members of St Philip and St James, Hodge Hill, could not have imagined the possibilities for celebration that lay ahead. Their church building, a much-loved and well-used multi-purpose community space built in the mid-1960s, had been rapidly demolished, the main roof having been condemned, and the cost of essential repairs approaching half a million pounds. When it was first built, it had been hailed as 'one of the most significant developments in post-war church architecture', designed by a radical team of church architects, profoundly shaped by an incarnational theology which understood God to be in the midst of daily life as much as Sunday worship. Lunch clubs and playgroups, badminton games and youth groups, all happened in the same space as services of Holy Communion, with no physical barriers or screens dividing 'sacred' from 'secular'.

Located just at the top of the large green triangle of Hodge Hill Common – a space that, historically, would have been allocated for the shared use of local tenants for pasturing their animals, and where neighbours might often meet up, catch up and do business with each other – the church building itself served as a similar kind of 'common' space, 'hosted' by the church, for the (socio-economically and increasingly ethnically diverse) residents of Hodge Hill to use for many and varied activities, but also a space of interaction and encounter. The loss of the building was felt sharply across the local area, in which there were very few other dedicated public 'bumping spaces' – and none at all on a similar scale.

That summer in 2008, the church congregation were homeless and grieving, unable to offer any comfort to bewildered neighbours as angry as they were that 'their church' had been so suddenly taken away from them. 'Business as usual' was more than 'interrupted'. How could they possibly now be 'the church at the heart of the community' without a place to call home, into which they could welcome others? How could they love and serve their neighbours without a space in which to first meet them? What on earth could 'mission' look like now? It was in asking those searching questions, staying with their discomfort, that the faint possibilities of a new way of being began to open up.

12

A Third Economy

In Chapter 5, we explored two different kinds of 'economy' that are powerfully shaping the Christian Church – especially the Church in England – in the early twenty-first century. We used the term 'economy' there to describe systems in which we participate with our bodies and our imaginations, and which shape:

- what we *value*
- what we *desire*
- what we *worry* over
- what we *celebrate* and delight in
- what we do with our *bodies*
- how we see and treat other *people* and other *non-human creatures*.

In Chapter 5, we described the economies of 'counting in', and of 'giving out', and explored some of the dangers and temptations associated with each of them. Here we will describe a third economy, with some recognizable similarities to elements of the first two, but also with some radical differences.

It would be very tempting to present this third economy as 'the answer' – as the 'promised land' we need to head towards once we've escaped the 'Egypts' of the first and second economies. But life is more complex than that. In reality, it is impossible to escape entirely from economies one and two, even if we really wanted to. Money can be useful for getting things done. Underneath the crude number of people 'in church' there are exactly that number of journeys of exploration, discipleship and commitment, exactly that number of clusters of gifts longing to be given, shared and received – and stories, too, of those who have died, moved on, or worse, given up. And from the second economy, an outpouring from the Church into the wider world of 'service' and 'proclamation' is first and foremost an expression of *love* for our neighbours: wanting to share with them some of the gifts for which we, ourselves, are thankful because we know they have sustained, enriched, transformed and even – in many different ways – saved our lives.

But what we've already explored is that these first two economies can also be profoundly distorting, even destructive, of our relationships with our neighbours – and, therefore, of our own individual lives and collective life as 'church' too. They can serve to reinforce, rather than overcome, the various kinds of 'obliviousness' – both within wider society, and within the community of the church – that we explored in depth in Chapters 3 and 4. So, the third economy we outline here is offered more as a 'corrective pull', to stand alongside the others in prophetic and life-generating tension.

Economy #3: 'being interrupted'

Figure 8: Economy #3

Like economy #2, this third economy values and longs for the growth of God's kin-dom, but unlike economy #2, the 'flow' is not just one way, outwards in service and proclamation. In fact, this third economy values something that economy #1 emphasizes – what the church *receives* (from the outside, in) – but it expands the possibilities for that far beyond what can be *counted* – money and people (as attendees). Pushing that a bit further: we tend only to count the things we're expecting, wanting, needing – the square pegs that fit into the square holes we're focused on. What we're talking about here, for the church to receive, are most often the things we're *not* expecting, wanting or needing – things that don't fit any pre-determined hole that we know we have.

The language for this is *gift*: God-given, unique, diverse, often surprising, mysterious even. Gifts that are clearly visible, bursting to be unleashed, offered and shared. And gifts that are so well-hidden that even the gifted one is not aware she has that gift to offer. Gifts that are so obviously delightful, beautiful, life-giving. And gifts that are profoundly uncomfortable, unsettling, challenging – gifts that often don't feel like *gifts* at all, other than with the benefit of hindsight, when we look back and see how we've learned, changed and grown as a result of letting that difficult 'gift' come to us *as gift*. Gifts within individual human beings, but also gifts that can be discovered in particular relationships, in groups and associations, in places and stories and traditions, in events and encounters and split-second moments. Gifts that might include:

- creativity and skill
- practicality and physical strength
- hospitality and friendship
- kindness and care
- story and wisdom
- questions and challenge
- vision and leadership
- silence and listening
- passion and patience
- and much, much more …

In this third economy, the Church is neither anxious about its survival and its scarce resources, nor overflowing in its own God-given (and often, let's face it, rather self-satisfied) abundance. Instead, it rejoices in its radical insufficiency – in its not wanting or needing to be everything – and its role as treasure-seeker: in the world not as a bright light that dazzles our neighbours (the 'power of the performer' at its worst), but more like an ultra-violet torch that seeks out and reveals what would otherwise go unnoticed.[1] And treasure-seeking not as a friendly continuation of the imperial, colonialist project of 'discovering' new places from which to extract precious resources for our own enrichment – but rather to *delight* in gifts-being-shared, whoever might be on the receiving end; to *encourage* others to unearth (but not 'uproot') gifts that have been lying dormant; and to *give thanks* for those gifts which, undemanded and often unexpected, we are blessed to receive.

---

1 This image is inspired by the story of the 'Flash Floss Feast' in Rubery, another estate parish on the south-west edge of Birmingham. Neighbours young and old got together under the underpass of a dual carriageway that divides the area and, among other activities, created artwork on the concrete walls and pillars with UV-chalk, which would only show up with ultra-violet light.

So how do we inhabit, participate in, this third economy, the economy of 'being interrupted'? It won't come as a surprise, if you've followed the journey of this book to this point, to read that what is needed is as much a '*not* doing' as any kind of 'doing'. But as much as many of us in the Church might actually get significant spiritual benefits from some 'sitting back and waiting', there is certainly a bit more required than just that. In the following sections, we'll outline something of a spectrum of 'ways of being' – let's call them 'tactics',[2] to be appropriately deployed at different times in different circumstances – that help make it possible for this third economy to flourish.

'Wilding' and other ways of doing nothing

When a particular species is threatened with extinction (the peregrine falcon, say), the standard 'conservation' approach is to do everything possible to micro-manage an environment for the benefit of that species: planting one kind of tree, bush or plant, and removing others; introducing one kind of insect and getting rid of others. It's all about targets and control. But the more-than-human world is almost always more complex than we realize: a whole ecosystem of different species need each other in ways beyond what we know or can even imagine. What we *do* to try and 'manage' an environment often has all kinds of knock-on effects that we hadn't expected or intended.

One family-run farm in Sussex decided to try a different approach: to let go, to stop their previous practices of industrial farming and land management, to vacate the driving seat, to even stop 'tidying up' the dead wood and fallen leaves, to leave animals to die rather than sending them away to be 'put to sleep humanely'. To just *let it all be*. Occasionally, they made strategic interventions – introducing free-roaming grazing animals like Tamworth pigs, Exmoor ponies and Longhorn cattle, for instance – but even those were seeking to go *with* the grain of natural processes rather than battling against them, like so much industrial farming.

The government inspectors were worried they weren't abiding by often strict guidelines for controlling some species of plants and animals. Neighbours started complaining it was getting messy, ugly, 'out of control',

---

2 We deliberately use the term 'tactics' here following a distinction made by the philosopher Michel de Certeau. A 'tactic', as opposed to a 'strategy', doesn't try to claim a 'territory' for itself, within which it can control how things happen. Instead, tactics are 'opportunist' and 'ad hoc' engagements that seek to make the most of the context and circumstances in which we find ourselves. See Michel de Certeau, *The Practice of Everyday Life*, trans. Steven Rendall (Berkeley, CA: University of California Press, 1988), pp. 29–39.

'wanton vandalism'. And in words that revealed deep links between Englishness, a neatly ordered landscape and the 'civilizing' project of empire, some complainants even suggested that while 'foreign' countries might have their wild-lands, untamed by human control, 'you don't feel it should be *here*'.

But something amazing happened. Butterflies started being seen (purple emperors), and birds heard (nightingales), that everyone thought had vanished entirely from the English countryside. The 'messy' scrubland that began to grow and spread around the farm estate turned out to protect the little tree saplings to enable them to grow bigger and stronger than if human beings had tried to protect them with plastic tubing. Worms began to cleanse the soil of harmful chemicals and replace nutrients that had been lost through years of using chemical fertilizer and even help the soil to trap and hold more CO_2 than the same amount of rainforest. And all of this happened in just a few years.[3]

The contrast with the metaphor of 'church planting', and its often very numbers-driven approach, is striking. Where 'planting' places all the emphasis on the agency of the 'planter', suggests that what is planted is introduced into the local habitat from beyond, and implies a heavily managed process with an eye always to efficiency and maximizing 'yield', 'wilding' or 're-wilding' instead places the emphasis on *what is already there* in the soil of a particular place, the seeds and spores that are already present, already doing their thing.[4] It has no clear idea of 'end product' – it doesn't aim to 'produce' a heath, a meadow or a forest, or to recreate a landscape that existed in the past – but seeks to open up, in the richly complex and mysterious ecosystem of a place, unimagined possibilities for the future.

And just as ecological re-wilding requires the humans involved often to sit on their hands and resist intervening, similarly a 'missional re-wilding' requires Christians actively to resist starting up initiatives and projects – usually with a hefty dose of the power of the provider, the performer and the possessor (see Chapter 5) – that 'fill the space' that might otherwise be inhabited by the initiatives of our neighbours. Just as, to enable others to speak, we need at the very least to stop talking for a moment, so in this third economy we need at the very least to stop, or resist, 'doing stuff' for us to notice, let alone encourage, what our neighbours might be doing or wanting to do.

3 Isabella Tree, *Wilding: The Return of Nature to a British Farm* (London: Picador, 2019).

4 We are grateful to Revd Dr John White for articulating this insight, and also to a blog post by Paul Bradbury, 'Wilding the Church', *Church Mission Society*, https://pioneer.churchmissionsociety.org/2019/06/wilding-the-church/, accessed 8 May 2020.

Such an approach stretches our understandings of the Holy Spirit: as not only living and active in the world today, within and beyond the Church, but also as something wild, beyond human control and understanding. This re-wilding way of being, doing and not-doing requires a trust in the Spirit at work beyond our consciousness, and a willingness to leave 'empty' space through which the Sprit blows as she will, breathing life into us, our neighbours (human and non-human) and our neighbourhoods in unexpected ways.

Looking for the gifts

We can notice and encourage better, though, when we have an idea of what we are looking for. It can help to name some of the kinds of gift in our neighbourhood that might be waiting to be unleashed, encouraged, nurtured, to help us be more intentional in our 'treasure-hunting'. This second tactic is close to the heart of what is often called Asset-Based Community Development (ABCD), which names at least seven different kinds of 'asset' that can be found in any neighbourhood – however that neighbourhood is described in terms of its financial wealth or indices of deprivation.[5]

- The gifts of the *place* itself: the interconnected places and spaces that make up *this* neighbourhood, enable us to say *'here* we are' – places for playing and exploring, places for hosting activities and growing things, places of beauty and wildness and wonder; and our wild, non-human neighbours (both flora and fauna); the rarely noticed ways in which they are making this place 'home', around us and in spite of us.
- The passions, knowledge and skills of local *residents*: what local people care about enough to produce action; the knowledge they can share with or teach others; the expertise that can practically help others.

---

5 One of the most striking and beautiful stories of a church pursuing an ABCD approach is found in Michael Mather's book, *Having Nothing, Possessing Everything: Finding Communities in Unexpected Places* (Grand Rapids, MI: Eerdmans, 2018). Al also wrote a short introductory theological reflection on ABCD for the Church Urban Fund in 2013, which can be found here: www2.twittorial.co.uk/research/theological-reflection-asset-based-community-development.

Cormac Russell of Nurture Development has been a wise companion on our journey in Firs and Bromford, and has recently published *Rekindling Democracy: A Professional's Guide to Working in Citizen Space* (Eugene, OR: Cascade, 2020), which brings much wisdom to the questions we explore here. Nurture Development have also produced lots of resources to support ABCD work: www.nurturedevelopment.org/.

- The power of local *associations*: the visible and hidden connections between people, from the parents and carers who gather at the school gate and the dog-walkers that bump into each other in the park, to the weekly litter-pickers' walk and the more formally constituted residents' association.
- The resources of public, private and voluntary-sector *institutions*: schools and council services, shops and businesses, community centres and places of worship.
- The local *economies* of exchange: anything that is shared and swapped, including for example, skills (gardening), time (babysitting), things (lending a lawnmower), as well as money.
- The *stories* of people's lives and of their evolving community: the stories told readily, and those that take years to be heard; the 'majority' stories that claim a widespread 'we', and the 'minority' stories of marginalization and dissent.
- The regular and evolving *traditions* (new and old) of the place: everything from summer tea parties to Halloween ghost walks, from spring adventures into the bluebell woods to Santa's sleigh touring the streets at Christmas (these are just a few examples from the Firs and Bromford neighbourhood – every neighbourhood's traditions will be very different!).

While most of these are in no particular order of priority, any adventure of treasure-hunting in a neighbourhood needs a *place* to begin. We need to get a sense of *where* we are talking about, when we are talking about 'here'. We also need to pay attention to the physicality of the place, to the built environment that humans have shaped and reshaped over time, and to the earth beneath our feet, the water, the trees, the air that we breathe – how they shape our living and moving, and how they are changing and being changed, by agents both human and other-than-human, both near and far away.

This 'finding our feet' has to go hand-in-hand with a second starting point: our human neighbours. We can only begin to see the *place* when we begin to see through other neighbours' eyes as well as our own. And we can only do that if we approach our neighbours with a desire to see and hear *them*: who they are, what gifts they have and how they see the neighbourhood's past, present and future. One of the vital arts required for this tactic is *how to ask a good question*. For example:

- 'What do you love most about this place?' (a question about the *place*, and about their *passion* for it).

- 'Tell me a story of a time neighbours got together to make something good happen' (a question about the *past*).
- 'Where are neighbours coming together here to make a difference?' (a question about the *present*).
- 'If you could find a couple of people to join you, what could you start in your neighbourhood?' (a question about the *future*).

It was the last of these questions that Phil was asked, on that Unsung Heroes celebration evening, to which he responded with his idea for a Bromford Theatre Group. He found a space within which he could express his passion for theatre, and offer his knowledge and skills in bringing people together to stage a performance. Encouraged down that road, he drew on other neighbours' passions and skills too, and the emerging group was just the kind of 'informal association' that can become the beating heart of a local community. While the local church (a long-established community 'institution') was not in the driving seat of this new venture, we were able to offer support (helping Phil put the script together, and access some funding), and our youth-work partner organization Worth Unlimited offered the venue, 'the Hub', in which the new theatre group could meet and rehearse. In the final perform- ance, local places and spaces were transformed from being merely the (unnoticed, often seemingly ugly) background to people's movement around the estate, into the 'stage' and 'scenery' of the passion play – in ways that brought to visibility some of their hidden beauty. And as neighbours found diverse ways to participate in the telling, contribute to the performance, exchange their gifts for a part in the event – from acting and costume-making, to catering and looking after the children of performers – as noted above, the story being performed brought out resonances with many of the personal stories of those involved, and some of the shared stories of our neighbourhood. Finally – the last of the seven 'assets' of an ABCD approach to community-building – what had come to birth was a new community tradition: something that people would talk about long after it was over, and that would be expected, looked forward to, in the years to come.

This proliferation of gifts, and many like it, should come as no surprise to treasure-seekers familiar with the workings of the Holy Spirit. When St Paul writes of 'the manifestation of the Spirit for the common good' (1 Corinthians 12.7) he could be describing precisely this sort of mutual sharing and development of community 'assets' in a way which – perhaps miraculously – creates something far greater than the sum of its parts. It is perhaps not too great a stretch to reframe the 'assets' of an ABCD model as gifts of the Spirit, already present in our (and every) community, awaiting discovery, recognition, connection and encouragement. God is here before us in the skills, talents, relationships, stories, traditions and the very persons of our neighbours. Part of the task of 'treasure-seeking' is to recognize with humility, and without seeking to take control, the unexpected ways, people and places in which God is alive and active.

'Hearing to speech'

A third tactic builds on those that we've explored already, and digs deeper into how we can be more intentional in making spaces for others to be 'heard to speech', as feminist theologian Nelle Morton succinctly put it.

Alongside Morton, another helpful guide here is Otto Scharmer,[6] whose work is largely in the domain of management theory, but whose insights have much wider application, and strong resonances with what we are exploring here, and our focus on how we as Christians engage with our neighbours, particularly when 'we' come to those engagements with more than our share of power and privilege.

Scharmer describes four different levels of the things we usually think of simply as listening. The first, most superficial level, he describes as 'downloading', or 'listening from habit'. At this level, we simply hear what we expect to hear – 'I knew you'd say that' – and anything potentially surprising or challenging just bounces off us, leaving us utterly unchanged in our opinions, judgements and understanding.

A second level, a little deeper, Scharmer calls 'factual listening' or 'listening from the outside'. At this level our mind is open to absorbing new information, noticing differences with what we already think we know, and learning.

Deeper again, Scharmer's third level is 'empathic listening' or 'listening within'. This involves not just an open mind but an open heart, opening ourselves to be touched emotionally, and to learn not just new information, but to see through another person's eyes.

But it is the deepest, fourth level that is most significant for us here. This level Scharmer calls 'generative listening', or 'listening from Source'. His language borders on the theological (note the capital S!), as he describes the possibility of listening with an open will, making space for something coming from the future to begin to emerge in the present – what Christian theologians would call an *eschatological* perspective, the way we talk about the kin-dom of God. Listening at this level is not a response to someone who is already talking, but a listening that is *prior to speech*

---

6 www.ottoscharmer.com/theoryu.

– Morton's 'hearing to speech' – creating the conditions for something to be articulated that has perhaps never been expressed before, that has potential to change radically both the speaker and the hearer, in not just heart and mind but across one's whole sense of self-identity. As Morton puts it: 'Speaking first to be heard is power-over. Hearing to bring forth speech is empowering.'[7]

Something like this kind of generative 'space-making' happens in counselling and psychotherapy – but Morton is describing something that is inherently more political. It is the opposite of the kinds of defensiveness and obliviousness, attached to different dimensions of privilege, that we teased out in Chapter 3. The one who is *heard* discovers power and possibility; the one who *hears* shares power in ways which open them to the possibilities of learning and being challenged – even the possibility of being changed in ways that we might name *repentance* – a possibility we will return to in Chapter 15.

Morton worked as an educator and community activist. 'Hearing to speech' was what she experienced, and intentionally practised, in her daily life and work, and she traced its impact not just at the interpersonal level, but in ripples that had the potential to spread wider and wider into the world:

> Hearing to speech is never one-sided.
> Once a person is heard to speech
> she becomes a hearing person.

Morton describes a chain reaction of hearing that sounds remarkably like the common Christian understanding of conversion and evangelism. With the latter, we often imagine that 'once a person has heard the gospel preached to them, she becomes a gospel-sharer with others'. For Morton, the roles of speaker and hearer are reversed: once a person is heard to speech, she becomes a hearing person with others. There is something infectious about hearing others to speech, the effects of which have the potential to spread far and wide, liberating people and shaking structures out of their unjust, distorted and apparently fixed 'realities'.

But it is significant too that Morton writes also as a theologian. 'Hearing to speech' is not just something that happens between human beings – it has its origin in God, the 'prior great Listening Ear ... an ear that hears ... our own'. The Gospel of John begins with 'In the beginning was the Word', but Morton recasts this as 'In the beginning was the *hearing*'.

---

7 Nelle Morton, *The Journey is Home* (Boston, MA: Beacon Press, 1985), p. 205. See also Rachel Muers, *Keeping God's Silence: Towards a Theological Ethics of Communication* (Oxford: Blackwell, 2004).

And in the new beginning of Pentecost, the work of the Spirit is that of hearing: giving birth, in the first Christians, to a language of liberation and new life.

This hearing work of the Spirit is and always will be ongoing. Jesus himself describes the process of the ongoing revelation of the Holy Spirit: 'I still have many things to say to you, but you cannot bear them now. When the Spirit of truth comes, he will guide you into all the truth' (John 16.12–13). The more we are prepared to listen – truly listen, with attention to our neighbours and to the Holy Spirit speaking through them – the more of this truth we may encounter, perhaps from the most unexpected sources. Still, there are truths we cannot yet bear to hear. By cultivating a habit of listening, by hearing one another to speech again and again, little by little we will come to glimpse more of God, to be able to bear and to hear more of the truth which sets us, our neighbours, and the whole creation free.

But again, we need to let go. With hearing to speech comes an acknowledgement that what is spoken may not be what we want or expect to hear, and a commitment to dwell in the uncomfortable tension of that. It is a kind of re-wilding of our mental landscape, a relinquishing of our cultivated frameworks and patterns of thought and behaviour, in order to create a messy, beautiful space in which the new truths we hear may take root and flourish. Allowing room within ourselves for that wild, uncontrolled flourishing is essential if we are to hear into speech the Spirit who so often speaks in sighs too deep for words, meeting us beyond whatever neat ideas of God we may have cultivated.

Flipping the axis

At the end of Part 1, we – especially those of us who recognize ourselves as multiply privileged – heard Jennifer Harvey's challenge to *dis-identify* with the 'social justice Jesus' who is 'the central power agent in his saga', and found ourselves sitting with Zacchaeus in his tree, on the receiving end of Jesus' challenging invitation to open ourselves to having our life interrupted, disrupted, changed radically (see bottom right corner of the axis in Figure 9). But we also took a crucial question into Part 2: 'What if Jesus *himself* is interrupted, disrupted, changed, by (at least some of) his encounters with those around him?' And by the end of Part 2, we uncovered in Mark's Gospel at least five examples of exactly this happening to Jesus – and all of them, importantly, in what biblical scholars identify as the 'active' phase of his life and ministry, before he is 'handed over' into his passion, suffering and death. In fact, in the story of the anointing woman, we saw that it was the woman's action that tipped Jesus into that second, 'passive' phase: she commissions him as the Christ-to-be-crucified, while at the same time giving him something in and through the ointment – love, commitment, *covenant* even – that will stay with him all the way to the cross and the tomb.

What our 'third economy' reveals is another possibility in our – the 'we' that is multiply privileged – relationship to Jesus. If we should, as Jennifer Harvey warns us, steer a wide birth from the 'heroic' activist approach to the question, 'What Would Jesus Do?' (top right in Figure 9), we might nevertheless catch at least glimpses, in Mark's Gospel, of a Jesus who is *radically receptive* to the interruptions, the gifts, the challenges of his 'others' (the top left corner of Figure 9). A Jesus less as the *Word* of God but, as Nelle Morton reframes it, as the *Hearing* of God, and who – sometimes instantly, sometimes with more time and even the odd misstep – recognizes and responds to the Word spoken, or embodied, by those 'others', or coming to life *in the space in between* him and them. *This* Jesus we might be justified in imitating. 'What might Jesus *hear*?', we could ask, instead. What might Jesus *notice*? How might Jesus *receive*? And, if one characteristic of this Jesus is that he is no longer 'centre-stage' – but is not merely identified with those perceived as 'needy' and 'lacking' (bottom left in Figure 9) – then *where* might Jesus be encountered?

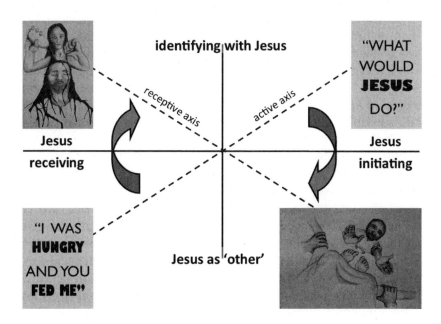

Figure 9: 'Flipping the axis' (shifting from 'active' to 'receptive')

Further reading

- Michael Mather, *Having Nothing, Possessing Everything: Finding Communities in Unexpected Places* (Grand Rapids, MI: Eerdmans, 2018)
- John McKnight and Peter Block, *The Abundant Community: Awakening the Power of Families and Neighbourhoods* (San Francisco, CA: Berrett-Koehler Publishers: 2012)
- Nelle Morton, *The Journey is Home* (Boston, MA: Beacon Press, 1985)
- Rachel Muers, *Keeping God's Silence: Towards a Theological Ethics of Communication* (Oxford: Blackwell, 2004)
- Andrew Rumsey, *Parish: An Anglican Theology of Place* (London: SCM Press, 2017)
- Cormac Russell, *Rekindling Democracy: A Professional's Guide to Working in Citizen Space* (Eugene, OR: Cascade, 2020)
- Isabella Tree, *Wilding: The Return of Nature to a British Farm* (London: Picador, 2019)

Questions for reflection/discussion

- Are there any elements of this third 'economy' which you recognize from your experience of church? Are there any that seem at odds with how the church currently operates?
- How easy or difficult do you find it to resist the temptation to always be 'doing stuff'? How can you cultivate ways of resisting that temptation?
- What do you see as the gifts in your neighbourhood? Is there anything you find it difficult to accept as a gift?
- Can you think of a time you have been 'heard into speech'? Or when you have heard someone into speech? How did that experience affect you?

Act 4

A Street Party

It's 9.30 a.m. on a Saturday morning in July, on the Firs and Bromford estate. A white van pulls up next to a green square, not much more than the size of a couple of tennis courts, edged on all sides by semi-detached and terraced houses, and blocks of 3-storey maisonettes. Out of the van, a man in his mid-20s and an older woman extract a bouncy castle and a generator, which they begin setting up on the green. It's not long before another car draws up, gazebos, bunting, a large water urn, games equipment and a giant Jenga set, among many other diverse items, packed tightly around its occupants.

As the gazebos go up, the visible busyness begins to draw neighbours out of the surrounding homes, some out of curiosity, but many others with a clear sense of purpose. A random collection of tables and chairs begins to assemble, and no sooner are the tables set down than they become home to a quickly growing array of sandwiches, samosas and pakoras, vats of meaty rice, and cakes of all shapes and sizes.

Although this street party has been advertised to start at midday, already by 10.30 a game of rounders has self-organized, and many of the chairs are occupied by neighbours of all ages chatting – often with lots of laughter, sometimes with more serious intent or compassionate care. While a number of people are clearly taking seriously the role of welcoming new arrivals, it's not immediately obvious who, if anyone, is 'running' the event, and it's quite apparent that many neighbours are meeting each other for the first time. Some adults lead arts and crafts activities with both children and other grown-ups. At one point a woman gets many of the assembled crowd on their feet and dancing in a high-energy Zumba session. At peak busyness, you might be able to count around 30 children and 40 adults enjoying the party in one way or another.

It's past 5 p.m. by the time the buzz begins to die down. The food has mostly been eaten, the chairs and tables begin to disappear with their owners back to their respective homes – but there are still enough people around to dismantle the gazebos, and scour each square metre of the green for litter. Two boys have to be persuaded, reluctantly, to relinquish two bats and a ball.

13

Life at the Edges

One of the key ideas in this book has been that of economies: complex systems that shape the ways we think, behave and interact with each other. In the previous chapter, the language of economy began to mix with the language of ecology or ecosystem: expanding our imagination to include the more-than-human world, with a deeper understanding not just of our interactions but of our interdependence as living creatures – that even includes (as we touched on briefly with the fig-tree story in Chapter 11) the gifts that can be given by parts of the ecology that are dying or apparently 'dead'. In this chapter, we want to shift our location a little, from somewhere right in the middle of an ecosystem, to somewhere in its borderlands, its edge-places.

The technical term for these edge-places is the *ecotone*: from the Greek words *oikos* (habitat, home, household) and *tonos* (tension). Between a lake (aquatic habitat) and a meadow (land habitat), for example, the edge-place or ecotone is the area along the shoreline where the two habitats meet and interact. The borderland between forest and heathland would be another example.

But these edge-places are not simply the boundary between one habitat and another, lines that you cross from one to the other like national borders. In these ecological borderlands, species from the two neighbouring habitats interact and intermingle, and a greater diversity and density of life is found there than in either of the two distinct habitats within themselves – making them places full of huge potential for new species to evolve and emerge, and unique 'micro-habitats' where rare 'niche species' are able to flourish.

The contrast between ecotones and human borderlands, then, is striking. The latter are so often fenced with razor wire and populated with checkpoints and armed guards. Areas of 'no-man's land' are demarcated precisely to *prevent* interaction across borders. Human history is bloody with memories of wars fought over borderlines, and imperial dreams of territorial expansion, of borders being pushed farther and farther back and ultimately eliminated altogether.

We are also used to talking about 'the edges', or 'the margins', as those places, communities and people-groups that are farthest away – sometimes geographically, often economically and culturally, and always politically – from the 'centres' of power, resources and decision-making. Margins can become 'cliff-edges' when lives and livelihoods are under-resourced, unsupported, precarious: the end result of the poverty of resources, relationships and identity that we explored in Chapter 2. And, as we saw there, in our collective imagination and public conversation such edge-places are all too often portrayed as 'lacking', 'defective', a 'problem'.

To reimagine edge-places as abundant with life and potential, then, demands a radical imaginative shift – especially if we do not have personal experience in the kind of permaculture gardening that seeks to mimic natural processes and maximize the benefits of ecological 'edge effects'. But according to Russian philosopher Mikhail Bakhtin, human cultures function much more like the fertile edge-places of ecosystems than the clearly bounded territories of countries edged by hard borders. A living culture, he wrote, has 'no internal territory', but rather its 'boundaries pass everywhere' – the interactions and intermingling of edge-places are what *makes* culture a living thing. Take the boundaries away, says Bakhtin, and culture 'loses its soil, it becomes empty, arrogant, it degenerates and dies'.[1]

Church in the edge-places?

What might this mean for what we usually call 'church'? In the first, 'counting in', economy of church life that we explored in Chapter 5, what mattered most were the countable things that came 'into church' (money and people), and the health or success of church life was measured by the size of its membership list and its bank balance – a very measurable kind of 'territory', the growth and expansion of which was something like the goal of the church's mission. The second economy, defined by 'giving out', was more relaxed about inhabiting the world beyond the church's own territory without trying to bring it all into what counts as 'church'. But here (as we teased out in Chapter 6) the territory of the church, as literally the 'place of worship', was vital as the place where Christians were fed and taught, formed and empowered, before they were able to go out and feed and teach others; mission, as 'service'

---

1 Mikhail Bakhtin, quoted in Romand Coles, 'The Pregnant Reticence of Rowan Williams: Letter of February 27, 2006', in Stanley Hauerwas and Romand Coles, *Christianity, Democracy and the Radical Ordinary: Conversations between a Radical Democrat and a Christian* (Cambridge: Lutterworth Press), 2008, p. 175.

and 'proclamation', happens as a *secondary step* to the prior formation that happens 'in church'.

But what if church and mission more resembled the life-generating interminglings in our ecological edge-places, or the interactions on the boundaries that, according to Bakhtin, keep a human culture alive? This is the question that Romand Coles – an American 'radical democratic' activist and political theorist – puts to the Christian community, from the outside. (Coles would not count himself as a Christian, but reads a lot of Christian writers with great enthusiasm and generosity.) What if church were a people, not 'called and gathered *prior* to encountering others', but a people just as profoundly and foundationally formed *at our borders, in our encounters with others*?[2] Rather than emphasizing – as our second economy would – the role of the church as speaker, eucharistic host, foot-washer and server, Coles suggests we discover the possibilities for the church as *listener*, as *guest* at other tables, and as in need of being *served* and having its feet *washed* by others in the edge-places beyond the church walls – and in the process to become more fully and faithfully *church* – a church that is at home not in its own 'territory' but precisely in those edge-places.

This would be a church rooted in the kind of encounters between Jesus and his 'others' that we explored in depth in Chapters 7 to 11. This understanding of 'church' would make it more difficult for us to think in the usual theological categories of *ecclesiology* (what the church is) and *missiology* (how the church is sent out) – and invite us to think more in terms of what South African theologian Klippies Kritzinger calls *encounterology*, the ways in which the church 'becomes flesh' precisely in and through its encounters – what Franciscan scholar Gillian Ahlgren identifies as being right at the heart of the way of life of St Francis and St Clare in thirteenth-century Italy:

> For Francis and Clare, encounter became an arresting way of life, open to all. In their experience, there was no one whose life would not be deeply enriched by deeper dedication to the way of encounter. Engaging the other with the intention to listen, to learn, and to connect is a mutually transformative practice that slowly changes everything. Encounter teaches us to honour the fragility and sacredness of our own humanity, especially as we come to know our common humanity together. When done in the conscious presence of the love of God, encounter creates sacred space in the human community. Encounter moves us from

---

2 Romand Coles, '"Gentled into Being": Vanier and the Border at the Core', in Hauerwas and Coles, *Christianity, Democracy and the Radical Ordinary*, p. 212.

observers of life to collaborators, with God, in the building up of the human community, the creation of a common home.[3]

What Ahlgren describes comes close to summarizing what we have called the third economy, of 'being interrupted', located in the edge-places, beyond 'territory', of encounters between human beings, and between human beings and the more-than-human world. She describes a way of making those edge-places *sacred*, making them *home* – a home we share with each other, a home we share with God.

Finding and creating 'bumping spaces'

'Hodge Hill Unsung Heroes', the celebration gathering where Phil shared his idea for a community theatre group, was the culmination of a few months of church members engaging in intentional conversations, active listening, in what we've learned to call 'bumping spaces' around our area: those places where people naturally come into close proximity with each other – whether or not they ever actually have a conversation. We hung out in the foyer of the Children's Centre, in the queue at the Post Office, in the parks often used by dog-walkers, at the bookies, the barbers and at the school gate. In some of those places, it seemed sensible, polite, or even safest, to ask for permission, or at least to explain what we were doing to those in charge of those spaces. Strangers hanging around at school gates, for example, are not always welcome! The fact that we weren't recruiting, 'selling' anything or asking for money did help. The idea that we were there simply to *listen* to people was almost always embraced enthusiastically.

Out of this process of getting to know our neighbourhood more thoroughly, volunteers from church started two significant, but very modest, local initiatives. The first we called 'Hodge Hill Cuppa': once a month at each of two local primary schools (with their permission, of course), towards the end of the school day, a few of us would set up a table in the playground, where parents and carers congregate to collect their children. We offered free tea, coffee, squash and biscuits, information about activities and events going on in the neighbourhood – and a friendly face and a listening ear. Over time, these 'pop-up' spaces of hospitality, not on our own 'turf', have become expected and valued by many – and often enables genuine encounters in spaces where people might not otherwise talk to each other.

---

3 Gillian Ahlgren, *The Tenderness of God: Reclaiming our Humanity* (Minneapolis, MN: Fortress, 2017), pp. 35–6.

The second modest initiative was a more 'solid' expression of what 'Hodge Hill Cuppa' was attempting to offer. It was sparked by the city council's decision to close the doors of the local Neighbourhood Office, a place where people had been able to walk in to get advice and support with housing and benefits issues. The initial idea behind what became 'Open Door' was to start a debt advice centre or a job club, along the lines of one of the nationwide franchises that were becoming prominent in Christian circles. But neither the franchise model nor the 'service provider' approach sat comfortably with us as a church, and what evolved, based in a small shop-front youth centre run by a local partner organization, was a weekly drop-in space that offered, first and foremost, a warm welcome and a cuppa, a place to sit and chat and make friends. Our volunteers would, if people wanted it, sit with someone and work through a form from the Department for Work and Pensions or put together a CV, but that was to be a secondary, rather than primary, purpose of Open Door. We were also profoundly committed to helping people identify what their gifts, skills and passions might be, and work out how they might be able to share them with their neighbours. Open Door became one of the first of a national network of 'Places of Welcome', a network which includes the value of *Participation* among its five 'P's.[4] The intention of Open Door was to chip away at the distinction between 'hosts' and 'guests', drawing and encouraging participants to join in the work – and the fun! – of hosting.

Unearthing the 'connectors'

A third kind of 'bumping space' has emerged as the church's involvement in community-building went deeper into the roots of neighbourhood life. Just like the fine, fungal threads that connect trees together in what has been called 'the wood-wide web' (see Chapter 11), we've discovered that many of the connections in a neighbourhood are hidden, below the surface, quietly channelling information and sharing life-sustaining resources. We have discovered people in our neighbourhood who wouldn't often be described as 'community leaders', because they're rarely the most visible, rarely 'up front', rarely the loudest voices in the room. But they *are* people who are known, liked and trusted by their neighbours, and they have the particular gift of noticing the gifts in others, and being unafraid to make connections between neighbours whose needs and gifts might fit together, but who don't yet know each other. We call them 'connectors'. And at the

---

4 See www.placesofwelcome.org.uk for the latest map of Places of Welcome nationally, and for more about their core values.

moment, we pay Paul, a resident of our neighbourhood and a member of our church community, to unearth those neighbours with the natural gift of connecting, and to support them to do it more intentionally.[5]

Every week, a team of 'street connectors' go out walking around different parts of our neighbourhood, knocking on every door they pass, seeking out doorstep conversations that might be an opportunity for 'hearing to speech' (see Chapter 12), inviting neighbours to consider what gifts they might possibly have to share with others in our neighbourhood. And often, one of the questions they ask people is whether they might be willing to be a 'host' for one of our small, 'micro-local' street parties (as described in Act 5 above). Supported by our regular connectors, street party hosts are the people who take responsibility for inviting their neighbours (usually around 50 households at the most), and kicking off the provision of tables and chairs, food and drink, for the party. What we have found is that once one or two hosts get the ball rolling, other neighbours begin to join in – not as consumers of something that has been put on *for* them, but as co-producers of something that they make happen together: these other neighbours also offer to bring furniture, make food, set up games and activities, and so on. The chain reaction that Nelle Morton named as 'hearing one another to speech' unearths and nurtures an economy of abundance, and a deepening and multiplying of connections. In contrast to our large-scale 'community events', where people attend in their hundreds – usually coming in their already-established groups of family and friends – and go away feeling happy, but rarely having got to know anyone they didn't already know, we've found that every time a small-scale street party happens, significant numbers of neighbours get to know someone from their street, by name, for the very first time – and that those friendships often deepen in the following weeks and months.

From 'body of Christ' to 'flesh of Jesus'

In our neighbour-led street parties, the church's involvement in community-building has 'gone deeper into the roots'. We might also say *submerged*. There is nothing about a street party that has the church 'stamp' on it, and the initiative, the leadership, the connecting and the hosting have all moved a significant distance beyond the church's agency, let alone control. The discovering and sharing of gifts, the welcoming of strangers, the

---

5 See https://streetconnector.wordpress.com/2018/11/10/engagement-comes-naturally-jos-story-of-being-a-leader-and-a-connector/ for the story of Jo, one of our most passionate connectors – and some of Paul's reflections on the role.

deepening of friendships, the breaking of bread and the sharing of wine (among many other forms of refreshment!) all have strikingly eucharistic resonances to them, but we would be over-reaching ourselves in a dangerously colonialist manner if we were to 'claim' such events as part of the distinct, boundaried 'body of Christ' that we often imagine when we think of 'church'.

But encounter, Gillian Ahlgren suggested, can 'create sacred space in the human community' – the kind of sacred, and transformational, spaces that we saw emerging in encounters between Jesus and some of his 'others' in Mark's Gospel. So how might we, as Christians, talk about such fertile edge-places in ways that speak also of God? Rather than 'body' language, with its relatively clear boundary between 'inside' and 'outside', we want to suggest the creative possibilities that arise if we play instead with the language of 'flesh'.

What does the word 'flesh' conjure up for you? The raw material from which bodies are made, perhaps? Something that goes deeper than 'skin', more than just the *surface*, but like skin names what can be uncovered and exposed, and also – like the ecotone – what *comes into contact*. Flesh is what *touches*, and *is touched* – it distinguishes one body from another, but it is also what joins us together. As such, flesh is the raw material not just of *bodies*, but also of love and joy and discovery – and of violence, shame and fear. Flesh is profoundly entangled with vulnerability. Flesh can be *marked*, wounded, and those marks and wounds can go deep, and can endure for a lifetime, even into death.

Is flesh gendered, raced, classed and aged? Only in so far as it is marked by its interactions, by what is done to it and how it is perceived, by the ways it has changed and *been changed* over time. 'The particular ways in which my *flesh* is shaped by the world depends on how my *body* is perceived in society', post-colonial theologian Mayra Rivera reminds us.[6] My flesh is shaped by what theorists of gender, race and class call 'the gaze': how my body – and bodies in some ways like mine – is looked at and seen, described and represented in the media, thought about and treated, by those who, in positions of power and privilege, 'set the rules of the game'. So the patriarchal 'male gaze' views women as (passive) sexual objects for the pleasure of the (active) male viewer; the racializing 'white gaze' looks for this or that bodily trait (skin colour being just one among others) and separates the world into 'those like us' and those who are 'different' and inferior; and in a similar way the 'middle-class gaze' looks for traits of behaviour, dress or voice to cast some people – 'the poor' – as crude, feckless, stupid or needy, in contrast to the self-

---

6 Mayra Rivera, *Poetics of the Flesh* (Durham: Duke University Press, 2015), p. 114.

styled sophisticated, cultured, cosmopolitan observer. There is also, as we explored in Chapter 5, a 'heroic', or 'missionary gaze', which views those who 'aren't like us' as lacking, in need of what we can provide for them or perform to them, or needing us to make *their* territory *ours* to manage or control because we know what's best for them.

The 'gaze', then, in all its various forms, observes from a distance, categorizes, and 'flattens' a world of complexity to simply 'how I see it', imagining somehow that 'how I see it' is identical with a universal, objective view of reality. In stark contrast, the political theorist Romand Coles (following in the footsteps of philosopher Maurice Merleau-Ponty) introduces the idea of 'intercorporeal illumination': seeing the world not solely through our own eyes, but through the interaction between *different* ways of perceiving the world; through the interaction of different bodies standing (or sitting, or lying!) in even subtly different locations. And seeing not to judge or control, but for our seeing and understanding to be transformed. There is, suggests Coles, a 'depth', a 'richness', a 'wildness' of truth that can never be glimpsed through the 'flattening', 'imperial gaze', but can only emerge through these 'intercorporeal' interactions.

Coles goes on to describe 'the flesh of Jesus' as that 'thick yet flexible, vulnerable, porous membrane' which 'at once joins with and distinguishes' what we usually call 'church' from what we usually think of as 'world'. The flesh of Jesus 'extends beyond the committed', not simply *into*, but precisely *as* the contact zones, the fertile ecotones, between 'church' and 'world'.[7] The deep, rich wildness of truth, rather than something the church possesses, or even *receives*, within its own secure 'territory', is in fact something that only *becomes flesh* in our interactions, our encounters, across the lines that would normally divide us: lines between 'Christian' and 'non-Christian', as well as lines defined by gender, race, class, age, geography, species and more. To paraphrase Gillian Ahlgren, we might say that, when done in the conscious presence of the love of God, *Jesus becomes flesh* in our encounters across difference, within the human community.

Seeing glory, in the flesh

For much of this book, we have focused on the Jesus we encounter through the narrative of Mark's Gospel. Our shift here to the language of 'flesh' is rooted in a different lens through which we see Jesus: the Gospel

---

7 Coles, 'Pregnant Reticence of Rowan Williams', pp. 191–2.

of John. 'The Word became flesh and lived among us' – 'moved into our neighbourhood', as *The Message* translation puts it – 'and we have seen his glory' (John 1.14). John, in turn, is surely recalling the words of the prophet Isaiah: 'And the glory of the Lord shall be revealed, and all flesh shall see it together' (Isaiah 40.5, KJV). We see God's glory in the flesh of God's creatures, and we see God's glory *as* the fleshy creatures that we are, together, in the edge-places of our encounters with each other.

Gillian Ahlgren's phrase, 'in the conscious presence of the love of God' is a call to *contemplation*, to habits of attentiveness that stay put, and look, and look again, seeking to *notice*, in the often unpromising, unsung and unnoticed, the often fragile, torn and vulnerable – in the flesh, we might say – to see God's glory. But if it is a call to *look*, then it is a call to *look together*, to lean in to each other in our shared search for what Romand Coles calls 'intercorporeal illumination'. Often, those moments of shared seeing will take our breath away. Often, they will move us to tears. Often, they will change us. Always, they will be moments of standing on holy ground. Just as with the practice of generative listening, this 'looking together' needs us to give it *time*, time for us to begin to receive its gifts and its challenges, time to let it begin to change us.

But when the moment, the encounter, has passed, what happens next? What do we 'do' with what has just happened to us, with the gifts and challenges that we have received? Where can we take them? These are the questions we take into our next chapter.

Further reading

- Gillian Ahlgren, *The Tenderness of God: Reclaiming our Humanity* (Minneapolis, MN: Fortress, 2017)
- Samuel E. Ewell, *Faith Seeking Conviviality: Reflections on Ivan Illich, Christian Mission, and the Promise of Life Together* (Eugene, OR: Cascade, 2019)
- Stanley Hauerwas and Romand Coles, *Christianity, Democracy and the Radical Ordinary: Conversations between a Radical Democrat and a Christian* (Cambridge: Lutterworth Press, 2008)
- Dorothy Lee, *Flesh and Glory: Symbolism, Gender and Theology in the Gospel of John* (New York: Crossroad, 2002)
- Mayra Rivera, *Poetics of the Flesh* (Durham: Duke University Press, 2015)

Questions for reflection/discussion

- Where are the 'edge-places' and the 'bumping spaces' in your neighbourhood/community?
- Think of someone you know who is a good 'connector'. What are the qualities you value in them?
- Can you think of an example of a time you have 'seen God's glory in the flesh'? What helped you to recognize it?

Act 5

The Community Talent Show

It was a Friday night in St Wilfrid's Community Centre, which had played host, for a while, to a monthly 'open mic night' and, more recently, a weekly family disco. Tonight, however, was extra special. The tables and chairs had been dressed up as if for a wedding reception, and balloons, streamers and lots of excited neighbours filled the main hall. This was the very first 'Firs and Bromford's Got Talent' live finals night.

Compèred by members of the Bromford Theatre Group, the evening included performances from local residents young and old, singing, dancing and performance poetry. Every performer had a story – a journey, a battle, to get on to the stage that evening. Many had struggled for years with chronic low confidence or anxiety. And yet, their courage and determination, their raw vulnerability and yet dignity and pride, was clear for all to see as they stood there before us, showing us something of their God-given passions and talents.

In the end, the 'competition' wasn't really a competition at all: each and every one of them was cheered on – willed on, hoped and prayed on – by each and every one of us in the audience, and we were heart-burstingly proud of all of them. We would have made them all joint winners if we could have done. Our role, collectively, was encourager, cheerleader, celebrant of the wonderful gifts of our neighbours – the wonderful gifts that are our neighbours.

14

From the Outside, in

In February 2020, the Dean of Winchester, Catherine Ogle, tweeted a photo of the cathedral crypt. Framed by the stone arches stood a solitary statue in lead, a life-size male figure with head bent, contemplating the water held in his cupped hands.[1] What was particularly striking about this photo was that the bronze man was knee-deep in water. The cathedral crypt had flooded (as it does most years) after weeks of heavy rain, a fate at that point common to homes, other buildings and land in countless places across the UK – one of many ways in which the effects of global climate change are beginning to be noticed, and felt more dramatically, on our own doorsteps.

---

[1] You can see photos of the statue at www.winchester-cathedral.org.uk/gallery/ant-ony-gormley-sound-ii/

The statue had been made by sculptor Antony Gormley, shaped on a cast of his own body. Gormley had, a few months before, staged an exhibition of his work at the Royal Academy of Arts in London, which included one piece called *Host*: in one of the grand nineteenth-century rooms of the gallery, with white walls and gilded ceiling, Gormley had covered the floor with a thick layer of Buckinghamshire clay and Atlantic seawater.[2] An 'invasion of the inside by the outside', is how the exhibition notes described it, quoting Gormley's own words. 'Is it an image of destruction – a devastating flood? Or of potential creation?'

This chapter explores that question for that vital, recurring moment in the life of the church when it gathers for worship. What might it mean to respond to the 'invasion of the inside by the outside' not with fear and defensiveness, but with welcome and the anticipation that it might contribute to us being 'made new'?

In Chapter 6, we explored the ways in which we often come to church (or at least, approach the four-fold structure of worship, *gathering – word – table – sending*) as worshippers coming to receive: coming in with empty hands, hearts (and tummies!), ready to be filled, equipped and energized to go out into the world to serve our neighbours and proclaim the gospel. In this understanding of worship, we *receive* from God, to *give out* to the world – our second, 'giving out', economy in a nutshell.

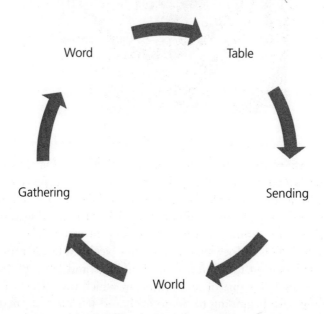

Figure 10: The 'cycle' of worship, revisited

---

2 See the exhibition guide at: www.royalacademy.org.uk/exhibition/antony-gormley.

154

But what might happen to our gatherings for worship if we reverse the flow – if we're as much formed by what we receive in our encounters with others in the edge-places of the world, as we are by what happens in church? How can the life of the *gathered* church be formed, transformed, and even *re*formed, by our missional engagements with our neighbours?

Gathering

Rather than gathering for worship as empty vessels, thirsty for a spiritual 'refuelling' after a week of giving out in the world, in this third economy we Christians will come to church overflowing with stories of encounter, gift and challenge from encounters with our neighbours. Where the second economy placed the emphasis on the final *sending* phase of worship, now we will pay much more attention to the *gathering*. It will be much more than simply the 'are we ready? then let's begin ...' to which we are often accustomed.

At Hodge Hill Church, we often begin worship by asking congregation members two questions, thinking about places, people or situations from the past week, either close to home or in other parts of the world:

- What do you bring with you, from your week in the world, that you want to say thank you to God for?
- What do you come with, that weighs heavily on you, that you want to bring to God in prayer and concern?

In different liturgical seasons of the year, we will often vary the questions, for example:

- In Advent – where is the world longing for light, and hope?
- In the Christmas and Epiphany seasons – where in the world have we caught glimpses of God's glory?
- In Lent – where in the world is thirsting for the water of life? Where have we been challenged this week, that we need to bring to God in confession?
- In the Easter season – where have we seen signs of resurrection life?
- On and after Pentecost – where have we seen the Spirit bringing life?

Then we invite people first to spend some time quietly reflecting on their own or, if they prefer, talking with one or two people nearby. Next we invite some of those who are feeling a bit braver to share within the wider congregation. The response is fascinatingly unpredictable. When we first introduced this into our 'gathering' liturgy, there were quite a few faces looking completely blank, or worried they had nothing to say. After a week or two, the 'buzz' in the small conversations grew in energy and volume, and would sometimes be hard to interrupt! When people are invited to share publicly, some weeks there will be next to nothing (even after a busy 'buzz' in small groups!), but sometimes it's like the flood-gates have opened and there will be a torrent of gratitude, compassion and concern.

In the church tradition of most of our congregation members, this 'speaking out' in church has been unfamiliar. We recognize for some church traditions it is much more commonplace. But for us it has gently revolutionized our worship, and how it links to our lives in the world. These gathering questions, alongside what we call 'fifth gospels' (personal invitations to congregation members to offer a two- to three-minute reflection on where, recently, they've encountered God, or how they've seen God 'at work' over a longer timescale), stand in the long and broad Christian tradition of 'testimony', shared in different ways by Quakers, Pentecostals and many others. But what we have tried to emphasize as we've explored it, is to resist the urge to fit these fragments of 'testimony' into any predefined framework: while it may be true for some people that before they first encountered Jesus their life was terrible, and after that encounter their life has been nothing but joyful, for most of us the story is much more complex, messy and unresolved. At their best, these are stories of being surprised, interrupted, challenged and stretched – and as they are told, and heard by others, the church as a whole is also surprised, interrupted, challenged and stretched.

In Hodge Hill, we are quite a liturgical church community – we value a significant element of structure to our worship, and familiar elements that are consistent from week to week. But within that familiar structure, we are also discovering the freedom to be able to 'faithfully improvise', following the prompting and guiding of the Spirit in our midst. For us that particularly means being attentive to what is shared in the 'gathering' – and how it could or should shape what follows in the rest of our worship together:

- What have we shared, and heard, that shapes what we should give thanks for today, and how we should do that?
- What have we shared, and heard, that shapes how we should say sorry today, how we should bring our prayers of grief and lament to God, how we should seek God's forgiveness and healing – for ourselves, for our church community, for our neighbourhoods, for the world we share?

- What have we shared, and heard, that shapes what and whom we should pray for today – in our prayers of concern and intercession – and how we should do that?

Word and table

How, therefore, would our third economy, the economy of *being inter-rupted*, reshape the ways in which we listen for God's word, and gather around God's table in church?

First, we can hold on to their significance – as the second economy emphasizes – as *practices that form us*: repeated words and actions, week after week, that mould and shape our habits of word and action, of thinking and feeling, of interacting and responding in other parts of our daily lives. But we might reimagine these church-based practices less as *filling* us up and more as *opening* us up.

Second (and really this is inextricable from the first suggestion), we can explore ways of reconfiguring both word and table as spaces of *gathering*, as much as they are also spaces of *equipping*; not so much 'professional catering', but more 'bring-and-share feast'.

So how might what we Anglicans call 'the liturgy of the word' in church become a space where we get to practise that *generative listening* which Otto Scharmer calls 'listening from Source', and Nelle Morton named 'hearing to speech'? Yes, as Bible readings are read, or acted out, we are listening for what God might be saying to us, a word that we trust will form us and transform us. But what if we are also being formed in the art of listening itself, in seeking to hear with God's ears, so that we might be more attentive listeners among our neighbours in the world? We mentioned Quaker and Pentecostal practices of keeping shared silence, and making space for congregation members to offer testimony. But are there other ways that this space can shape us as deep listeners?

Perhaps some of the suggested approaches to Bible stories that we offered at the beginning of Part 2 – much more participative than a con-ventional 'sermon slot' – might help us deepen the art of 'hearing one another to speech'? But if the liturgy of the word is truly to become a 'bring and share feast', then we need also to find ways of asking questions such as:

- Where in this Bible passage do we hear echoes of encounters we've had with our neighbours?

- Where have I seen God present or active in the world in similar ways to how God is present or active in this passage? What verbs does God have in this passage that are also verbs I've witnessed in the world?
- What story could we share from our life in the world that might resonate with what we're hearing in this passage?
- What questions might a particular neighbour (held for now in my mind and heart) ask of this passage, if they were here?
- What am I learning from particular neighbours that resonates with this passage today?

When we come to gather around the communion table, different questions and opportunities arise. As we are fed with the bread and wine, the body and blood of Christ, how might that also deepen in us a hunger and thirst to sit around other tables with our neighbours, receiving the hospitality they are longing to offer us, and the food and multitude of other gifts they are wanting to share with us? How can the 'foretaste of heaven' we enjoy in church whet our appetite for the heavenly banquets of many other dishes that are served up in kitchens and community centres, in mosques and gurdwaras, on bus journeys and at school breaktimes, in picnics in the park and around the drinks machine at work?

Perhaps it is in the little details of our bodily interactions in the Eucharist – the way our eyes meet with the one offering us food and drink, the way we open our hands to receive, the way we taste and savour and swallow and give thanks for what we are given – might giving these things more of our regular, mindful attention slowly sculpt our bodies, mould our embodied habits, for similar interactions in our daily lives? Surely in the sharing of communion we are learning expectation, patience, cooperation, humility, receptive openness, joy and gratitude ('Eucharist' literally means *thanksgiving*, after all), and much more, that could profoundly shape the way we behave at other tables, at other meals, at other moments of sharing and receiving.

But might it be possible too, at least sometimes, for the celebration of communion in church to include the taking, and giving thanks, and breaking and sharing of some of the gifts that we have brought with us, received from our neighbours? The unexpected curry brought round by a Muslim neighbour celebrating Eid? A slice of the home-made cake, or the leftover Greggs pastries, first shared at the weekly community lunch? Might such offerings, brought to the eucharistic table, help us give thanks for those other places of sharing and bread-breaking – those 'altars in the world', to use Barbara Brown Taylor's phrase?[3] Might they train us in a

---

3 Barbara Brown Taylor, *An Altar in the World: Finding the Sacred Beneath our Feet* (Norwich: Canterbury Press, 2009).

greater attentiveness not just to the gifts from our neighbours, but to the gifts our neighbours *are* to us?

Sending

'Go in peace to love and serve the Lord' are the words of 'dismissal' in most Church of England communion services. We observed, in Chapter 6, how much the final *sending* section of our liturgies tends to focus on going out *fed*, *equipped* and *energized*, to *feed*, *serve* and *proclaim* to our neighbours. Little tweaks of language can make a big difference here. What if, for example, we were sent out with:

> Let us go in peace
> to *meet* and love Christ in our neighbours.

Or

> Let us go into the world,
> *seeking* and sharing Christ's peace.

And just as with our *gathering* liturgies, different seasons of the year offer opportunities to stir in us a renewed openness to encountering God in our encounters in the world, in ways that transform us:

> keep us ever watchful,
> that we may be ready to meet Jesus.
> (from a post-communion prayer for Advent)

> May Christ, the Light of the World,
> reveal in all creation glimpses of his glory
> (from a blessing for the Epiphany season)

> God of resurrection,
> we have met you here
> in words of life and bread broken and shared.
> As we go out into the world,
> open our eyes to see your presence,
> open our ears to hear your voice,
> and open our hands to receive you with joy,
> that all creation might shout ALLELUIA!
> through Jesus Christ our Lord. **Amen.**

Alleluia! Christ is risen.
He is risen indeed. Alleluia!
Where compassion is earthed
Christ is risen!
Where generosity overflows
Christ is risen!
Where trust takes root
Christ is risen!
Where friendship grows
Christ is risen!
Where hope blossoms
Christ is risen!
(post-communion prayer and closing responses for Easter season)

Reversing the 'orders'

The Church of England talks about the different 'orders' of ministry within the body of Christ: the *laos* (a Greek word, often translated as 'laity', but meaning 'the whole people of God'); deacons (Greek *diakonos*, meaning 'servant' or 'minister'); priests (or presbyters, Greek *presbuteros*, meaning 'elder'); and bishops (Greek *episkopos*, meaning 'overseer'). Although the Church of England, in its official documents (such as the liturgies for ordinations), does its best to describe these 'orders' as different gifts brought to the whole, of equal value, all too often it slips into hierarchical thinking. The orders themselves, after all, come as 'layers' overlaid on each other – when you are ordained into a new layer, you retain all the previous layers too – so it is difficult to avoid the idea that more layers means, well, *more*.

Even in recent years, as the Church has rediscovered and re-emphasized the critical role of the *laos*, the whole people of God, as the primary ministers and messengers of the gospel,[4] the *economics* of church life has more often than not emphasized a power dynamic where money, resources, strategy and direction flow from the 'centre' ('the diocese', focused on the bishop) out to the 'edges': first to the parishes, focused on the priest; then further outwards – as we've seen in Chapter 6 – to the wider congregation, who are encouraged and empowered to 'go out' yet further, in their mission and discipleship in 'the world'.[5]

---

4 See for example the Church of England's 'Setting God's People Free' report and work that has followed from it, www.churchofengland.org/SGPF.

5 The Church of England's 'Renewal and Reform' programme, intended to reshape the church for the twenty-first century, has included a huge shift in the way money is dis-

But what if we imagined the flow differently? What if we were better able to notice, value and celebrate the things that flow in the opposite direction, from the outside and the edges, inwards towards what we've called the 'centre(s)' – beyond the things that are most often counted, the money (for 'parish share' or 'common fund') and church attendance data?

Starting with the (more-than-human) world

What if we started at the edges, in the edge-places, the ecotones, of the world? What if we started by dwelling in those places, and letting them form us, in contemplation and wonder? What if we started by listening to what Pope Francis has called 'the cry of the earth' – the ways in which the earth and other-than-human creatures raise their voices in celebration and resistance to injustice[6] – and attending to the embodied wisdom, the rhythms and the connections, of the ecosystems of which we are a part? What if, like the American grass farmer Joel Salatin, we were to make a habit of getting down on our tummies to get the ant's-eye view of the world;[7] like permaculture gardeners, to reshape our technologies and our ways of life to imitate and follow an ecosystem's inbuilt processes; or like practitioners of re-wilding, to step back and see what the other-than-human world will do without our interference?

And then (as we explored in the 'third economy' of Chapter 12), we might attend similarly, in the 'bumping spaces' of our neighbourhoods, to our human neighbours: not as 'potential Christians' (let alone 'potential financial givers') or 'empty vessels' waiting to be filled, but as abundantly gifted, by God, with wonderful, surprising, awkward, unsettling, transformative gifts. Gifts that our neighbours are longing to share with us, or that they are already sharing, if we would only open our eyes to notice. Gifts that can teach, feed, unsettle and enliven us. How richly blessed would we find ourselves to be, when we begin to receive such

---

tributed, but again with high degrees of centralized decision-making. Of all the money distributed by the 'Strategic Development Fund' so far, the largest proportion has gone into the planting of 'resource churches': big, well-resourced churches often located in city centres, intended to generate a 'missional flow of ministry' to the places of the city where resourcing is deemed most needed (with some churches labelled, explicitly or implicitly, as 'needy' or even 'failing'). (See www.churchofengland.org/about/renewal-reform)

6 Pope Francis, *Laudato Si': On Care for our Common Home*; see also eco-justice principles of the *Earth Bible*, in Celia Deane-Drummond, *A Primer in Ecotheology* (Eugene, OR: Cascade Books, 2017), p. 31.

7 See for example Michael Pollan, 'Sustaining Vision', https://michaelpollan.com/articles-archive/sustaining-vision/

gifts through encounters with our neighbours – and especially with those neighbours who, seen through a purely financial lens, have little that can be counted?

The laos *as the (receptive) agents of mission*

Who, then, is the 'we' who do the listening in the world's edge-places? We have used the language of the *laos* as 'the whole people of God', but we should be more modest with such language: many of our faithful neighbours might describe themselves as 'people of God' too; we are talking here about that sub-section of God's people, who specifically seek to follow the way of Jesus. Formed and transformed in the edge-places, as much if not more than we are 'in church', we will both understand the *laos*, dispersed in the world, as the church's primary agents of mission, but also that mission as first and foremost a *receptive* endeavour: of opening ourselves to notice and nurture, to listen and draw out, to celebrate and affirm, to be challenged and changed. It's a kind of 'evangelism', as we noted in Chapter 12) that can be infectious: once a person is heard to speech, she becomes a hearing person for others. Such encounters should also send followers of Jesus, like the disciples on the Emmaus Road (Luke 24.13–35), running with haste back to our fellow-believers to share breathlessly what we have heard and seen.

Deacons as 'threshold-crossers'

If two of the most significant gifts of ordained ministry are to *symbolize* and *enable* the ministries of all members of the body of Christ, then the role of the deacon emerges with a new clarity, beyond the traditional understanding of being 'servants' of the church. Jess Foster, a 'distinctive deacon' (i.e. permanent) in the diocese of Birmingham describes her vocation: 'My calling became clear to me when I was asked where I saw myself standing in church. I said I don't see myself standing at the altar but at the *door*. I see my calling as enabling people to come into church, but also enabling people to go out into the community to build relationships that are mutually transformative.'[8] In Jess, who has developed a rich ministry particularly through her friendships with people of many different faiths, we see the deacon both as *enabler* of the two-way flow between church and world – enabling people, stories, encounters to 'cross

---

8 Jess Foster, 'No ordinary ministry', Church of England website, www.churchofengland.org/life-events/vocations/no-ordinary-ministry#na, accessed 8 July 2020.

the threshold' – but also as *making visible* to others the transforming power of encounters in the world.

Priests as 'story-gatherers'

Rather than being those responsible for feeding, equipping and sending out the people of God from church, the role of the ordained priest might instead be to enable and symbolize the ways of *gathering* that we have explored in this chapter: holding open the liturgical space to 'hear to speech' those testimonies of moments of transformation in the world, and to find ways of enabling those testimonies to enrich, challenge and transform the whole of the church's gathered worship. For those of us who find ourselves in that position, a vital part of our role is to embody this gathering in our *own* lives, to open ourselves up to be changed by what we hear – and also, within the 'economy' of the wider church, to both symbolize and enable the 'speaking towards the centre' of what we have seen, heard, touched and experienced 'on the edges'. Our aim should be for us not to be the spokespeople for our congregation members, but to find ways of enabling them to speak with their own voices to the wider church; to share their gifts with, and present their challenges to, the wider church, born of their lives in the world, and encounters with their neighbours.

The listening ministry of the bishop?

Although neither of us has any first-hand experience of 'bishopping', we have nevertheless caught glimpses of others doing it. As 'chief pastors' (a phrase from the ordination service), their role is also one of 'gathering together', but at a diocesan level, and also to speak, teach and lead the Church in mission. In recent years, their role in 'overseeing' has often been translated into the language of organizational management, setting the 'strategic direction' of their dioceses, albeit – hopefully – with theological underpinnings. But what if we were to shift these weighty tasks into receptive mode?

What if, instead of focusing on a bishop's role as *teacher*, we attended to the *listening* ministry of the bishop? What if bishops saw their role, first and foremost, as that of paying the most profound attention to what the people and parish churches within their dioceses are witnessing, and wanting to say to, and share with, the wider Church? What if, alongside their role in distributing the central resources throughout their diocese, they committed to gathering up the abundant gifts and challenges that come from the people of God dispersed across that diocesan area, and reflecting on, and seeking to embody, how those gifts and challenges might transform the body corporate? What if they, rather than 'speaking for' their dioceses in the corridors of power, were to find ways, again (for a bishop is also a priest and a deacon), of both symbolizing and enabling those voices from 'the edges' to find a hearing in such 'central' places?

From the 'inside edge'

All of these suggestions, so far, have been about looking for a 'counter-flow', of encounter, gifts and challenges, testimony and wisdom, in the opposite direction to that which tends to dominate our imagination and our day-to-day life as church: attending to what might come 'from the outside, in'. But what about those who have been faithfully on the 'inside' of church, but have experienced themselves repeatedly pushed to the edges, marginalized, silenced, rendered invisible – not (only) by wider society, but by the church itself?

Writing for and within the Church of England, Sam Wells suggests that the Church's 'renewal' and 'reform' will come, not from the Church's 'centre', but from those it has historically and structurally marginalized – and that this will only happen with a movement that is more profoundly unsettling than that implied by the word 'inclusion'. Those of us who are already comfortable need to be prepared to be radically disrupted by those who have not yet been recognized as part of 'us':

Prophetic ministry is not about condescendingly making welcome alienated strangers. It means seeking out the rejected precisely because they are the energy and the life-force that will transform us all. If we're looking for where the future church is coming from, we need to look at what the church and society has so blithely rejected ... The church is founded on and comprised of stones that the builders rejected. The challenge for the church is to see Jesus in the face of the ones we have rejected. And to let the Jesus we discover in them become our cornerstone.[9]

---

9 Sam Wells, 'A Future that's Bigger than the Past: Renewal and Reform in the Church of England', www.churchofengland.org/sites/default/files/2018-01/A%20Future%20that's%20Bigger%20than%20the%20Past%20-%20Renewal%20and%20Reform%20in%20the%20Church%20of%20England.pdf, accessed 8 May 2020.

Sam Wells names race, class and gender in his article as three dividing lines in human life, down which the Church's 'exclusionary attitudes ... have malformed ministry and mission'. We would want to name sexuality, dis/ability and age as three more.

One of the interactions between Ruth and Al which sparked the collaboration of this book was Al's suggestion, in a blog post, that children – in their 'wonderings', insights and questions – 'have a vast and mysterious capacity to interrupt and disrupt, deepen and enrich, our reflecting and our worshipping in ways that speak of God'. Ruth picked up that suggestion and developed it further, with some wondering questions of her own.

> What if relationships between adults and children within the church were less about who can teach what to whom, and more about what we can all learn together from, and about, God?
>
> What if children, including the youngest children, shaped the worship and structures of the church?
>
> Church, at its best, puts Jesus in the centre. And Jesus, in one of his clearest pieces of teaching, puts a child in our midst, and tells us 'change, and become like this'. A church which truly followed that teaching, a child-like, child-centred – dare we even imagine child-led – church, would radically disrupt the structures of power within and beyond the church. It would break down all our adult-centred notions, of 'them and us', of 'how things are done', of 'what works' and 'what's possible'. It would tell a new story, sing a new song, about who we are and who God is. It would be a Magnificat sort of church – raising the humble, putting down the proud, and proclaiming the glory of God.
>
> Come, Holy Spirit ...[10]

Ruth's wonderings are less about finding ways of enabling those at the 'edges' to come towards the 'centre' – although that, in itself, would be a good first step. She is pointing us to something more radical: relocating our collective attention, so that the places we have thought of as 'edges' become the holy ground on which, together, we discover the glory of God, and therefore become the new 'centres' – but multiple, interdependent, disruptive, transformative 'centres' – of our listening, learning, discerning, gathering, sharing, worshipping, deciding and world-changing – through the power of the Spirit in our midst.

---

10 Ruth Harley, 'Church "upside down": what if...', *becausegodislove* blog, 1 May 2018, https://becausegodislove.wordpress.com/2018/05/01/church-upside-down-what-if/, accessed 8 May 2020.

That is what we are advocating throughout this book. That is what we are seeking to flesh out, through the Bible studies at the book's core, through the earthed stories that punctuate the more descriptive chapters, and through the more practical possibilities offered in this final part of the book. That is what returns us now, with Jesus, to the places of cross and resurrection, to look at them again with fresh eyes.

Further reading

- Nadia Bolz-Weber, *Accidental Saints: Finding God in all the Wrong People* (Norwich: Canterbury Press, 2015)
- Sara Miles, *City of God: faith in the streets* (Norwich: Canterbury Press, 2014)
- Heidi B. Neumark, *Breathing Space: A Spiritual Journey in the South Bronx* (Boston, MA: Beacon, 2003)
- Barbara Brown Taylor, *An Altar in the World: Finding the Sacred Beneath our Feet* (Norwich: Canterbury Press, 2009)

Questions for reflection/discussion

- Which parts of the cycle of worship (gathering, word, table, sending, world) feel most significant to you, and why? Are there any you would like to explore further?
- If the 'flow' between those elements is reversed, does that change your perceptions of them, and if so how?
- How do you feel about the concept of 'orders of ministry'?
- If the 'orders of ministry' are reversed, as we are proposing here, how does that affect your perception of them, and of your place within them?

Act 6

Unheard Voices

Al

The conversation happened over a generous roast dinner. The vicar and the curate were in the middle of a series of 'one-to-one' visits (which were rarely one-to-one!) to members of the congregation, exploring together questions such as, 'What brings you joy?', 'Where have you caught glimpses of the kingdom of God?', 'What's the most important thing for you about your faith?' and 'When has church been at its best?'

In most homes, a cup of tea and a biscuit came as standard. In Faith's[1] house, it was the full works. While some conversations tailed off quite quickly, here we could have easily talked for hours. The food and the insights both came abundantly.

And then there was silence. Not an entirely comfortable silence, but a pregnant silence nevertheless. There were things that needed to be said, that had not yet been said.

Faith said how much she valued the way Sunday services began in Hodge Hill: when everyone is invited to think about what they're thankful for from the past week, and what they want to bring to God in prayerful concern. Usually, people have a conversation in twos or threes, and then the braver among us will share something out loud, with the whole congregation. Sometimes this can be quite brief. On other occasions, it can be like opening the flood gates.

But Faith described how this simple invitation had given her – and other members of the congregation of African-Caribbean heritage especially – an opportunity to be heard in a way that she hadn't experienced for years. For her contribution to be valued. For her to be seen.

I was stunned. This was several years into my time in Hodge Hill, and it was the first time I'd picked up any sense that Faith or other African-Caribbean members of the congregation had been feeling unheard, unvalued, invisible. My main motivation for introducing the by now well-established gathering ritual into our liturgy was a much more general concern: to help congregation members connect their experiences in their

---

1 Not her real name.

daily lives with what we did together in Sunday worship. I'd not remotely intended it as a way of making space for particular, unheard voices to be able to speak. I'd not even noticed there was a problem – and now I was kicking myself for my obliviousness.

Since then, we've done further intentional work together as a congregation. With Faith's enthusiastic collaboration, we've been much more deliberate in gently encouraging people of colour in the congregation into speaking, 'hosting' (distributing communion, for example) and leading roles; we've gathered together some small groups of white people and people of colour to read and discuss books on racism and 'white fragility', and to share with each other our experiences, reactions and some deep and often ambivalent feelings. Faith talks about the 'huge boost in confidence' she's experienced through these 'new beginnings'. But the wounds are still there: wounds of hurt and division that have been inflicted, and borne, over many years; wounds that have not yet been able to come to full, public expression; wounds that still, at times, have salt rubbed into them rather than soothing balm; wounds that are far from healed.

15

At the Cross

When it was noon, darkness came over the whole land until three in the afternoon. At three o'clock Jesus cried out with a loud voice, 'Eloi, Eloi, lema sabachthani?' which means, 'My God, my God, why have you forsaken me?' When some of the bystanders heard it, they said, 'Listen, he is calling for Elijah.' And someone ran, filled a sponge with sour wine, put it on a stick, and gave it to him to drink, saying, 'Wait, let us see whether Elijah will come to take him down.' Then Jesus gave a loud cry and breathed his last. And the curtain of the temple was torn in two, from top to bottom. Now when the centurion, who stood facing him, saw that in this way he breathed his last, he said, 'Truly this man was God's Son!'

There were also women looking on from a distance; among them were Mary Magdalene, and Mary the mother of James the younger and of Joses, and Salome. These used to follow him and provided for him when he was in Galilee; and there were many other women who had come up with him to Jerusalem. (Mark 15.33–41)

Where is God?

At least two questions demand our attention in Mark's narrative of Jesus' crucifixion. First, where is *God*? And second, where are *we*? They are connected together, in a third question: *who hears* Jesus' cry of god-forsakenness?

To the first question, Christians have responded in a variety of different ways.

Some have suggested that Jesus was not really 'godforsaken' at all: that his words here are simply the beginning of a prayer, Psalm 22, that he then went on to pray to its end, moving from godforsaken lament to confidence, trust and praise. Jesus' faith, and his relationship with God, remain strong. Others have suggested that, as a vital part of God's saving 'plan', 'the Father turns his face away',[1] unable to look at the one who takes upon his shoulders the sin of the world. God the Father absents himself in this moment of tragic, but necessary, desolation.

Each of these suggestions, for us, begs a question. To the first, we wonder if it really takes Jesus' words with the seriousness that Mark's narrative seems to be urging on us – or whether, like curious bystanders, we are mishearing him. From Jesus' anointing (at the beginning of chapter 14) to his death (at the end of chapter 15) he is left, as former archbishop Rowan Williams puts it, 'more and more visibly alone, repudiated by more and more persons and groups. The [male] disciples run away from him, Peter denies that he knows him, the High Priestly council condemns him, the Roman governor and the soldiers reject and abuse him, and he ends on the cross crying out that God too has abandoned him.'[2] The paradox, the mystery, of the crucifixion is that, in Jesus' godforsaken cry, Mark means us to hear the very voice of *God*. In this Jesus, here – pushed out to the very edges of human society, condemned, isolated, dying, godforsaken – Mark wants us to *see* God – 'the crucified God'.[3]

In the second suggestion considered above – the idea that in this moment, in the darkness of the cross, God turns his face away, absents himself – we hear an answer that emerges, barely seen or heard, from the comparable darkness of Auschwitz; from Jewish theologians' wrestling with God's apparent silence, hiddenness, *absence* even, in the midst of the

---

1 From the Stuart Townend song, 'How deep the Father's love for us'.
2 Rowan Williams, *Meeting God in Mark* (London: SPCK, 2014), pp. 55–6.
3 Jürgen Moltmann, *The Crucified God* (London: SCM Press, 1974).

genocidal dehumanization, terror and destruction of the Holocaust. In a striking observation, Jewish feminist theologian Melissa Raphael notes that post-Holocaust theologies of God's absence have tended to focus on a God 'who promises protection and then, empirically, fails to deliver it' – on a God who 'can no longer be trusted'. But instead, she argues, what is to be distrusted is not *God* but a particular – patriarchal, 'heroic' – way of *imagining* God: 'God's silence in Auschwitz was the silence of an omnipotent God-king who was never there in the first place, but ... who reigned in the minds of those who required divine sanction for their own hierarchical rule.'[4]

In the space left open after *that* God's departure, Raphael directs us to the unheard and overlooked stories of courageous, persistent physical care, by women and among women, in Auschwitz. Where the Holocaust attempted – often successfully – to isolate human beings from each other and desecrate their personhood to the point of erasing it, the testimonies of many women in Auschwitz describe how moments of touch, wiping, and washing – even the barest, most ineffective gestures towards genuine washing – became moments of restoration of relationship and personhood, for the living, the dying and the dead. Where the image of God, among her human children, was becoming increasingly, violently 'de-faced', the apparently ordinary, barely perceptible actions of these women were, defiantly and persistently, enabling the glory of God's face to be reflected back into the world.[5]

Returning to Mark's crucifixion narrative, what might we now see, as we look again, in the company of Melissa Raphael and the women of Auschwitz? Might we notice, and wonder at, the women 'looking on from a distance'? The female followers of Jesus who had accompanied him all the way from Galilee to Jerusalem, and who will accompany his body all the way to its tomb, to see where it has been laid, so that they might return, with spices to anoint it, when the Sabbath is over (Mark 15.47—16.1). While the most noticeable trajectory of Mark's narrative is of Jesus' abandonment, there is another barely perceptible story. The women's story of staying and watching, their solidarity with the crucified one, their accompanying his body to the tomb, their determined returning after the Sabbath pause, is all of a piece with the prophetic labour of love of the woman who interrupted the Bethany dinner party with her costly perfume – who, as Jesus said there, 'anointed my body beforehand for its burial' (Mark 14.8). In *their* staying, might we discern *God's*

4 Melissa Raphael, *The Female Face of God in Auschwitz: A Jewish Feminist Theology of the Holocaust* (London: Routledge, 2003), p. 52.
5 Raphael, *Female Face of God*, pp. 66–70.

staying?[6] Might we dare suggest, with Melissa Raphael, that the women here – like the woman with the haemorrhage who encountered Jesus on the road – know something that Jesus does not: that it is only the heroic, interventionist, patriarchal 'God-king' who has absented himself? And it is in the women's 'hearing Jesus to speech' (as Nelle Morton put it, at the end of Chapter 12) – hearing even his cry of godforsakenness – that we might discern the enduring *presence* of the God who is, in Morton's words, the 'prior great Listening Ear'.

Where are *we*?

Where we are born into privilege, we are charged with dismantling any myth of supremacy. Where we were born into struggle, we are charged with claiming our dignity, joy, and liberation.[7]

There is, then, in this final act of Mark's drama, an entangling of the threads that we have followed through these chapters. The one who is powerful and who has resisted power is now on the cross utterly power-less. The one who, in his society, was structurally privileged as a man, and a rabbi, is silenced. The one who so often in Mark's story has been the busy, active, initiator – albeit with a few, significant, interruptions – is here nailed down to the ultimate passivity: dying and death. And at the same time, the women on the margins of their society, on the margins of Jesus' story – who have largely, even in Mark's disruptive, revolu-tionary narrative, gone unnamed, unheard, glimpsed briefly and then disappeared without a trace – it is those women who have nevertheless along the way emerged as bold enough to interrupt, disrupt, school and commission Jesus, and are here the ones who 'hear him to speech' one last – or, perhaps, not-quite-last – time.

So where, in this part of the story, are *we*? To answer that question, as black feminist author and activist adrienne maree brown reminds us, we need to pay attention again – for the not-quite-last time in *this* book – to the dividing lines of structural privilege and power in the world we share: to the ways in which we are divided from each other, and indeed divided within our*selves*, down lines of gender, class and race – as well as age,

---

6 See for example Rita Nakashima Brock, *Journeys by Heart: A Christology of Erotic Power* (New York: Crossroad, 1996), pp. 89–100.

7 adrienne maree brown, 'Report: Recommendations for us right now from a future', http://sublevelmag.com/report-recommendations-for-us-right-now-from-a-future, quoted in Nora Samaran, *Turn This World Inside Out: The Emergence of Nurturance Culture* (Edinburgh: AK Press, 2019).

dis/ability, sexuality, geography and even creaturely species. Because, to identify with the *women* in this scene, we need to have lived something of the struggles they had lived: the multiple forms of marginalization that rendered them anonymous, silenced, appearing only at the edges of stories centred elsewhere. And perhaps there are dimensions of our identity, in which we have undergone exactly such struggles. In which case, we will find ourselves among this small group of faithful women watching near the cross, and we will discover – before too long – that the good news of resurrection is entrusted to *our* ears, to *our* lips, into *our* hands.

But where our own identities are enmeshed in one or more of the forms of privilege structured into our society, where do those dimensions of our lives find our place in this critical moment of the Gospel story? If we are to take seriously those aspects of who we are that identify us as male, or white, or middle-class – or straight, or cis-gendered, or able-bodied, or adult, or from the global North, or human in this more-than-human world – who is there in this scene with whom we might identify?

The answer to that question, we want to suggest, might possibly be found in the Roman centurion. He is, after all, a very visible representative of multiple dimensions of privilege: 'race' (while we know nothing about his skin colour, his identity as Roman citizen functions in many ways similarly to whiteness), class (as not just a Roman citizen but a senior army officer), and gender (as a man). In his role, he is – perhaps apart from Caesar himself – as powerful a representative of the oppressive, occupying Roman empire as you can imagine. He is invested in the system, in its endurance and its expansion: he actively contributes to it, and very obviously benefits from the privileges it accords him.

And yet what happens, for this centurion, at the crucifixion of Jesus of Nazareth, at the death of a Jewish rabbi, condemned by his own leaders for blasphemy and put to death by the Roman authorities to keep the peace, the *Pax Romana*? From the one verse (15.39) we've quoted here, and from his brief confirmation to Pilate that Jesus is indeed dead (15.44–45), we know next to nothing. Scholars are not even sure if his words in verse 39 are affirming Jesus as 'the Son of God' or, more modestly, 'a son of god'. But let us imagine, for a moment or two, that in his utterance here he caught at least a glimmer of the first of those possibilities: that after everything he has witnessed, he has come to the point where he knows that the title commonly used for the Roman emperor, 'Son of God', is better used of the dead Jew hanging in front of him. Let us begin to imagine what such a radical change of allegiance might look like: an act of treason – of 'traitor-hood' – even more dramatic than Zacchaeus' abandonment of his tax-collecting role, and the wealth and power that he had accrued with it (that we began to explore in Chapter 6).

In the remainder of this chapter we invite you to join us, and this Roman officer, on a journey not just of 'being interrupted' but of slow and painstaking transformation – personal, relational and structural – that begins here, at the foot of the cross. It is inevitably a journey of the *imagination*. But it is a journey also fleshed out by the countless testimonies, from across time and space, of those who – as adrienne maree brown puts it – born into privilege, have sought to dismantle the myths and structures of supremacy, alongside those who, born into struggle, have claimed their dignity, joy and liberation. It is not a *linear* journey: it is one in which we will attempt to look both ways at once, double-back on ourselves, and admit – often – that we don't in fact know the way. But these, too, are precious gifts for this way of travelling, gifts perhaps even more necessary than we realize.

Relocation

'*Where* we live', says theologian of race Willie James Jennings, 'determines in great measure *how* we live.'[8] We saw, in Chapter 3, how much our *location* can shape our obliviousness, particularly in relation to class, race and climate change denial. And we have seen, in Part 2 and the preceding chapters of Part 3, how much a relocation – chosen or unchosen – can open up the possibility of all kinds of transformative encounters.

The Roman empire stretched far and wide, but it is likely that our centurion might well have been a long way from home: every day, in his job, he would have been encountering Judaean Jewish women and men, and many other 'others', in a cosmopolitan city like Jerusalem. He did not have to make any special effort to seek out 'bumping spaces' in which such 'others' might cross his path. For some of us, relocation might need to be more intentional: deliberately finding and spending time in the social and cultural 'ecotones' that are accessible to us: on our doorstep, or requiring a longer journey; either 'in the flesh', or in online spaces where encounters-across-difference are made possible. We almost certainly also need to relocate more into our *ecological* ecotones – the bumping spaces between the human and more-than-human world – and we will return to focus specifically on how that relocation might happen in our final chapter.

---

8 Willie James Jennings, *The Christian Imagination: Theology and the Origins of Race* (New Haven, CT: Yale University Press, 2010), p. 287.

But it is in one very particular place that the Roman centurion's eyes are opened – at the site of Jesus' crucifixion – and there are profound ironies about this location that, significantly, disturb our normal geographies of 'centre' and 'edge'. The scene takes place beyond the edges of the city – Jesus has been pushed to the very edges of society, to even the edges of human life, to a *wilderness* place where the 'human waste' of the city and other-than-human creatures make their home. It is at the edges of this Roman's world too and, yet, in the act of crucifixion it is, at least temporarily, a 'centre' of Roman power: he and his empire are demonstrating their control to anyone who might be looking on. Nevertheless, in Mark's telling of this event, it is the apparently powerless *Jesus* who is centre-stage and the supposedly powerful Roman centurion who experiences himself as profoundly decentred. Might we also wonder, in the light of our reflections at the beginning of this chapter, if it is in fact the 'hearing space' between Jesus and the women looking on and listening from a distance, that is revealed as the new centre of divine presence? There are parallels here with the story of Jesus' encounter with the Syro-Phoenician woman. There, on the edges of Jesus' world, the woman took Jesus' 'No' and turned it into a 'Yes'. Here, at the edges of this Roman centurion's world, what happens between Jesus and the women takes the Roman empire's violent 'No', and transforms it into the beginnings of a 'Yes'.

Relinquishing

Relocation, on its own, can often make no difference at all. Interruptions can happen – even interruptions as dramatic as the one at Golgotha – but they don't, in themselves, spark change. Every day up until that Good Friday, the centurion could easily have gone about his work in Jerusalem without ever encountering one of the city's inhabitants on terms that would surprise, disrupt or challenge him – just as many of us who are multiply privileged can walk through our own cosmopolitan city centres, and sit in our urban coffee shops, without having those privileges disturbed in the slightest. As well as physical relocation, then, a certain kind of relinquishing is demanded of us – both in our openness to being interrupted, and in our response to interruptions when they happen. It is a necessary 'letting go' – of our attachment to the securities that our privileges give us – that can only ever be partial, incomplete. But it needs to begin somewhere.

For the centurion, the most obvious way in which he might begin to 'exit' the unjust systems of empire would be to resign from his job, as a leader in the army of occupation. Easy to say, but at what cost? Beyond the trappings of status and power, questions of livelihood: can he get another job? Can he still support his family? And deeper, more existential questions too: could he make a bigger difference, by staying on the inside and working to reform the institution? When the institution in question is the army of the Roman empire, exiting is probably the only viable option. Many of our institutions are rather more morally ambivalent – the Church included, centred as it is on loving God and neighbour, and yet inescapably entangled (as we have highlighted, in Chapter 4 especially) in colonial, racist, classist, patriarchal structures, both historical and contemporary, as well as the distortions that come with 'mission' thinking (that have been our focus throughout). But if our institutions are in any part entangled in forms of oppression, injustice and obliviousness, our guiding questions must surely be: if we don't leave, then *what*? And if not now, *when*?

It can be comforting to tell ourselves we'll change an institution from the inside, when we eventually get into a certain position of power within it – but our participation in institutions forms us and *de*forms us along the way: we build relationships, we do deals, we make compromises, we become enmeshed in the systems with less and less room for manoeuvre, or the imagination to do so. Even the idea that the higher up the hierarchy we go, the more power we have to change things, is a product of hierarchical thinking that is both distorting of our imagination and relationships and, in many ways, a lie. In the words of self-described 'black, lesbian, mother, warrior, poet' Audre Lorde, 'the master's tools will never dismantle the master's house'.[9] It isn't an option, for example, for men to embrace some kind of imagined 'benevolent patriarchy' (consider the equivalent idea, of 'benevolent racism'): the choice is either to collude with such hierarchical systems, or resist them – and the latter requires a radically different way of living and relating. We will return to that thought, in the next chapter, when we contemplate resurrection.

So, if our centurion is not to immediately tender his resignation, where can he begin? He can relinquish particular roles and refuse certain tasks – imagine if others then followed his lead! He can resist certain kinds of behaviour: talking about his 'others' in ways that are demeaning, stigmatizing, dehumanizing. In his relating to his 'others' he can relinquish the kinds of power that he has, perhaps, taken for granted: always being the one to speak first, and to have the last word; being the 'initiative-taker'; controlling the space, the terms of interaction; and, perhaps when he is in more benign mode, resisting the temptations to provide and perform for his 'others'. All of these are forms of resistance, *within* the systems in

9 Audre Lorde, *The Master's Tools Will Never Dismantle the Master's House*, Penguin Classics (Harmondsworth: Penguin, 2018).

which he is enmeshed, but also ways of 'exiting slowly' from them. None of them are without risk, or cost: any of them could, in an institution which expects high levels of obedience and loyalty, get him court-martialled and kicked out of the army. But even if he were no longer an army officer, he would still remain a *Roman*: his 'slow exit' from the systems of empire would still require a lifetime's journey.

Receptivity

As we explored in Chapter 12, once we begin to take a step back, resist the temptations to 'do stuff', and let go of some of our defensiveness when interrupted and challenged, we can begin to notice forms of life, agency and interconnection 'growing wild', beyond the boundaries of the spaces we try to manage and control. We also teased out some of the ways in which our intentional *stopping*, *looking* and *listening* to others can, at best, make space for new, unexpected possibilities and truths to emerge.

Imagine, then, a third dimension of the journey of change for our Roman ex-centurion. He has *relocated* – intentionally or unintentionally – into 'bumping spaces' where encounter with his others is at least a possibility. And he has begun the process of *relinquishing* his grasp on those behaviours that he previously relied on to entrench and reinforce his position of power and privilege. But now, in this space, he needs to be attentive and receptive: he needs to open himself to *listen*, to the possibility of being repeatedly interrupted, and to the possibility of receiving the gifts and challenges of those around him in ways that will change him.

This is, however, much more easily said than done. When power and privilege distort our relationships, being truly receptive to our 'others' requires a complex negotiation of *distance* and *trust*. The two are inter-twined, because my coming closer to you requires a deeper trust between us, and yet for trust to grow between us we need a certain amount of inti-macy. And the negotiation of the two, in turn, takes *time*: we talk a lot, in our community-building work in Hodge Hill, about going 'at the speed of trust'[10] – and building trust mostly happens with painstaking slowness.

Trust grows, first, when those of us who are privileged *listen* to what our 'others' say to us, directly, without jumping instantly into 'defensive' mode. But how do we learn that art? We might do well to compare Robin DiAngelo's description of the 'defensive moves' of white fragility (Chapter 3), with Jesus' responses in the five encounters from Mark's Gospel

---

10 A phrase used often by Cormac Russell (see note in Chapter 12).

we explored in Chapters 7 to 11. DiAngelo pointed us to the ways those of us who are multiply privileged unintentionally deploy our emotions – anger, fear and guilt, for example – as well as our capacities for arguing, staying silent and leaving the room, to maintain our defensive walls. In a different dimension of privilege, we encountered Darren McGarvey's observations on the ways in which working-class voices are often silenced by being 'dismissed', 'discarded' or explained away as being due to 'mental health problems'. McGarvey even highlights the semi-conscious responses of 'disgust' and 'revulsion' in relation to class (but they could equally apply across other structural dividing lines) that those of us who consider ourselves 'progressive', 'inclusive', 'liberal' or whatever, would rarely dare contemplate, unless we were truly prepared to be fearlessly honest with ourselves.

In Jesus, we do see a reactive, self-centred anger (cursing the fruitless fig tree because he's hungry), and a bald, 'othering' dismissal (refusing the Syro-Phoenician woman's request because she's 'not one of us'). But we also see a willingness to be stopped 'mid-flow' and a curiosity to find out more about his interrupter (on the road and the woman with the haem-orrhage), an openness to be challenged and to change his mind (with the Syro-Phoenician woman), and a readiness to see the God-given giftedness and significance of people, and their actions, that others have already written off (with the anointing woman, and the little children).

Robin DiAngelo helpfully outlines some verbal 'tactics' for responding less defensively, in ways that are more open to engaging with, listening to and believing our 'others', and to grappling, processing, reflecting and learning within ourselves:[11]

- I appreciate this feedback
- This is very helpful
- It's my responsibility to resist defensiveness and complacency
- This is hard, but also stimulating and important
- Oops!
- It is inevitable that I have this pattern. I want to change it
- It's personal but not strictly personal
- I will focus on the message and not the messenger
- I need to build my capacity to endure discomfort and bear witness to the pain of racism [or other forms of division, marginalization and injustice]
- I have some work to do.

---

11 Robin DiAngelo, *White Fragility*, pp. 141–8.

Imagine our Roman centurion – or ex-centurion – responding in this way, the next time he encounters a challenging interruption from a member of the occupied nation he had been sent to keep under control. Imagine him responding in such a way not just to a Jew, but to a 'working-class' Jew, a *female* working-class Jew, even. Imagine what that will begin to do to his ways of looking at the world, being in the world, and relating to those around him. He will indeed realize he has 'work' to do – and by no means easy work either. What that 'work' might look like is the focus of the fourth dimension of the journey of change.

Repentance

Our Roman ex-centurion might have had his worldview turned upside-down at the foot of the cross. He can become the best listener in the world. He can earn the trust of those who, until recently, would have hidden in fear when they saw him approach. He can begin to hear and understand their lived experiences, an 'intercorporeal illumination' (see Chapter 13) beyond anything he had understood or imagined before. But he is not, cannot become, 'one of them'. Whether he stays in or leaves the Roman army he remains, inescapably, a Roman, part of the economy and politics of the oppressive empire. There is 'work' that he must do, as a Roman, and with his fellow Romans, if his conversion is to make any difference to anything.

This 'work' is what is often called repentance. It is inescapably *personal* – it's about me, and my entanglement in distorted ways of being and relating. But it must also be *communal* – work that I undertake with those with whom I live and interact from day to day. And it must be *structural* – work that changes the institutions, systems and structures in which I participate, however unwillingly or unconsciously.

If this work involves reshaping the *present* and the *future*, then it must begin by remembering the *past*. It requires us to work through our personal histories, to discern where we have personally contributed to, and benefited from, privilege and injustice. But it also requires of us to work through our *collective* histories (including our *churches'* histories): histories of empire, colonialism, slavery and racism; histories of class exploitation, profit, inheritance and property ownership; histories of patriarchy, gender violence and the gendered division of labour; histories of child abuse, institutional dishonesty and the silencing of children's voices; histories of the destructiveness wrought on our planet and our creature-kin who share it with us by the systems of human consumption. As we list those histories – even the barest of their headlines – the weight of them can quickly feel overwhelming, paralysing. None of us can deal with them as a whole. We need to begin somewhere: to pull at one thread, and slowly see what unravels.

In Hodge Hill, a small group of us – made up of both white people and people of colour – committed to reading together the books *White Fragility* (Robin DiAngelo) and *We Need to Talk about Race* (Ben Lindsay), as a way of beginning conversations about race in our church community, our own lives and our society. Listening to each other's experiences and testimonies, and reading the words of others beyond our group, have gone hand in hand. Those of us who are white have committed both to listening attentively and non-defensively, but also to resisting the temptation to lean on our sisters and brothers of colour for our learning, advice, guidance and moral support. As white Christians, our desire has been to discover some of our obliviousness (to our whiteness, to our neighbours of colour, and to racialized injustice more widely), identify some of our addictions to the status quo, relinquish some of our defensiveness, and work towards living anti-racist lives in church and society. As a group together, we have also begun to explore ways of challenging our wider local church community to tackle the white-dominance and racism that is part of its history – but which also infects its present.

What of other dimensions of privilege and injustice? Some of us also want to read Darren McGarvey's *Poverty Safari* together, to help us think more deeply about how *class* shapes and deforms our imaginations and relationships – but for the moment, that thinking is happening in more practical, embodied ways, in our relationships with our neighbours on our estate. We're also maintaining an ongoing alertness to the ways sexism and patriarchy infiltrate our thinking, our language and liturgy, and our ways of being together as church. Enabling and supporting children to be agents and leaders in the centre of church life is another 'work in progress' currently, and that process is happening in yet other ways (see Act 2 above). We are also discovering, from our young people primarily, how we as a church can become more active in resisting our addictions to consumption, car travel, other forms of environmental destruction, and engage in positive ways in the global movement to tackle climate change. As a community we are learning, slowly, to be realistic about what any of us have capacity for at any one time, and to give each conversation, each bit of exploration, the time and particular kind of attention it needs – and not to be paralysed by guilt when we know that our responses, our efforts, are far from perfect.

Structural repentance: two examples

What about the *structural* level of repentance? In 2006, the Church of England's General Synod agreed unanimously to make a corporate apology for the Church's complicity in sustaining, and profiting greatly from, the British colonial slave trade, just under 200 years since that trade was abolished in British law. 'The Body of Christ', said then archbishop Rowan Williams, 'exists across history and we therefore share the shame and sinfulness of our predecessors, and part of what we can do ... is prayerful acknowledgement of the failure that is part of us, not just of some distant "them".' While acknowledging that repentance must be more than 'words alone', however, the synod stopped short of committing to any kind of reparations – financial or otherwise.[12] The bicentennial commemorations of abolition the following year also gave much attention to the stories of white abolitionists, and little to the agency and resistance of the slaves themselves, and of black abolitionists such as Olaudah Equiano. Fourteen years on, in 2020, another debate took place in General Synod, and another apology was issued. This time, synod committed to lament and apologized for the 'conscious and unconscious racism experienced by countless BAME [black, Asian and minority ethnic] Anglicans' from the Windrush generation to the present day, and to come up with a plan of action to 'stamp out' any such racism in the future, including commissioning research to assess the impact of that racism on church members lost, churches that have been closed, and vocations missed.[13]

By way of comparison, in 2017 and 2018 the Council for World Mission (CWM) – which includes the United Reformed Church (of England and Wales) among its members – held four 'Legacies of Slavery' hearings in the UK, Ghana, Jamaica and the USA, attending to its historical complicity in the Transatlantic Slave Trade, and the legacies of that trade in present-day racial injustice, and exploring ways of making reparation, and discovering 'anti-imperial models of Christian mission in today's world'. Like the Church of England, CWM's work has included corporate apology and commitments to racial justice, but has also proposed divesting from corporations which have unpaid legacies of slavery or who exploit poor, black and vulnerable communities, and a £7 million 'Jubilee' of financial reparation, to assist member churches working on

---

12 Stephen Bates, 'Church apologises for benefiting from slave trade', *Guardian*, 9 February 2006, www.theguardian.com/uk/2006/feb/09/religion.world, accessed 8 May 2020.

13 Adam Becket, 'Synod apologises to *Windrush* generation for C of E racism', *Church Times*, 11 February 2020, www.churchtimes.co.uk/articles/2020/14-february/news/uk/synod-apologises-to-windrush-generation-for-c-of-e-racism, accessed 8 May 2020.

racial justice and an investment fund to resource black-led businesses. It is important to consider, we would suggest, why the Church of England has decided to 'free-up' millions of pounds of its historic assets to 'invest in the future' (focused on the numerical growth of Church of England congregations), but has so far been unwilling to contemplate financial reparations for its past.

Such is the kind of 'work' of personal, communal and structural repentance that we can imagine our Roman ex-centurion exploring with his fellow Romans: not just in terms of race and empire, but through the lenses of class and gender too. We who are multiply privileged might do likewise, attending also to the fault-lines that distinguish by age and species, as well as sexuality and dis/ability. But if relocation, relinquishing and receptivity mark different dimensions of the *beginning* of a journey of change, where might that journey take us? In the next three sections, we will revisit each of those dimensions, and explore what further possibilities those 'beginnings' might enable us to imagine. Our journey was never going to be a straight line – we might think of it more as a (probably erratic) 'spiral', circling and recircling the different dimensions of the 'beginnings' we have explored, each time enabling us to go a bit deeper.

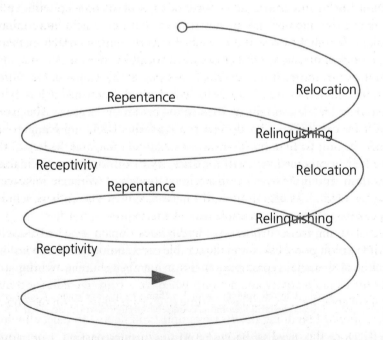

Figure 11: The spiral of repentance

Relinquishing – revisited

Can we imagine, first, the possibility that our Roman man's attempts at non-defensive listening, and his willingness to grapple with the part he has played within the oppressive empire, has slowly and, however piece-meal, begun to build trust with some of those who have up until now been his 'others'? Can we imagine this Roman discovering a liberation movement, a motley crew of other renegade Romans and courageous locals – courageous, not just to dare to work with the 'enemy', but to risk becoming outcasts in their own communities for doing so? That movement might even be one of those communities (some might call them 'churches') that have been popping up all over the region and beyond, inspired by, centred on, the crucified rabbi whose death turned his life upside-down. And if we've got that far, can we go a little further to imagine our Roman offering his time, energy and skills to that movement, that community, for the dismantling of the empire and all of its multiple oppressions?

Such is the work of an 'ally', crossing and subverting the dividing-lines drawn by injustice. But critical to being an ally is knowing *what work is not ours to do*. For someone like our Roman, with the character and formation for a senior role in the army that remains part of who he is, it might not be out of character for him to jump at opportunities to be the 'fixer', the 'mender' of the destruction that he and his empire have wreaked. He might even find himself, for very understandable reasons, accepting invitations to take up senior leadership roles in our imagined resistance movement. But *he cannot be the one that brings about salvation* – not for the oppressed society he is living in, not even for himself. That would be to put himself firmly back in the centre of the story. The great-est gift he can bring is to deepen the journey of relinquishing he has already begun: to find creative ways of *stepping back*, of 'clearing' the space he has occupied, to enable the agency of others. Here, 'solidarity' takes flesh as *amplifying* – to his fellow Romans – what he is hearing from his 'others', as cheerleading from the sidelines when others venture to speak and act, and as multiple acts of passing on.

This last phrase is deliberately ambiguous. When those of us with multiple privilege are asked to take on roles and responsibilities, when we are invited to make a contribution (for example, speaking, writing, and other forms of creativity and action), when we are given credit for things that have gone well, we need every time to consider *passing* on the oppor-tunity: *should* I be doing this (for example, joining an all-male, all-white panel)? Does this need to be *me*? And to consider passing it *on*: could this be someone else? Is there someone whose rootedness, experience and expertise easily outstrips mine, but has been overlooked for precisely the reasons we've discussed throughout this book? (For example, when a journalist approached Al to ask for a quote on working-class vocations in outer estates, rather than speaking directly to someone with a working-class background and a track record in encouraging working-class vocations.)

There is another dimension to this 'passing on' too: the Latin word at the root of the word *tradition* means both 'handing over' and 'betrayal' (words held close together in most retellings of the Last Supper). In our acts of 'passing on', we are both *breaking with the traditions* and *betraying the systems* that privilege some over others because of race, class, gender and so on. We are also, in small but significant ways, involved in creating *new traditions*, where the expectations of who does, and who can, are radically transformed.

Relocation – revisited

Second, we might track the ex-centurion's journey of change back to the question of relocation. He has already, we should remember, been relocated far from home, and is accustomed to inhabiting the bumping spaces of cosmopolitan Jerusalem. At the place of Jesus' crucifixion, he finds himself and his world radically decentred – a decentring that continues as he discovers the paths of relinquishing and repentance. But let us return to where this chapter began: to the place from which the female followers of Jesus 'look on from a distance'. Let us imagine, now, that weeks, months, perhaps years after the darkness of that Good Friday, our Roman and these women have heard about each other, encountered each other even, through those underground networks of anti-imperial resistance and followers of the way of Jesus. But what if he decides he wants to *join*? What if he wants to become 'one of them'? What if he wants to pack up his home in the Roman garrison and move into the neighbourhood of the Jewish acquaintances he hopes might possibly become his friends?

Willie James Jennings, whom we encountered earlier as a theologian of 'race', invites us to consider seeing the journey of faith as a 'reaching out' to near and distant neighbours – 'the *joining* of peoples now separated by violence, poverty, or race' – and a 'reaching down' to 'join the land', the earth and all its creatures. Jennings is not afraid to talk about the 'erotic' nature of Christian existence, rooted in a doctrine of creation as divine and human *touch*: this 'space of joining' means 'the opening of lives to one another in love and desire', 'a joining of peoples not only to each other but also to the God who calls them to touch his body'.[14]

---

14 Jennings, *The Christian Imagination*, pp. 286–8.

Jennings' vision is radical, but it is also cautious and clear-eyed. He refuses to use the language of 'reconciliation' because, he says, such words can all too easily be used as 'ideological tools' of the powerful and privileged, and can pretend that these processes can unfold without disrupting *our* timescales, *our* identities and *our* agendas. It can be all too tempting to want to jump to reconciliation without the painstaking processes of truth-telling, truth-hearing, relinquishing of power and repentance, that are needed to avoid reconciliation being a superficial change, imposed on those with less power by those who retain all the benefits of the status quo.

If there is to be some kind of 'joining', therefore, between the Roman ex-centurion and those who not long ago lived in fear of him, then such a joining cannot be an *invasion*: the colonizing of what was 'home' by the more powerful outsiders, taking control with their own vested interests, agendas and rules. Neither, realistically, can such joining be like joining a *club*, where those already on the inside are used to setting the rules, and where new members are 'included' on the expectation that they learn to 'fit in'. There are plenty of churches that operate just like this – but the change imagined here is much more radical and far-reaching than that. If anything, Jennings' vision of joining perhaps comes closest to the *intimate* joining of two people together in mutual love and care through marriage, or other forms of chosen family: something resembling John's version of the crucifixion scene, where Jesus joins together his 'beloved disciple' and his mother, a new household to last beyond his death (John 19.26–27). But if you've made it this far through this book, it's unlikely that you will contemplate the image of *marriage* – at least in its culturally dominant, heterosexual expression – without asking of it the *power* question. In a society that is far from free of the gendered distortions of patriarchy, different expectations of men and women, and unequal power dynamics between the genders, what might such an image mean for our vision of joining?

And this is where I (Al) must confess that, on first writing this chapter, I jumped to Jennings' vision of 'joining' far too quickly. For someone whose identity carries multiple privileges, but who longs for a different world – a world of equality of dignity and power, and relationships of mutuality and reciprocity – it's a profoundly attractive vision, seductive, even. Like the early days of falling in love, it can be easy for some of us to imagine that we are *there* already – or that we can float there effortlessly in an instant, merely by uttering those three words 'I love you', sealed with a kiss.

But the only kiss in Mark's Gospel is that given by betrayer to betrayed. And that, we want to suggest, is the hard ground on which any such joining must be contemplated. Nelle Morton's language of 'hearing *one another* to speech', which we have used repeatedly in this book, emerged among circles of *women*. It assumes a mutuality and, largely, an equality of power – and we might want to question even that, through lenses of race and class, for example. But feminist theology is dangerous in the hands of men, if such conditions of equality and mutuality are *assumed*, but are not, in fact, the reality. And that has at least three crucial implications for any of our imagined 'joinings'.

First, while it might be the person with more structural privilege who makes the approach, the decision to go any further down this road of deepened intimacy must be firmly in the hands of the 'other'. Just as in a heterosexual relationship where the man has taken the initiative, and all other forms of privilege (race, class, age, dis/ability, and any forms of role-related power) might be equal, the woman's capacity to say No must be defended, enlarged, strengthened in all possible ways. The female followers of Jesus reserve the right, however trustworthy this Roman ex-centurion has proved himself to be, to tell him to go away and find other people to befriend.

Second, as feminist theologian and ethicist Karen Lebacqz has argued, women seeking loving heterosexual intimacy have to learn the art of 'loving your enemy'. Whatever the track record of an individual man, however gentle, attentive and self-aware he might be, the reality is that all of our relationships are – subtly or not so subtly – infected with the distortions of patriarchy. Thus, as Lebacqz puts it, heterosexual women 'must seek intimacy precisely in an arena that is culturally and experientially unsafe, fraught with sexual violence and power struggles'. Even in private, women and men play out 'roles' in our relationships that have been shaped in public, and those roles need attending to in every negotiation and renegotiation of those relationships. Lebacqz uses the startling term 'enemy' to highlight how the man's role in a male-female relationship is always played out in ways that either collude with, or have to consciously resist, publicly-embodied patriarchal expectations and power dynamics. 'Loving your enemy', for Lebacqz, therefore requires of the female partner a very specific kind of *forgiveness* – consciously taking the risk that she will find a safe space with *this* man, despite the widespread violence of patriarchy – while holding fast to the necessary tools for ongoing *survival*, not least a 'hard-boiled honesty' that is determined to see through any 'shallowness, hypocrisy and phoniness'.[15]

---

15 Karen Lebacqz, 'Love Your Enemy: Sex, Power, and Christian Ethics', *Annual of the Society of Christian Ethics* 10 (1990), pp. 3–23, www.jstor.org/stable/23560724, accessed 12 June 2020. Lebacqz quotes womanist theologian Katie Geneva Cannon's observation that for black women to survive, throughout the history of the USA, has

Third, and perhaps just as startling, for any imagined 'joining' between the Roman ex-centurion and the women who witnessed the crucifixion, we might reach for both the language and the practice of *safeguarding* that is still, shamefully, not yet a non-negotiable 'given' in our church communities and institutions. Treating our Roman man as the 'ex-offender' that he is, any sense of him being able to 'join' a community that includes those he may have harmed, however indirectly, requires not just the capacity for that community to say 'No' to his joining, but also an agreement – constantly monitored and regularly reviewed – as to what he can and can't do, which roles and responsibilities he may take on, and which must be out of bounds. It requires of him an ongoing *external* accountability, to both his 'others' within the community and his Roman peers, and a relentless *internal* accountability as he pursues his lifelong journey of relocation, relinquishing, repentance and change.

Receptivity – revisited

Last, then, with these safeguards established, it may be that the 'schooling' for our ex-centurion that began at the cross might be further deepened through more profoundly receptive interaction with his 'others'. Beyond the bumping spaces of initial encounter, in a 'safe-enough' space beyond the all-seeing eyes and heavy-handed control of the Roman empire, we might just begin to imagine possibilities of mutual en-*trust*-ment, carefully attentive to power, that perhaps resemble the scenario described here by political theorist Emily Beausoleil:[16]

A formerly homeless theatre workshop participant searches out the right characters for his tableau; he scans the group, and points to me. He places me in the scene; he lifts my arm and shapes my hand into a dismissive wave; he adjusts my hips and torso; he sculpts my face with his fingers, gently, until I am scowling scornfully. He crouches low, cowering in front of where I stand, and we hold this image. I hold this stance, I become this character. I feel in my body how he sees people like me, I feel in my body that I am this character. My arm begins to ache; I try to look for cracks in the mould to overwrite this position of scorn, but I am frozen in character before the group. I am implicated.

required of them the qualities of 'hard-boiled honesty, dual allegiance, down-to-earth thinking, and seeing through hypocrisy', to 'face life squarely, front and center, without reverence or protection by the dominant powers in society' – see Katie G. Cannon, *Black Womanist Ethics* (Eugene, OR: Wipf and Stock, 1988), p. 89.

16 Emily Beausoleil, 'The politics, science and art of receptivity', *Ethics and Global Politics* 7:1 (2014), pp. 19–40.

Beausoleil's description here is of a power-full encounter, in many different senses: the power over her body, at least temporarily, that she gives to the 'formerly homeless' man; the 'gentle' power with which he sculpts her; the power of the stance that he gives her in relation to his own 'cowering' position; the power of the profound understanding that she, quite immediately, 'feels in her body', her 'frozenness', her 'implicatedness' in yet more social, economic and political power relationships in wider society that produced both the man's homelessness and the social scorn that he had to bear; and finally, the power of Beausoleil's story-telling on us, her readers, as we wonder – or know all too well – where we might fit into the tableau she describes.

This interaction deepens the kinds of 'intercorporeal illumination' we have already explored: seeing ourselves through the eyes of another, understanding ourselves through what they have to say to us, placing ourselves literally in their hands. It takes Otto Scharmer's 'generative listening' a step further: here, we open ourselves to receiving a kind of knowledge, empathy, understanding *in our body*, as much as in our 'mind', 'heart' or 'will' (the locations Scharmer identifies for his different levels of listening). Beausoleil describes the kind of intimate interruption that Jesus experiences with the anointing woman of Mark 14 (see Chapter 9), and the kind of 'knowing in her body' that the woman with the haemorrhage had when she touched Jesus (see Chapter 7).

The en-trust-ment of this moment must be *mutual* because it asks a lot both of the formerly homeless man, and of the female academic. Even when the one offering themselves to be 'sculpted' has, structurally, in relation to the 'sculptor', more privilege and power in multiple dimensions, the radical reversal of that power that is required in this context opens them up to the risk of the sculpting touch being inappropriate, disrespectful, and even abusive. This kind of willed vulnerability on both sides is something that can never be commanded or expected, must always be freely chosen, often requires a third party to 'manage' the space carefully, and needs to be surrounded by wider circles or structures of safety and support. But at their best, if such spaces can bring deep revelation of our 'implicatedness', then they might also enable the possibility of radically reimagining our relationships to each other, and the world which both shapes us and is shaped by us.

After his affirmation of Jesus as 'son of God' (in Mark 15.39) and his brief encounter with Pilate (in 15.44–45), we hear no more of the Roman centurion. He has his moment of revelation, and then disappears from the story.

We follow the body of Jesus a little further, but only as a dead body, carried to the tomb.

If the power of the Roman empire is stripped naked, at the cross, so too are our imaginings of an all-powerful God-king. There is no hope, no future, Mark tells us, to be found in either of these. Nevertheless, as we glimpsed in this chapter's beginning, there is something that endures. Something that defies despair, and the dispersal orders of the powerful. Something that gives hope to the possibility of 'joining' that we have only barely been able to imagine here. Something that goes by the name of resurrection.

Further reading

- Rita Nakashima Brock, *Journeys by Heart: A Christology of Erotic Power* (New York: Crossroad, 1996)
- Willie James Jennings, *The Christian Imagination: Theology and the Origins of Race* (New Haven, CT: Yale University Press, 2010)
- Audre Lorde, *The Master's Tools Will Never Dismantle the Master's House*, Penguin Classics (Harmondsworth: Penguin, 2018)
- Melissa Raphael, *The Female Face of God in Auschwitz: A Jewish Feminist Theology of the Holocaust* (London: Routledge, 2003)

Some reading specifically on dismantling privilege (in addition to the suggestions at the end of Chapter 3 and in the various sections of Chapter 4):

- British Quakers, *Owning power and privilege: Toolkit for action* (2018), www.quaker.org.uk/our-work/social-action-training-and-tools/toolkit-for-action-2
- Council for World Mission, *Unmasking Empire* (2018), www.cwmission.org/wp-content/uploads/2018/10/CWM-UNMASKING-EMPIRE-FINAL.pdf
- Mary Elizabeth Hobgood, *Dismantling Privilege: An Ethics of Accountability*, revised edn (Cleveland, OH: Pilgrim Press, 2009)

On gender:

- Carter Heyward, 'Men Whose Lives I Trust, Almost', in Stephen B. Boyd, W. Merle Longwood and Mark W. Muesse (eds), *Redeeming Men: Religion and Masculinities* (Louisville, KY: Westminster John Knox, 1996)
- Grayson Perry, *The Descent of Man* (Harmondsworth: Penguin, 2016)
- Mark Pryce, *Finding a Voice: Men, Women and the Community of the Church* (London: SCM Press, 1996)

- Nora Samaran, *Turn This World Inside Out: The Emergence of Nurturance Culture* (Edinburgh: AK Press, 2019)

On race:

- Jennifer Harvey, *Dear White Christians: For Those Still Longing for Racial Reconciliation* (Grand Rapids, MI: Eerdmans, 2014)
- James Perkinson, *White Theology: Outing Supremacy in Modernity* (New York: Palgrave Macmillan, 2004)

On safeguarding:

- Rosie Harper and Alan Wilson, *To Heal and Not to Hurt: A fresh approach to safeguarding in Church* (London: Darton, Longman and Todd, 2019)

Questions for reflection/discussion

- When you read the crucifixion narrative(s), who do you identify with, and why?
- What sort of possible future(s) can you imagine for the Roman centurion?
- Of the four 'stages' identified in this chapter (relocation, relinquishing, receptivity, repentance), which do you find easiest to identify with and which do you find most difficult?
- Can you think of examples, either from your own experience, or from other stories within the Bible, or from books, TV or films, of each of these four stages?

Act 7

An Easter Eve Encounter

It was Easter Eve, not long before sunset, and a small group of us gathered in Comet Park, bringing blankets and folding chairs, lanterns, flasks of hot drinks, and the makings of a fire around which we would sit.

We were there to enact a version of the ancient 'Easter vigil', a service dating back to the earliest days of Christianity, in which, in the dark hours preceding Easter morning, Christians gather outside around a fire to remember 'the mighty acts of God' – in creating the world and bringing liberation to the people of Israel – after which the new Easter candle is lit, leading the congregation into the church to celebrate afresh the good news of Jesus' resurrection.

Ours was not the first fire to be lit in Comet Park that spring. Six days before, a petrol-fuelled fire had destroyed some newly installed play equipment – a climbing-frame and a couple of big swings – that had been enjoyed by local children for just a few short weeks. 'The kids' themselves had been blamed by many locally for the fire: an act of futile self-sabotage. But there was also a quieter, darker rumour circulating that adult residents of neighbouring houses, who had not been consulted about the building of the new play park, were in fact responsible – reasserting their right to live in privacy and undisturbed peace.

So, we gathered, that Easter Eve, on the charred circle of earth where the short-lived climbing frame had briefly stood. Most of us, however, were too caught up in grief and shock at recent events, to be able to make much sense of the task to remember 'the mighty acts of God'. Instead, we sought to enter more deeply into the Easter Eve of the very first disciples – the friends of Jesus who knew nothing of the significance of that evening, other than the fact that it was the second evening after they had witnessed their friend and teacher crucified, dead and buried. There was no tomorrow for them – only a dark yesterday. And in solidarity with them, we shared our own stories of hopes dashed, of loves lost, of futures foreclosed, of dark nights aching for dawn to come.

In the midst of our story-telling, we had visitors. Curious young visitors – a family of children (no adults) ageing from about three years old to late teens, the headscarf on one of the girls suggesting they were Muslims.

They were disappointed, bewildered, angry even that the new play equipment had been destroyed. Who would do such a thing, and why? They had come to the park to play – what were they supposed to do now? They came with these questions to us – this odd-looking group of adults, sitting in a circle, illuminated by lanterns and firelight – but they also wondered, out loud and directly, what we were doing there. We told them we shared their disappointments and bewilderment – we too had hoped that the park was a sign of a new beginning for our neighbourhood, of something good happening here for local young people. We too were sad, frustrated and angry. We explained that we had been telling stories together, and that we were Christians, remembering an equally bewildering experience of loss from many, many years ago. We invited them to join us in the circle, if they wanted to.

They were more interested in the contents of a small, plastic box under one of our folding chairs. 'What's in there?', they asked, pointing at the little round balls of soil and clay. We explained that they were seed bombs, made earlier in the week at one of our all-age activity days, that at the end of our gathering that evening we were going to throw into some of the more inaccessible and unpromising places around our estate, with the hope – the far-fetched hope – that a little new life, a few wild flowers, might in time spring up. They were stunned.

'Wow, do they really work?'

It was possible, we said.

Could they have some?

'Of course!'

How much did we want for them?

'Nothing – have them as a gift from us.'

'Seriously?!'

Seriously.

They went away, hands full of seed bombs, voices lightened by the prospect of throwing things that might, just possibly, bring a little life, colour, beauty and hope.

16

Resurrection

When the sabbath was over, Mary Magdalene, and Mary the mother of James, and Salome bought spices, so that they might go and anoint him. And very early on the first day of the week, when the sun had risen, they went to the tomb. They had been saying to one another, 'Who will roll away the stone for us from the entrance to the tomb?' When they looked up, they saw that the stone, which was very large, had already been rolled back. As they entered the tomb, they saw a young man, dressed in a white robe, sitting on the right side; and they were alarmed. But he said to them, 'Do not be alarmed; you are looking for Jesus of Nazareth, who was crucified. He has been raised; he is not here. Look, there is the place they laid him. But go, tell his disciples and Peter that he is going ahead of you to Galilee; there you will see him, just as he told you.' So they went out and fled from the tomb, for terror and amazement had seized them; and they said nothing to anyone, for they were afraid. (Mark 16.1–8)

At the end of the Community Passion Play, after Jesus' cry of god-forsakenness, and the Roman centurion's grief-stricken 'altar call', after the deep, thick silence that seemed to drown even the constant roar of the traffic on the M6 above our heads, a voice broke into song:

Now did you want to see me broken
Bowed head and lowered eyes
Shoulders fallen down like tear drops
Weakened by my soulful cries
Does my confidence upset you
Don't you take it awful hard
'Cause I walk like I've got a diamond mine
Breakin' up in my front yard
So you may shoot me with your words
You may cut me with your eyes
And I'll rise ... I'll rise ... I'll rise ...
Out of the shacks of history's shame
Up from a past rooted in pain
I'll rise ... I'll rise ... I'll rise ...

The words, set to music by the American singer-songwriter Ben Harper (half Jewish, half African-American and Cherokee ancestry), were written in 1978 by African-American poet, writer and civil rights activist Maya Angelou. Like the story of the state execution of a first-century Palestinian Jewish teacher, both music and poetry had made quite a journey to be 'heard to speech' in an abandoned corner of an outer estate on the edge of twenty-first-century Birmingham, England. But their defiant hope resonated profoundly with the take-no-shit attitude of those who had gathered that day around the very first Bromford crucifixion scene and, in the way that resonance works, amplified something that was stirring in this neighbourhood: something that might be named hope, or determination, or possibility, or even resurrection.

Revealing the 'background'

One of the hallmarks of the kind of 'radically receptive' church that we've been edging towards over the course of this book, is that it does not believe it is *creating* the kin-dom of God, but *discovering* it already present in the neighbourhood, and responding receptively and creatively to that ongoing discovery. The idea of God continually present, independent of any of our efforts, is crucial to becoming a less anxiety-driven, less self-centred church. If the kin-dom of God is already among us, in our neighbourhoods, then the calling of the church is not to 'grow the kin-dom' or 'build the kin-dom' or 'bring in the kin-dom' but to *see*, to *know*, to *receive* the kin-dom, and then to live as people who know that reality. More than any other moment in the Christian story, it is the resurrection of Jesus that highlights this *interruptive* nature of God's kin-dom: it is, by its very definition, not something we can do for ourselves, but comes to all of us as gift, as challenge, as world-changing disruption.

One way to try to make sense of this is to borrow from the feminist philosopher and theologian Mary Daly her concepts of 'Foreground' and 'Background'. Daly defines the Foreground as 'the male-centred and mono-dimensional area where fabrication, objectification and alienation take place'. This is what we have described in Part 1 – as we have examined the racism, classism, sexism and ecocidal anthropocentrism which beset both our society and our Church – and which came to focus in the 'gaze' which 'flattens' reality, to which we attended at the end of Chapter 13. In contrast, Daly defines the Background as 'the Realm of Wild Reality; the Homeland of women's Selves and of all other Others; the Time/Space where auras of plants, planets, stars, animals, and all Other animate beings connect'. This is the dimension of reality which we would want to equate with the kin-dom of God (though we recognize that Daly would not accept that equivalence), and that we have been seeking to tease out in Part 3. It is the dimension of reality in which the *shalom* of God prevails, characterized by justice and integrity, in which every part of creation – including us humans – finds its right place and is at peace. And it is always present in the Background, just waiting for us to look beyond the Foreground of privilege, oppression, conflict and competition, and receive it.

In contrast to the mere 'instants' by which Foreground time is measured and which offer only a pale imitation of reality, Daly speaks of 'Moments', within which the Background breaks through, interrupts the Foreground, and we glimpse it more clearly. Such Moments present themselves to us as 'windows and doors through which we leap and race into the Background'. The passages of Scripture we have explored in Part 2 are some such Moments, when Jesus' openness to being interrupted enables the Background, the kin-dom he has come to proclaim, to be seen and heard. We would suggest that the 'Acts' which we have interspersed throughout the book are also such Moments – windows through which we have glimpsed God's kin-dom of *shalom* present in the Background of our own neighbourhood. For Christians, the resurrection of Jesus is the greatest of all Moments. Seen through the wide open door of the empty tomb, and in the strange-yet-trustworthy new life encountered in the Easter garden, the resurrection reveals most clearly the Background as the kin-dom of God, and exposes most fully the sinful, harmful, death-dealing Foreground as a sham.[1]

---

1 Mary Daly, *Outercourse: The Be-dazzling Voyage* (London: The Women's Press, 1993), pp. 1–6.

Yet, in Mark's resurrection story, the briefest of all four Gospels, the resurrection is only known by Jesus' *absence*: 'he is not here', 'he is going ahead of you'. And the story breaks off abruptly. The women who witness this moment of absence flee from the tomb and 'say nothing to anyone, for they were afraid'. If this is a Moment, a 'window or door' through which the women 'leap and race' into the wild, abundant life of the Background, then it is a Moment which has barely begun.

Nevertheless, it is still a beginning. And we should not underestimate the ways in which 'terror and amazement' all too often accompany such beginnings. Once seen, the Background can't be *un*seen: living into the story of that revelation can and should inform every aspect of how we live and how we perceive the world. Having once glimpsed the Background, we should never again ignore the many smaller windows on to it which we encounter. Acknowledging the Background – acknowledging that there is more to reality than the broken Foreground we see most easily – is profoundly disruptive. It invites us into the uneasy tension of living between the world as it *is* and the world as it *should be*, in the now-and-not-yet of God's kin-dom. The Moments in which we perceive the Background interrupt our Foreground ways of living. They may provoke in us a discontent or restlessness which, if we sit with it rather than closing the door on what has interrupted us, will reveal itself to be holy.

In Part 3 of this book we have proposed, and attempted to flesh out, a different 'economy' from the economies we observe currently prevailing within the Church. A Church which is radically receptive, which is willing to be interrupted and to embrace interruption as a gift will, we suggest, also be one which is more alert to the wild, interconnected, abundant life of the Background, more ready to embrace and rejoice in the resurrection Moments in which that Background reality of God's kin-dom becomes more fully present to us, through the gift of our neighbours.

In the spirit of Mark's Gospel, this final chapter will resist the urge to neatly tie up the many loose ends that have been unravelled and teased out over the course of this book. Here, we will offer just a few more glimpses of resurrection, Moments through which we ourselves have only just begun to step, falteringly, following in the wake of those who have, more confidently, leapt and raced before us. At best, like Mark's ending, these 'windows and doors' will offer themselves as an invitation, a challenge, to each of us, to accompany the women and other Others as they run from the tomb, and to discover for ourselves where their footsteps take us.

Resurrection is for losers: where are we, now?

... where we walk in the world with unearned privileges it is our role to unlearn and 'dismantle the myths' of entitlement, to reconnect with empathetic capacities dulled by acculturation into dominance, and to become accountable ... Where we walk in the world as targets of systemic violence, we are tasked, as [adrienne marie] brown writes, 'with claiming our dignity, joy, and liberation'.[2]

Nora Samaran riffs on the words of adrienne marie brown that framed Chapter 15. Resurrection is for those whom the systems of the world have rendered the 'losers'. It is no coincidence that Mark's resurrection narrative is all about the women. There are no men to be seen at this point, Jewish, Roman or otherwise: they will find their place in the resurrection story only *later*, as *recipients* – second- or third- or fourth-hand – of the good news. Resurrection for the *privileged* can come (as both Jesus and St Paul remind us, frequently) only through the painstaking process of losing everything that the systems of the world have persuaded us we are entitled to – even our heroic fantasies that the power and responsibility to 'change the world' are somehow in *our* hands – and receiving the world-changing news from, embracing the company of, seeking solidarity with, those for whom 'losing' has been a taken-for-granted part of life. For many of us, resurrection must mean hearing *after*, following *after*, speaking *after*, acting *after* – after Jesus and our other Others, our other neighbours, who have begun the journey ahead of us.

Jack Halberstam, queer theorist and author of the book *The Queer Art of Failure*, seeks to wean us of our addiction to succeeding, achieving, winning, and calls us 'to recognize that "empathy with the victor" invariably benefits the rulers'. Instead, he repeats the invitation to us, that we have already seen offered to both Zacchaeus and the Roman centurion, to become traitors to the empire, to dis-identify from the winners, and 'to discover our inner dweeb, to be underachievers, to fall short, to get distracted, to take a detour, to find a limit, to lose our way, to forget, to avoid mastery'. 'There is something powerful in being wrong, in losing, in failing,' he argues, playfully, tentatively suggesting that 'all our failures combined might just be enough, if we practice them well, to bring down the winner.'[3]

---

2 Nora Samaran, *Turn This World Inside Out: The Emergence of Nurturance Culture* (Edinburgh: AK Press, 2019), p. 12.

3 Jack (Judith) Halberstam, *The Queer Art of Failure* (Durham, NC: Duke University Press, 2011), pp. 120–1.

Just as Eucharist, reimagined from the outside-in, might not just feed us to feed others but also deepen in us a hunger to *receive* from our neighbours, so the possibility of resurrection, for those of us who are multiply privileged, must surely depend at least in part on us acknowledging our own deep needs, and other parts of us that lie buried in our depths. It was only in the midst of a nine-month course of psychotherapy that I (Al) was helped to realize that one of the powerful drivers of my passion for community-building was my own deep longing for friendship and community – a longing that found some of its significant roots in childhood experiences of conflict and fear of abandonment, a total ineptitude at romantic relationships as a teenager, and the experience of divorce as a young adult. None of these are solely my story to tell publicly here, but it is enough to say that reconnecting with them in recent years has enabled me to enter more wholeheartedly into Halberstam's 'queer art of failure', in ways that have enabled me to see in my present relationships much that I had not seen before.

It is perhaps important to sound a note of caution here. Embracing the 'queer art of failure' may be a very different experience when approached from a position of multiple privilege, than from a position where privilege in some dimensions intersects with oppression in other dimensions. It is a well-documented phenomenon that a woman's 'failure' is likely to be seen as in some ways representative of women in general, whereas a man's failure is not generally read as representative of men – and can even sometimes be deployed strategically (through superficial apologies and assurances that they have 'learned from their mistakes') to increase their 'social capital'. The same is true in the dimensions of race and class. This creates an added layer of complexity and tension for women, black people, or working-class people who seek to engage with the 'queer art of failure', while simultaneously resisting the narrative that would co-opt our failure as in some way representative of our gender, race, or class, in ways which may be damaging to others who share that characteristic. The liberating power of being a 'loser' is not just for white, middle-class men, of course. But we must acknowledge that our 'position' in the very hierarchies we are seeking to subvert will itself influence our experience of that subversion.

Remaining

If 'losing' is a prerequisite for resurrection, so too is *grieving*. Halberstam's playful account of losing needs to sit alongside the 'hard-boiled honesty' (Katie Geneva Cannon's term) that squarely faces all the ways in which losing – being overlooked, silenced, pushed to the edges, demeaned, exploited – is painful, traumatic and often deadly. Injustice – the kind of structural privileges that we have teased out in this book – quite literally kills. And even on the privileged side of those gaping divides and false hierarchies, injustice profoundly distorts and wounds our humanity, the image of God within us. It is not understating this reality, then, when we name it as *collective trauma* – albeit unequally distributed, and differently experienced. Trauma: 'an event or series of events that are too much to bear', as trauma theorist Arlene Audergon defines it. Such experience, she goes on to say, 'is beyond the "edge" of what is possible to perceive and respond to, beyond what we are able to include in our identities, as individuals or communities'.[4]

When we have touched, in this book, on the denial present – explicitly or implicitly – in so many of us with regard to catastrophic climate change, we suggested that 'cultural trauma' might be a significant factor in that denial (see Chapter 3): a 'homesickness' or 'solastalgia' that has much in common with the 'post-imperial melancholia' that lies deep under the collective – and overwhelmingly white – British drive towards Brexit. A refusal to acknowledge the reality (past, present and even future), and an inability to mourn what is no longer there (or will, soon, not be there any more). Something similar could be said of racism and white 'fragility', a class-based indifference to the cruelty of austerity and the stigma of poverty, 'toxic masculinity' and the ongoing effects of patriarchy, church decline and institutional anxiety: none of these can be addressed pragmatically as a 'problem to be solved', or through a purely intellectual argument, without missing the profoundly powerful emotional levels at which they also function. For those of us whose identities bear various kinds of structural privilege – who suffer from the kind of 'empathy deficits' we explored in Chapter 3 – we need to find ways of confronting, and learning to grieve, the losses we have been complicit in inflicting on our 'others' which are intimately entangled with the losses we have inflicted on ourselves.

Grieving

The women followers of Jesus who gathered to keep vigil near the cross, and who determinedly return to the tomb, are a witness not just to the deadly violence of the empire, but to the vital task of grieving in the midst of trauma. With trauma, time does not behave in the linear way we often

---

4 Shelly Rambo, *Spirit and Trauma: A Theology of Remaining* (Louisville, KY: Westminster John Knox, 2010), p. 18, quoting Arlene Audergon.

imagine it to. As trauma theologian Shelly Rambo explains, 'the past does not stay, so to speak, in the past. Instead, it invades the present', presenting us with experiences that were barely comprehensible in the past, and in the present might still escape comprehension. Survival (a word we saw Karen Lebacqz use, in the previous chapter, in the context of 'loving your enemy')

> is not a stage in which one gets beyond death; instead, death remains in the experience of survival and life is reshaped in light of death – not in light of its finality but its persistence. Persons who experience trauma live in the suspended middle territory, between death and life.[5]

The women who stay at the cross, who go to the tomb for the burial, and who return there persistently, show us something of what Shelly Rambo means by 'witnessing from the middle': not looking for ways of 'getting over' or 'moving beyond', and being suspicious of 'the rhetoric of "re" – rebuilding, restoring, recovering'. But instead *remaining*: dwelling in the midst of the experience of trauma, and attending to 'what remains', both in terms of the traumatic experience and its ongoing effects, but also in terms of a persistence, a survival, of life, of hope, of love.

Shelly Rambo challenges 'linear readings' of the cross and resurrection which place 'death and life in a continuum': death behind, life ahead; life emerging victoriously from death. While this way of reading, she acknowledges, can at its best 'provide a sense of hope and promise for the future', it can also 'gloss over the realities of pain and loss, glorify suffering, and justify violence'. The quest for a 'redemptive ending', she warns us, 'the drive to perfection, wholeness, and newness as goals for human life', can exclude too much of the ongoing lived experience in which life and death remain 'peculiarly entangled'. Such goals exclude too many people, and other-than-human creatures too, for whom the complex ambiguities of 'what remains' are stubborn, persistent, unavoidable.

Instead, Rambo directs our attention to the space '*between* cross and resurrection' – what the Christian tradition calls the 'Holy Saturday' space, between Good Friday and Easter Day – where we will find, if we look attentively and patiently enough, 'a new way of being … a form of life that is not triumphant', but rather 'life configured *as remaining*', 'love making its way through death'.[6] And here, in this 'space between', we might just sense what Rambo describes as the dual movement of the Spirit: 'tracking the undertow' and 'sensing life'.

---

5 Rambo, *Spirit and Trauma*, p. 25.
6 Rambo, *Spirit and Trauma*, pp. 143ff.

'Tracking the undertow' and 'sensing life'

This dual movement that Rambo charts is worth letting unfold a little further. The 'undertow', she reminds us, 'refers to an underlying current that lies beneath the surface of the water. Though waves move toward the shore, the undercurrent pulls in the opposite direction. This pull is not visible, but its force can be great.' Rambo calls us 'to track the movements of the Spirit's witness to the undertow, to death's pull in life' and to a theology of 'the deep' – the Hebrew word is *tehom* – that 'attends to the losses, grief, and the chaos of life', realities which 'remain but, in and through the Spirit ... are witnessed'. 'Tracking' the undertow involves 'discerning what does not rise to the surface. It accounts for the force of institutions and persons that do not want certain truths to be told.'[7] It names the kind of painstaking 'work' that, in the previous chapter, involved a combination of 'receptivity' and 'repentance'.

But alongside 'tracking the undertow', Rambo calls us also to the work of 'sensing life', recalling Jesus' promise that the Spirit will lead the disciples into truth: 'Jesus tells the disciples that they will not understand the events that will take place; but they will, in the Spirit, be guided in relationship to them'. The 'life' that is to be 'sensed' is 'not miraculously new but instead is a mixed and tenuous process of remaining'. The Spirit's witness is 'to forms of life that are less discernible, more inchoate and tenuous, than visible and secure'. These barely discernible forms of life bubble up, we might say, even as the undertow's downward pull persists. 'Sensing' their emergence, therefore, requires *imagination*, 'an encounter with what is not [yet] recognizable':

> In this encounter, there is a movement to reorient oneself in relationship to what is not immediately familiar. This movement involves interplay of the senses in an attempt to find one's way. Sensing is a way of aligning oneself in the face of what is unknown... trying to grasp a sense of things in the darkness, attempting to move toward life without knowing its shape.[8]

7 Rambo, *Spirit and Trauma*, pp. 160–1.

8 Rambo, *Spirit and Trauma*, pp. 162–3. Rita Nakashima Brock also explores the ways in which 'the Christa-community' endures through the death of Jesus, in *Journeys by Heart: A Christology of Erotic Power* (New York: Crossroad, 1996), pp. 89–100.

An example: embracing the tasks of climate grief

How might this 'remaining' look in practice, in relation to some of the forms of obliviousness and division that we have explored? Christians involved in the climate justice movement – particularly through Green Christian and Christian Climate Action – insist on the need not just for safe spaces for truth-telling (something we explored at length in the previous chapter), but also spaces for grieving. They point to examples such as the dramatized funereal processions of Extinction Rebellion's 'Red Rebels', the International Day for the Remembrance of Lost Species, and invitations to Britain's churches to offer 'grief circles' and other spaces for mourning and regenerative pastoral care. Grief is less of a linear journey, they suggest, and more a series of tasks that we can either reject or embrace (see the table below, developed by the Climate Psychology Alliance).[9]

Embracing the tasks of grief	Rejecting the tasks of grief
Accepting the reality of the loss, first intellectually and then emotionally.	Denial of: the facts of the loss; the meaning of the loss; the irreversibility of the loss.
Working through the painful emotions of grief (despair, fear, guilt, anger, shame, sadness, yearning, disorganization).	Shutting off all emotion, idealizing what is lost, bargaining, numbing the pain through alcohol, drugs or manic activity.
Adjusting to the new environment, acquiring new skills, developing a new sense of self.	Not adapting, becoming helpless, bitter, angry, depressed, withdrawing.
Finding a place for what has been lost, reinvesting emotional energy.	Refusing to love, turning away from life.

Both climate scientists and eco-theologians alike are justifiably cautious about the language of *hope*, while warning us away from the cliff of *despair*. Hope can too easily slide into a false optimism in our collective ability to change with the necessary speed, or in the arrival of a magic

9 Paul Bodenham, 'Beyond hope and despair', in Jeremy Williams (ed.), *Time to Act: A resource book by the Christians in Extinction Rebellion* (London: SPCK, 2020), p. 128.

'technofix' – what eco-political theologian Catherine Keller calls hope's 'ex-cepting itself' from attending to 'the thick copresence of what matters'. Hope as denial or avoidance, she suggests is better pronounced 'hype'. Similarly, despair can cause us to give up entirely, 'surrender to all the "too-lates"'. These twin temptations can be seductive, not just in the face of climate catastrophe and the extinction of countless species of life, but also amid the rising tide of divisive, 'us-and-them' right-wing politics, and also for Western Christians seeing the crumbling of our much-loved church institutions. What is required, instead, is what Donna Haraway names 'staying with the trouble': learning to be truly present to our reality, with all its losses and fears, divisions and injustices, as well as its joys and gifts and connections. And learning to be truly present with each other, as the 'mortal critters' who together share planet Earth, whose pasts, presents and futures are utterly intertwined – but pasts, presents and futures which are also 'unfinished', open, as Shelly Rambo puts it, to 'moving towards life without knowing its shape'.[10]

An example: a 'Year of Lamentation' for slavery and racism

Another example comes from the diocese of New York, in the Episcopal Church of the United States of America (ECUSA), as Christians there – both white people and people of colour – sought to grapple with their entangled history, experienced very differently, of slavery and racism. A 'Year of Lamentation' formed the first year of a three-year programme of lamentation, repentance and apology, and reparation in the diocese. It was, said one participant, '*an opportunity for black and white Christians to grieve together. Many people made that journey and were transformed by it.*'

One church in the diocese, St Mark's in east Manhattan, used a liturgy in every Sunday service for the year, in which the congregation acknowledged before God 'the pervasive presence of racism in our country's origins, in our institutions and politics, in our diocese and its churches, and in our hearts', and then went on to repent of 'the many ways – social, economic, and political – that white supremacy has accrued benefits to some of us at the expense of others'. The adoption of the liturgy exposed deep hurt and rifts within this one congregation, as Cynthia Copeland, congregation member and co-chair of the diocesan Reparations Committee testified: 'Some people are new to conversations about white

---

10 Catherine Keller, *Political Theology of Earth: Our Planetary Emergency and the Struggle for a New Public* (New York: Columbia University Press, 2018), pp. 89–90, 168.

supremacy, privilege, and power, and it's difficult to talk about what that means. Those who have most trouble are those who take it personally; no one wants to be accused of being racist. It's only when we reframe it and say, "Look, we are all part of a system, we all breathe the same air," that people can start to relax and really engage.'[11]

Here, repentance (which we teased out at length in the previous chapter) is entangled with lamentation. This is not just about hearing, 'seeing' and understanding differently – it goes deeper into the wells of our individual and collective emotional lives. Lamentation seeks to give voice to – to 'hear to speech' – collective grief at past and present division and injustice, and the wounds, destruction and death that those have caused and continue to cause. And somehow, in grieving together the poisoned air that we all breathe, the air itself begins to clear, our 'breathing-together' begins to come more easily. How might things look if we approach the class and race divisions exposed by Brexit, or the changing shape of the institutional Church – as well as the history of slavery and racism, and the global environmental crisis – with such a determined commitment to 'staying with the trouble', attending to the silenced voices, and to our silenced wounds and griefs?

Recycling

When Europeans brought sheep and cattle to Australia they also brought European plants on which these animals could graze. In doing so, they rebuilt a European ecosystem in which they could always be the top predator; grass-sheep-man. But they did not bring decomposers and the native Australian decomposers – used to the dry and stingy dung of kangaroos – left the wet and piling dung of the European grazers where it fell. The dung began to accumulate. In some places it was feet deep and, like the water in the stories of floods, it kept rising. Flies took over where the beetles had failed, but slowly and unpleasantly. The Europeans, despite their intentions, had created a new ecosystem, one in which the ball-rolling dung beetles had been replaced by flies that batted at farmers faces, flies that rose like haloes everywhere the farmers went. The piles of excrement and clouds of flies were the evidence of the value of decomposers (and of some decomposers over others). They

---

11 Rosie Dawson, 'Slavery: "Apology without cost would be empty"', *Church Times*, 7 June 2019, www.churchtimes.co.uk/articles/2019/7-june/features/features/slavery-apology-without-cost-would-be-empty, accessed 8 May 2020.

were a measure of what the Europeans should have been grateful for in their farms back home but had not known to thank.[12]

Throughout this book we have tried to bring to light ways in which our collective imaginations – particularly the imaginations among those of us who benefit from structural privileges – are formed and deformed in ways that leave us with amnesia about our histories, and areas of the world's life of which we are oblivious, and which push certain groups of people and other-than-human creatures to the edges of our attention, and the edges of systems of power. At its most extreme, people and other-than-human creatures are treated simply as resources, commodities to be colonized and exploited, used and consumed, disposed of and discarded. But in so doing, in our inescapable interconnectedness and interdependence those of us who are multiply privileged are overlooking, repressing and discarding parts of the life, the 'flesh' (as we put it, in Chapter 13) of which we ourselves are a part. As the story of the European settlers in Australia and their missing decomposers reminds us, many of our fellow creatures of which we are often oblivious, are in fact essential to the functioning and thriving of our whole ecosystems. They are our *kin*. And not only them, but the often-hidden processes they are part of – of death and decomposition – are not in *opposition* to those processes by which plants and other animals grow and flourish, but are themselves equally vital parts of the cycle of life. Blessed are the decomposers.

Over-accepting and reincorporation

Community gardener and theologian Sam Ewell, drawing on the language of Pope Francis, talks about God's 'preferential option for the discarded' and, starting with the necessity of food waste within the food cycle, extends this 'preferential option' out to include also those places, people and ways of living, that are so often discarded in our societies and church communities. This resonates with Sam Wells' reflections (that we touched on at the end of Chapter 14) on the 'stone that the builders rejected', in relation to the church's own foundations. And, in fact, Ewell builds on Wells' twin ideas of *over-accepting* – embracing events and interactions that come to us, and retelling them within a larger story (what we saw the Syro-Phoenician woman doing with Jesus' 'No' in Chapter 8) – and

---

12 Rob Dunn, 'What if God were a maggot?', in *Scientific American* blog, 20 December 2012, https://blogs.scientificamerican.com/guest-blog/what-if-god-were-a-maggot/, accessed 8 May 2020.

reincorporation – drawing upon discarded yet vital elements of the past as resources for improvising in the present – as vital practices of the church.

The startlingly abrupt ending of Mark's Gospel, many scholars believe, is an intentional invitation to *recycle*: to go back to the beginning of the Gospel and start reading it again, with our eyes opened wider in the light of what we now know. It is only through the 'opening' of the empty tomb, we might say, that we are able to see and understand more clearly parts of the preceding story that formerly went unnoticed: glimpses of the kin-dom that Jesus proclaims, glimpses of possibility that anticipate resurrection – including, but by no means limited to, the stories that we explored in Part 2:

- the possibility of kinship between strangers, revealed by the interruption of the woman with the haemorrhage;
- the possibility that our prejudices can be challenged and changed, our horizons broadened, revealed by the disruptive persistence of the Syro-Phoenician woman;
- the possibility of enduring presence through suffering and death, revealed by the prophetic interruption of the woman with the ointment;
- the possibility that our hierarchical imaginations might be overturned and dismantled, revealed in the disruptive presence of little children;
- the possibility that even in dying fig trees and rapacious mustard plants, life is shared and passed on through a web of hidden interconnections, and disrupted ecosystems can be 'turned over', reconnected and renewed.

This whole book has, in some sense, been an exercise in reincorporation: remembering parts of the Christian community's founding texts that have often been overlooked or too easily 'flattened' by a gaze that refuses to be interrupted and disrupted by them.

But what of interruptions and disruptions that come to us from beyond the biblical text? What of the testimony of Renford McIntyre and tens of thousands of others from the Windrush generation, against the racist 'hostile environment' policy of the UK government? What of the story of Khadija Saye, and the 70 others who died in the Grenfell Tower fire, and all the residents of tower blocks, estates and other low-income neighbourhoods across the country, whose gifts and talents are overlooked and whose identities are stigmatized because of where they're from? What about the witness of 17-year-old Samantha Hanahentzen, for whom the #MeToo movement was the encouragement she needed to speak out on her experience of being sexually assaulted? What about Greta Thunberg's relentless holding to account of the world's most powerful leaders, her insistence that they listen to the science on climate change and species extinction and respond accordingly? And what about the cloud of witnesses within the community that we call 'church', who have spoken up against that institution's history of obliviousness to, and abuse of, both human beings based on divisions of race, class, gender or age, and our other-than-human kin too?

A critical assumption for Wells' theology is that 'the Christian story is larger and greater in depth and scope than the smaller stories that present themselves'.[13] When the Church is presented with a challenge, it already has all the resources it needs to be able to respond, and among other things this can help the Christian community deal with suffering in ways that avoid either attempting to *escape* suffering, or being *overwhelmed* by suffering (a similar dilemma to that of 'technofix or despair' that Catherine Keller laid out in response to environmental crisis, above). However, as we've seen repeatedly in this book, the Church's story – at least, the story that the Church has lived out – has so often proved itself to be narrow, distorted and partial. The Church's desire to 're-narrate' every 'smaller story' within its ongoing narrative, to 'accept' what happens to it 'without losing the initiative' (Wells' words),[14] can all too easily be just another way of defensively reinforcing the privileges it enjoys within the current status quo. Just as it was not Jesus, but the Syro-Phoenician woman, who practised over-acceptance in her encounter with Jesus, so it is often not the *Church*, but the Church's 'others' – those who are outsiders to, or have been pushed to the edges of, the institution – who are the 'decomposers'. And it is the Church itself, and its story, that are often in need of being decomposed.[15]

Being decomposed

In *This is God's Table: Finding Church Beyond the Walls*, Anna Woofenden, a pastor in the outskirts of Los Angeles, tells the story of a community of people – wealthy and poor, old and young, housed and

13 Samuel E. Ewell, *Faith Seeking Conviviality: Reflections on Ivan Illich, Christian Mission, and the Promise of Life Together* (Eugene, OR: Cascade, 2019), p. 226, quoting Samuel Wells, *Improvisation: The Drama of Christian Ethics* (Grand Rapids, MI: Brazos Press, 2004), p. 143.

14 Wells, *Improvisation*, p. 133.

15 Although St Paul's story is most commonly read through his Damascus Road moment of conversion, he also demonstrates an *ongoing* struggle of repentance akin to the process of decomposition. When he reflects, in Philippians 3.7–9, that 'whatever gains I had' he has come to regard as 'loss' and as 'rubbish', in order that he might be 'found in Christ', we wonder if he is pointing us to the ways in which our own entanglements with structural privilege (both inside and beyond the Church) are in need of decomposition.

unhoused – that found itself, quite unexpectedly, forming around garden-ing, eating and worshipping together. One of the focal points of Garden Church became the compost pile:

> ... it takes all sorts of things that are leftover, done, used, and dying – food scraps, peels, dried leaves, stale bread, even your shredded news-paper – and turns them into rich soil. It doesn't have to be fancy, it just needs to be purposeful. You put it all in a bin and let nature do its thing.[16]

The more Woofenden learned about the mysterious processes of decom-position, the more the compost pile became not just a focal point of Garden Church's gatherings, but a focal metaphor for their understand-ings of God: the Divine Composter, who calls us to surrender both our despair at what we can't change, and our temptations to heroic imagin-ings about what we think we *can* change, and interrupts, disrupts and breaks them down to the point that the things we once clung to rigidly become 'as mushy as an overripe banana':

> She takes all that has been, all that we've used, our best bits and our slimy bits, the endings in our lives and the pain of loss, the tantalizing crumbs from our joyful moments and the leftovers we've kept for too long. God takes *all* of that and says, 'Okay, great, let's see what we can do with it next!'[17]

Decomposition, we might say, is the opposite of the kinds of desperately melancholic, nostalgic clinging to the hardened memories of imagined 'good old days', that we have diagnosed underneath Brexit, that can paralyse us in the face of environmental crisis, and that often afflict the life of the Church. The role of the decomposers is to interrupt, disrupt, break open, chew over, and regurgitate what we might otherwise cling to, in ways that do not allow anything to remain the same. It is another glimpse of the often-hidden work of the Spirit.

(Re)discovering

As the story of Garden Church testifies, in the disruption of the decom-position process an environment is being created in which the most unlikely of juxtapositions and connections – things and people finding

---

16 Anna Woofenden, *This is God's Table: Finding Church Beyond the Walls* (Harri-sonburg, VA: Herald, 2020), pp. 129ff.

17 Woofenden, *This is God's Table*, pp. 129–32.

themselves 'alongside' each other – and interdependent sharing become possible. This unexpected 'throwing together' Sam Ewell names 'subversive cohabitation': 'a way of "dwelling" together for the sake of seeking the kin[-]dom, in order to receive, experience, and share ... the good news of "abundant life"'.[18] The rotting compost pile presents us with another of Daly's Moments, a window or door into the possibility of 'creating a common home' in the edge-places and bumping spaces of our society that we explored in Chapter 13. Or to put it another way, this is where we see the 'joining' of torn flesh – of 'peoples now separated by violence, poverty, or race', of human and other-than-human creatures and the earth itself – that we saw Willie Jennings anticipate in Chapter 15 and that, as we teased out there, requires an ongoing negotiation of distance and trust, and is inextricable from a 'hard-boiled honesty' that refuses easy reconciliations.

Here, perhaps, we glimpse the significance of the double sending at the empty tomb: the female disciples are sent with a message to the male disciples; and the message itself is a sending to both women and men together, to go back to Galilee, where they will see Jesus. This is both a re-forming and reconfiguring of *community*, the community of Jesus-followers (with the women, this time, as its initiators), and a returning and a restarting 'back home', back at the beginning, back in Galilee, an edge-place, far from the centres of power. Each of these aspects of the shape of resurrection is worth considering in a little more detail.

'Community' begins at the edges

The resurrection community, on the one hand, is not a given. It doesn't just appear, fully-formed and ready for action. Instead, it is a possibility that lies ahead, a gift that comes from God's future – what Christian theologians call an eschatological reality – for us to reach towards, fail towards, stretch towards, like branches of a tree stretching towards the sun.

But on the other hand, the resurrection community is already present, in the Background, under the surface, if only we are attentive enough to search for it: like the hidden network of roots and fungal filaments that connect trees together for their mutual flourishing and defence. 'It turns out,' says Catherine Keller, 'that there are entire undergrounds forming in the ground beneath, down there in the dirt with the dehumanized and the non-human', an 'expansive commonality' that black political theorists Stefano Harney and Fred Moten name 'the *undercommons*': a 'we' who

---

18 Sam Ewell, *Faith Seeking Conviviality*, pp. 248–9.

'are disruption and who consent to disruption', who 'preserve upheaval', who are sent 'to renew by unsettling, to open the enclosure', to 'falsify the institution', to 'make politics incorrect' and to 'persist in resistance and self-organization'.[19] Here we catch glimpses of the kind of 'liberation movement' that we hinted at in the previous chapter: living within yet *underneath* the surveillance and control of the empire.

The resurrection community is *not yet*, but has also already begun: it is not waiting for *us* – especially we who benefit from the structural privileges of the empire – to be its beginning. For those of us who call ourselves Christians, part of the self-identified resurrection community called 'Church', Mark's resurrection story sends us back to the edges of the world *we* know, to rediscover – or discover for the first time – the sprawling connections of community and teeming life already there among our often-othered neighbours, human and other-than-human. *We* need 'them': our smaller 'we's, narrowed by our divisive, semi-oblivious 'us-and-them's, need to discover a bigger 'we', beyond even our better moments of human solidarity. As Donna Haraway starkly reminds us, 'staying with the trouble' requires us somehow to '*inherit* the trouble' as '*ours*', to 'reinvent the conditions for multi-species flourishing, not just in a time of ceaseless human wars and genocides, but in a time of human-propelled mass extinctions and multispecies genocides that sweep people and critters into the vortex'.[20] And the *beginning* of that 'staying' is for us to return to our edge-places, to look and listen attentively to whom, and to what, lives and moves there, and to know those places, that life, those voices, as the beginning of a new 'we': 'Our animal kin cannot do our politics for us. But we cannot now do the political without them – which is to say, without admitting their humming, roaring, barking, buzzing input.'[21]

Where are the male disciples?

Mark tells us nothing of the next chapter of the story for the male disciples, scattered and hidden after Jesus' arrest and crucifixion. Neither Mark's narrative, nor the logic of resurrection itself, allows them any room to reform the Jesus-community on their own initiative: they are

---

19 Catherine Keller, *Political Theology of Earth*, p. 30; quoting Stefano Harney and Fred Moten, *The Undercommons: Fugitive Planning and Black Study* (Wivenhoe: Minor Compositions, 2013), p. 20.

20 Donna Haraway, *Staying with the Trouble: Making Kin in the Chthulucene* (Durham, NC: Duke University Press, 2016), p. 130.

21 Keller, *Political Theology of Earth*, pp. 168, 86–9.

utterly dependent on the faintest of possibilities, that they might somehow hear the women's message (the women who 'said nothing to anyone'!) and respond. And this faint possibility must surely require at least five conditions, each of which we have explored at length in these last few chapters.

First, they will need to learn the art of *remaining*. They will need to find ways of staying in the company of the women who returned from the tomb, in terror and amazement, long enough for them to find the courage, and the words, to be able to tell of what they have seen and heard.

Second, these men will need to practise a *receptivity* for which they have not, in Mark's Gospel, been renowned. As well as the patience required to hear their terrified co-disciples to speech, they will then need to dig deep to find the verbal, intellectual and emotional resources to trust what they hear. They will need to resist firmly the defensive, dismissive habits that come attached to structural privilege – and that Luke's Gospel displays to us in all its ugliness, where the women's words 'seemed to [the men] an idle tale, and they did not believe them' (Luke 24.11). How many women, with how much persistence, would it take, we wonder, for their #MeToos to break through the male disciples' fragile defences?

Third, then, if and when they do hear and believe the women's testimony, these male disciples must be prepared to follow them in relocating to Galilee, as the messenger at the empty tomb had said. In one sense, this might be the easiest of steps: it is simply *going home*, for them. But for them to encounter the risen Jesus there, they must surely go home with fresh eyes: 'to arrive where we started / and know the place for the first time', as T. S. Eliot once put it.

And that must surely require them to continue trusting the women as their guides, not settling back into the old familiar ways of being 'in charge'. They must relinquish any temptations to take over, to colonize spaces, connections and stories that are not their own. Admittedly, their social position is more ambivalent than that of the Roman centurion: seen through the lenses of class and race, they are not among the 'privileged', neither do they possess any of the military power of an officer of the Roman army. But their investment, as men, in a patriarchal ordering of society is not something they will be able to shed overnight.

Discovering what feminist philosopher Grace Jantzen has named 'trustworthy community'[22] will depend, for the men at least, on discovering different forms of trust and authority to those they have been accustomed to. The ongoing work of repentance, for them, will require them to be prepared to let go of their familiar androcentric (male-centred) ways of

---

22 Grace Jantzen, *Becoming Divine: Towards a Feminist Philosophy of Religion* (Manchester: Manchester University Press, 1998), pp. 210–11.

thinking, relating and acting, their very identities as men within their social contexts, to be 'decomposed' within the new relationships that have been presented to them as gifts – as challenges, as interruptions – of Jesus' resurrection.

Murmurations of starlings and wormhole solidarities

A Murmuration of Starlings! Gorgeous, mysterious, no one in the lead, everyone in the lead ... Each one is managing 'uncertainty in sensing' by attending to seven other birds, thus optimizing 'the balance between group cohesiveness and individual effort.' There is probably more to understand ... Which seven do they pick and why? Proximity, pheromones, sparkle in a feather? Among one bird's seven, how many of those are attending to at least some not in the same seven as the first bird? What is happening when the seven becomes part of 700? What tips them to and fro as they go hither and yon?[23]

As Catherine Keller ends her book, *Political Theology of the Earth*, so we near the end of ours: with a murmuration of starlings – thousands of birds, swooping and diving together in coordinated flight. Those of us who are multiply privileged are *not* being called to 'step up' to lead movements of change and resurrection in the world. We *are* being called, like Zacchaeus and the Roman centurion, to let the work of relocation, relinquishing, repentance and reparation begin in us, and to 'call out' others who share our privileges to join us, as we continually search for ways of pulling down the scaffolding of the structures that have privileged us, separated us, and kept us oblivious from our neighbours. And we *are* called – this is the gift of the resurrection for us – to let the pattern of our discipleship be profoundly shaped by the small group of women who journey with Jesus to Golgotha, who accompany his body to the tomb, and who return (to the tomb) and return (to the male disciples) and return (to Galilee): attending to their attending, to their 'sensing' of life and direction; attending to their turnings and returnings; and seeking to do likewise. The resurrection calls us to become starlings, reading the movements of our multitude of 'others', and joining in as followers, allowing ourselves to be swept up and whirled around.

Such whirling will start with the edge places, and with the neighbours that are close at hand, and swarming above our heads, and connecting under our feet. But it will also, inevitably, whirl us beyond the local, draw

---

23 Catherine Keller, *Political Theology of Earth*, pp. 179–80, quoting David E. Roy and Barbara J. King.

us through webs of connection to places and people and creatures from whom we imagined geographical distance had separated us utterly. Across such divides, Romand Coles points us to the possibility of 'wormhole hope': 'shortcuts' and 'bridges' across 'impossibly abyssal stretches of regular space and time' (akin both to the 'wormholes' proposed by theoretical physicists, and to Mary Daly's Moments), which spark connections and energies for hope-full, co-created change that would seem impossible 'according to the normal coordinates we often take to exclusively define the real'. Coles points us to the apparently 'miraculous connections' that can be traced between apparently disparate periods and places of intense struggle, and challenges us to remember past 'intensities' in ways that cultivate within us a more profoundly attentive readiness to embrace what is coming to life in the present and future.[24] Such wormhole hope, wormhole *solidarity*, can be glimpsed in the ways the words of an African-American poet from 1978 echoed resonantly around a Birmingham outer estate in 2013, bringing hope and possibility into new expression.

Living together on our overheating planet, the number of 'climate refugees' permanently displaced by desertification and flooding – and other climate-related phenomena that we once called 'natural disasters', but we can now see more clearly as entangled with politics, economics, racism, colonialism and environmental destruction – will continue to grow, at a rapidly increasing rate. We are increasingly finding ourselves, says Coles, aware of the ways we are 'indebted to the initiatives and struggles of people in other places', and of the need for a 'receptive generosity and enhanced hospitality toward those coming unexpectedly into the places we are trying to make home'.

As we become more deeply conscious of our 'wormhole solidarities', so too we need to be determined in cultivating what Coles calls a 'hospitality for weightless seeds', acknowledging what ecologists now understand: that the 'ecological commingling among nearby and vastly separated places' is 'absolutely indispensable to the distinctive fertility of each and every place'.[25] We need each other, and each other's gifts and challenges, whether we are separated by great distance, or we find ourselves unexpectedly as next-door neighbours. Hospitality to climate refugees will be, for those of us who for the moment remain settled – and yet *un*settled by the changing dynamics of our world – an exercise not just of a penitential 'working through' of the ways in which our actions are complicit in the displacement of distant neighbours. It will also require a radical receptivity to those neighbours when they arrive on our doorstep: acknowledging

---

24 Romand Coles, *Visionary Pragmatism: radical and ecological democracy in neo-liberal times* (Durham, NC: Duke University Press, 2016), pp. 180–7.

25 Coles, *Visionary Pragmatism*, pp. 187–91.

not only their need of home in a space we have thought of as 'ours', but also their role as bringers of the gifts and challenges of 'disruptive grace'. In so doing, we will need to discover new stories of what it means to be a *neighbourhood*, and also new stories that stretch far beyond neighbourhoods and which pay little attention to national borders, of what it means to be connected to each other, and to find in each other our life and our future.

Respiring

> respire /rɪˈspʌɪə/ *verb*
> gerund or present participle: respiring
> 1. breathe
>   *'he lay back, respiring deeply'*
>   (of a plant) carry out respiration, especially at night when photosynthesis has ceased.
>   *'lichens respire at lower levels of temperature and moisture'*
> 2. (archaic) recover hope, courage, or strength after a time of difficulty.
>   *'the archduke, newly respiring from so long a war'*

Jesus said to them again, 'Peace be with you. As the Father has sent me, so I send you.' When he had said this, he breathed on them and said to them, 'Receive the Holy Spirit.' (John 20.21–22)

In their book *Coming Back to Life*, eco-philosophers and teachers Joanna Macy and Molly Brown offer a 'guidebook' to a form of group-work in which they have been engaged from the 1970s, helping hundreds of thousands of people around the world 'find solidarity and courage to act, despite rapidly worsening social and ecological conditions'. Through what they call 'the Work that Reconnects', rooted in the words of the Hebrew prophets and the life of Jesus, but also 'worked over and illumined' by Buddhist principles, they seek to bring people 'into fresh relationship with our world, and not only arouse our passion to protect life, but also steady us in a mutual belonging more real than our fears and even our hopes'.[26] At its heart is a spiral journey, through four successive and recurring stages.

The spiral begins with *gratitude*, a remembering that all these other 'mortal critters', human and other-than-human, exist alongside us – even those that sting us, annoy us or unsettle us, even those that want to kill

---

26 Joanna Macy and Molly Brown, *Coming Back to Life: The Updated Guide to The Work that Reconnects* (Gabriola Island, BC, Canada: New Society, 2014), p. xxiii.

us, those we want to kill, and those, if we're honest, we quite enjoy eating – not as resources to be used, not as possessions we have rights over, but as gifts, as kin. Beginning with gratitude, we slowly begin to overcome our habits of obliviousness to our creature-kin, and begin to learn to be present to them in ways that *let the pain in*: that open for us a 'way in' to grieving the pain of suffering others, and our own pain, our heartbreak for the world as it is, with all its divisions and losses.

In practising gratitude and honouring our pain, we begin to *see with new eyes* – to know more genuinely and more deeply our interconnectedness to all that is – and then to *go forth* to act on what we now know, not with some kind of fail-safe blueprint, but trying and risking failure at every step, needing to remember to practice gratitude, again, to hold us steady when we are tired or discouraged. And so the spiral, the turning and returning, begins again.[27]

Macy and Brown's spiralling more than resembles what Mary Daly describes as the 'Spiral Paths formed by Moments/Movements of participation in Be-ing', through which 'One Moment leads to an Other'.[28] They touch on each of the disorderly 'windows or doors' into resurrection that we have described in this final chapter: finding our place among the 'losers' so we can receive resurrection as *gift*; committing to remain in the places of trauma and loss so that we can begin to *grieve*, and in the grieving, begin to 'sense' where life is to be found; and opening ourselves to being decomposed, that we might (re)discover community and solidarity with all our Others, in ways that whirl us forward, back and around. These resurrection moments, too, name not a linear process, but a circling, a spiralling, a turning and returning to where we have been before, but returning differently. If we were to slow this spiralling down to the speed of trust – which we must – we might even find it something like *breathing*.

Breathing is something of a universal necessity. But for those of us whose identities are entangled in structural privilege, even our breathing requires particular kinds of attentiveness.

We take a breath
to resist the temptation to seize the initiative.

We take a breath
to avoid being the first to speak.

---

27 Macy and Brown, *Coming Back to Life*, pp. 67–8.
28 Mary Daly, *Outercourse: The Be-dazzling Voyage* (London: The Women's Press, 1993), pp. 4–5.

We take a breath
so we are better placed to hear others to speech.

We take a breath
to relax our defences,
to be better able to receive
interruptions,
challenges,
criticisms
as gifts.

We take a breath
to stay put,
to look,
and look again,
and to notice
the glory
in our common flesh.

We take a breath
to enter
into a shared unspeaking
with those human and other-than-human kin
who do not speak in words,
with those who have been silenced,
with those fighting for breath
because there is a knee on their neck,[29]
a hand on their throat,
or because the air they inhale
is poisoned with toxic chemicals,
or because
they are breathing their last,
crucified by today's empires.

We take a breath
to 'stay with the trouble',
to let in the pain,
to be interrupted by the losses,

---

29 These words were written (by Al) in the wake of the murder of black American man George Floyd by white police officers in Minneapolis, on 25 May 2020. Floyd was filmed lying on the ground, with a police officer's knee pressed down on his neck, gasping 'I can't breathe'.

with cries too deep for words,
to breathe them in
and breathe through them,
to let them pass through our hearts,
'making good rich compost
out of all that grief'.[30]

We take a breath
to let the work of relinquishing
and repentance
and reparation
begin in us,
to let the decomposers
and the processes of decomposition
do their thing,
break open,
chew over,
regurgitate,
reincorporate,
breathe.

We take a breath
to let ourselves be stretched
even to aching point
into wormhole solidarities
beyond our familiar horizons.

We take a breath
to ready ourselves
to follow after
and among
our respiring
con-spiring
'mass of swarming neighbours',[31]
a 'force field
of speechlessly breathing bodies',
catching a breath
in shared silence,[32]
stretching the Moment,

30 Macy and Brown, *Coming Back to Life*, pp. 276–8.
31 Tom Dewar, in a global #TogetherApart conversation, April 2020.
32 Keller, *Political Theology of Earth*, pp. 164, 167.

opening the window,
leaping and racing
together,
blown on the wind of the Spirit,
into the Background Realm
of Wild Reality
that is the kin-dom
of God's *shalom*.

We take a breath
to pass up the last word.
And so here is our ending.
And our beginning.

Breathe.

Further reading

- Rita Nakashima Brock, *Journeys by Heart: A Christology of Erotic Power* (New York: Crossroad, 1996)
- Romand Coles, *Visionary Pragmatism: radical and ecological democracy in neoliberal times* (Durham, NC: Duke University Press, 2016)
- Mary Daly, *Outercourse: The Be-dazzling Voyage* (London: The Women's Press, 1993)
- Samuel E. Ewell, *Faith Seeking Conviviality: Reflections on Ivan Illich, Christian Mission, and the Promise of Life Together* (Eugene, OR: Cascade, 2019)
- Jack (Judith) Halberstam, *The Queer Art of Failure* (Durham, NC: Duke University Press, 2011)
- Donna Haraway, *Staying with the Trouble: Making Kin in the Chthulucene* (Durham, NC: Duke University Press, 2016)
- Stefano Harney and Fred Moten, *The Undercommons: Fugitive Planning and Black Study* (Wivenhoe: Minor Compositions, 2013)
- Shelly Rambo, *Spirit and Trauma: A Theology of Remaining* (Louisville, KY: Westminster John Knox, 2010)
- Jeremy Williams (ed.), *Time to Act: A resource book by the Christians in Extinction Rebellion* (London: SPCK, 2020)
- Anna Woofenden, *This is God's Table: Finding Church Beyond the Walls* (Harrisonburg, VA: Herald, 2020)

Questions for reflection/discussion

- Can you think of examples of 'Moments' which reveal the 'Background Realm of Wild Reality' – either from your own experience, from Scripture, or from books or films?
- 'Resurrection is for losers' – how do you react to this (playfully provocative) phrase? And why?
- We have used a number of metaphors in this chapter – window and door, a murmuration of starlings, compost heaps, and more ... Which (if any) of these metaphors help you to grapple with the idea of resurrection? Can you think of other metaphors that would work for you and your community?

Act 8

An Easter Day Walk

Al

It was another Easter Eve – 2017, not long after the Brexit vote, and the election of Donald Trump as US President – when I received a text message from one of the city councillors in the next-door ward to our own, a young Muslim woman, and passionate community activist. Could I, and any sister and brother Christians I could muster, meet her the next day, in the afternoon, to visit some shops on the Alum Rock Road where, the week before, Britain First (a far-right, anti-Muslim group) had made their threatening and hostile presence felt (intimidating shoppers and shopkeepers in the name of a 'Christianity' represented by the big white cross they brought with them)? Could we come and show our solidarity with our Muslim sisters and brothers, sharing in peace together after our Easter celebrations?

How could I say no? What an invitation – and on Easter Day of all days! And so, after six hours of Easter morning services and breakfasts (many of us in Hodge Hill manage to fit in at least three breakfasts on Easter morning!), a small group of five of us headed down to the Alum Rock Road to meet Councillor Mariam, with some of the local neighbourhood policing team – who then acted as both our guides and travelling companions as we walked up a road which, for some of us at least, was unfamiliar.

As we walked and talked together, we were taken into a handful of Islamic bookshops and gift shops and were introduced to those who worked there. We received warm welcomes and generous hospitality, we listened to a little of each other's stories, and together we found ourselves sharing in a process of mutual encouragement, strengthening and peace-making – even perhaps in the beginning of the healing of some of the wounds of the previous week.

In each of our encounters, those of us entering one of the shops would greet those inside with the Arabic words of the traditional greeting between Muslims: 'as-salaam-alaikum'. Words which in English mean, simply, 'peace be with you'. Those we greeted would respond, 'wa-

alaikum-salaam', receiving and returning the greeting, acknowledging the presence of the God of peace between us. Sometimes our hosts would be the ones initiating the greeting, and it would be us on the receiving end. This was a 'walk of witness' like no other I had ever been on: 'witness' in the double sense of both being there, seeing, hearing, receiving something, and also of testifying, pointing to something that we believe to be true. It evoked for us Christians deep resonances with Easter stories from the Gospels (including stories we had heard that very morning), of Jesus appearing to his fearful friends behind locked doors, breathing on them and saying 'peace be with you'. Perhaps it also had echoes of that encounter on the beach where Peter's three-fold denial of his friendship with Jesus was reworked into a three-fold affirmation of love, at Jesus' gracious and challenging invitation.

Most profoundly, perhaps – and it hit me at the end of our time on the Alum Rock Road, when we were invited into a cafe and given copious amounts of hot tea and samosas – it reminded us of the journey of two of Jesus' grieving disciples, heading back to their home village of Emmaus, and encountering Jesus both on the road as a stranger, and as the guest-turned-host as he broke bread at their table. Being interrupted, being transformed, by the risen Jesus, as the embodied presence of God's peace, between us in encounters of greeting, welcome, hospitality, friendship and peace-making.

Act 9

A Walk in the Woods

There's a small patch of woodland in the middle of the Firs and Bromford estate. An outsider visiting the neighbourhood would be very unlikely to find it. For many years, even the majority of local residents didn't know it was there. There's only one path through it, from one end to the other, and it's well hidden: up the hill a little from the Bromford end of the neighbourhood (built on the flat ground of the former racecourse, leading to the banks of the River Tame), and separated by a high tree-lined cliff from the upper ground of the Firs end.

In early 2020, plans were coming together locally to put in a major funding bid to create an 'arts, heritage and well-being trail' through the neighbourhood, with the stated intention of encouraging more local residents to get out walking, and discover the estate's hidden beauty spots. Part of the funding would pay for professional artists to work with local people to create permanent and temporary art installations in the woods.

And then the COVID-19 pandemic hit the UK. At the height of the pandemic, the country was in 'lockdown'. For over two months, every member of every household, other than those in vital 'key worker' roles, had to stay at home 24 hours a day, 7 days a week, with the exception of a weekly shopping trip for essentials, an hour of daily exercise, and short trips to help vulnerable neighbours – always from a safe, non-infectious, 2-metre distance.

And suddenly, the woods burst into life. For many local residents, it became the place of their daily walk. Neighbours who had never met before would encounter each other in the woods, and take time to talk together. The bluebells came out, and gave the wood a glorious carpet of colour. Woodpeckers were heard high up in the trees. And things started appearing. A rope swing, and then another, and another. A complete set of dining table and chairs (complete with candlesticks, plates and cutlery, and a modest chandelier swinging from a tree branch), slightly off the beaten track, hidden in the trees, as if the wood's hidden residents had set up their own version of the Mad Hatter's endless tea party. And then a 'thank-you' jar, paper and pens, to encourage people to share what we were grateful for.

Some people said it wouldn't last, and they were right. The table was burnt (although remained stubbornly intact), and the diverse additions to the setting were scattered. Repeatedly. But Firs and Bromford's creative, resilient neighbours returned, again and again, to restore what was scattered, and bring new creations to refresh and renew the scene.

After a particularly definitive act of destruction at the table, an alternative location was found for this spontaneous focal point of community. An old tree, at one end of the wood, became host to streamers, wind chimes and bird feeders, a 'creative table' for children, painted stones all the colours of the rainbow, and more. And the 'thank-you' jar returned, and was stuffed full once again.

Throughout the 'lockdown' phase of the pandemic, the doors of the local church building were firmly shut, and its congregation – unable to gather together, even online, when so many were without internet access – fasted, for months, from sharing in the Eucharist. And yet here, in the woods, a breathing-space emerged: an unplanned, uncoordinated site of communion and thanksgiving.

Epilogue

In Conversation – COVID-19, the 'Great Interruption'

We were nearing the end of the process of writing this book, when the UK was hit by the COVID-19 pandemic. Suddenly, 'being interrupted' took on a whole new meaning! Gradually we started to reflect, separately and together, and with our friends, colleagues and neighbours, on what sort of 'interruption' this might be – for us, for our neighbours, for our communities, for the Church, for the world. We started an email exchange, which led to the conversation below, recorded on Zoom in May 2020, during lockdown.

We have divided the conversation into four sections, although – as tends to happen in any conversation – there is a certain amount of overlap and returning to earlier ideas,. Those four sections are:

- Writing, interrupted – we reflect on the process of writing this book, how that process has been interrupted by the pandemic, and how that interruption has shaped our thinking and writing.
- Exposing existing realities – we reflect on how the pandemic has exposed existing assumptions, power structures and inequalities, both in society and within the Church.
- Liturgy, interrupted – we explore the pandemic interruption in terms of liturgical time, eucharistic living, and what ministry might look like in a time of lockdown.
- Breaking down and building up – we explore a range of questions about being a neighbour and building trust in uncertain times, and about the place of death, decomposition and change in the Church.

We have tidied up the transcription of our conversation only slightly, just cutting out some of the inevitable 'er's, 'um's and repetitions. We are very aware that it captures only one very particular moment, from a very particular location and perspective(s), but we hope it may be a prompt for reflection. At the end, we have included some questions for reflection on your own experience of the 'great interruption' caused by the pandemic.

Writing, interrupted

Al   Is it worth just starting by reflecting a bit on how we've got to where we've got to? I was struck, I think it was last week, by realizing that it was the anniversary of me writing a blog about what would happen if we reversed the normal flow of church life and started from the outside in. And then you picked up on it and said, 'Yes, and ... and *children*'. And let's reflect on that. And turning the church upside down.

Ruth   Yes, that has been quite a process. I remember reading that blog post. And thinking: 'Oh, yes. That's what I've been thinking.' But actually in articulate words, that I can say something in response to. And I think that's been quite characteristic of the process all the way through, from my point of view, reading and saying 'Yes. *And also*, here's another thought.' And certainly the way we've emailed back and forth about this epilogue stuff has been like that.

Al   I've really appreciated and enjoyed both hearing the 'yes', because I think I've spent quite a lot of time with this stuff thinking, 'Does this make sense? Does it work?' and also being conscious of trying to write consciously from a position of privilege, multiple privilege, thinking, 'Actually is this speaking truth when heard through the ears of someone who shares *some* of those privileges but also doesn't share all of them?' So hearing the 'yes' from you, but the 'yes, *and* ...', I think has been profoundly helpful because it's stretched it, and stretched *me*, and tested some of the places where maybe it's not quite getting at the truth, but I think also it's felt like it's opened this huge new wealth of life and diversity within that. I think some of your 'yes, and's have been about 'yes, and what about *this* dimension of life as well?' And going right back to the beginning, the question of adults and children was one of the areas that was for me a sort of example, but not the stuff that I'm particularly focusing on at the moment. And actually, you were saying, 'Well, what if we do focus on that? And what then opens up by exploring *age*?' Because all the different dimensions aren't the same. Or they don't neatly map on to each other in the same way.

Ruth   I think you're right, the more dimensions that have entered the conversation, the more complex it's got, but also the more it's felt like we're getting towards something that's quite important and true. I think one of the things I've really enjoyed has been the ways that the writing process has reflected what we're writing about.

I feel like we've engaged in a process of over-accepting, in quite a good way. I really like that metaphor – the 'yes, and ...' For me, it's been quite helpful to be doing that as part of the writing process, as well as writing about the possibility of doing it.

Al   Absolutely. Have there been any bits of it that have felt difficult?

Ruth   I think I've certainly come at it with a fairly hefty dose of imposter syndrome, which is how I approach most of life to be honest. Despite your very enthusiastic 'yes, ands ...', I still, at the back of my mind, think, 'But who really wants to hear what I've got to say about this? Why do I think I've got anything to say? And what have I got that's worth listening to?' I think some of that is some internalized stuff, and some of it is probably just me, and some of it I guess is probably just inherent to the process of writing a book.

Al   Yeah, I get that. There's that similar, maybe not identical, feeling myself. I think one of the things I've really valued is that I went all through my PhD research and then into this phase of publication thinking, 'Does anyone actually want to read this or hear this? Is this actually interesting? Is it new or has everyone said it before?' So, I think having companionship in that, coming from different places and saying that there's something worth doing here, has been really helpful. I think in some ways it's had to slow the process down more. But in a good and important way. And certainly, in this last phase of life, the process has been slowed down in all kinds of ways well beyond our control. And I think another thing that it has done for me is reminded me how we're never really going to finish it neatly. I think that the joy of 'yes, and...' is that it's making something richer and more variegated. But the other side of that is, you know that there is never going to be a satisfactory point where we'll say, 'Right, we've done this.'

Ruth   Yes, there's always another 'and' to go! And also, I'm very conscious that there are things that we've said 'That is a "yes, and ..."' which we *could* go down, but we're not going to.' We can't fit all of the dimensions of this into this piece of work.

Al   Absolutely. That's certainly something that, if we haven't done it already, we need to acknowledge before we finish. [We've named two further areas in particular – the experiential lenses of dis/ability, and of being LGBTQI+ – which both have a lot of overlap with what we've explored here, but which will need a different space to this to tease out the particular insights and connections that they bring.]

Actually, there's something about embracing the finiteness of some of these tasks, but also acknowledging the unendingness of all of the main things that we've said are important in this. But it isn't a process of being finished. It's a bit like the Benedictine vow of conversion, as being something that isn't about a *moment* [that is, an instantaneous conversion], but it's something that we need to pursue for the rest of our lives. And I guess an invitation to others to engage in a similar journey.

Ruth   Yeah, absolutely. I think one of the possibly slightly unexpected dimensions of it, for me has been how formational it has felt. The extent to which the process of thinking about this stuff is changing who I am and how I relate to the church and the world and my own vocation, in really helpful ways, and in ways that I hope will go on changing.

Al   Do you want to say any more about that?

Ruth   It's been really helpful for me that the way in which we're writing, and the content of what we're writing, and the way in which we're doing stuff in Hodge Hill, are all very bound up together. To me that feels a bit different from a more distant process of theological reflection. If I experience something, then theologically reflect on it, and then act differently, that's one thing. But this feels much more entangled and enmeshed, and much more two-way. It feels like what we're doing is affecting how we're writing, as well. It's much more messy.

Al   And there's something quite experimental about that isn't there?

Ruth   Yes, I think improvisation is key. And improvising again is that 'yes, and ...', that acceptance of what you're being offered. Also, I think part of the formational thing for me is that it is making me more and more somebody who improvises. The practice of writing like that, and working like that, is making me more like that.

Al   I can certainly resonate with your sense that actually practice and reflection have been interwoven in this. That sense of having a sustained conversation about 'how do we do this?' has meant that I've been much more attuned to asking that, when moments of decision-making have to happen. So, the ways in which we've tried to do church in the midst of COVID-19 – I think some of them were probably ingrained enough as instincts here anyway, but some of them I think have been helped by having this ongoing process of thinking 'how does church work differently?'

We've reflected a bit [together] about the fact that even the process of writing the book has been interrupted by the crisis of

Coronavirus hitting the world. I think for me that's often been felt as immensely frustrating, even at times quite painful. So I think I've wrestled with that a lot, and certainly in our household I've found myself realizing that some of the time I take for granted normally – being on my own in the house, in my study with the door closed, with no interruptions other than the phone that I can put on silent for a while – is not part of life at the moment.

Ruth Yes, and I think it's more. It is about having that physical space and time. But it also feels to me very much like my headspace has been disrupted and interrupted. I definitely think Virginia Woolf was on to something with the whole concept of a room of one's own, and that's more than literal. I am missing my literal space, as in my favourite spots in the library at Queens, but it's more this sort of internal room of one's own, of being able to shut the other stuff out and focus. It's made me think a lot about that. I read an article saying that male academics are submitting a lot more articles for publication since lockdown, and female academics are submitting a lot fewer articles for publication since lockdown, and it doesn't take a great stretch of the imagination to work out why that might be. But really, that's just a microcosm of the whole history of intellectual thought. And of course, it's not just about gender. It's all these other dimensions that we've looked at, certainly race, but particularly, I think, class as well. When you look at models of study for university students during this situation, which assume that people do have a space of their own in which to study, then again, there's a whole assumption of privilege. I think it's quite helpful in a sense, although it's certainly not comfortable, to have those sorts of things, those sorts of assumptions interrupted.

I guess one of the assumptions that's been interrupted for me in quite a big way is the assumption that writing uninterrupted will produce something *better*. But I don't think that is the case, actually. I think the interruption has been part of the process and will be part of what comes out of the process. That's not a bad thing; and it's not a bad thing to be saying in quite an upfront way that being uninterrupted is not the great goal of the intellectual process. I was quite shocked when I saw some clergy online saying that one of the reasons they wanted to be allowed into their churches to say the Office was that when they were home, they got interrupted. I remember thinking, 'Well, isn't that just *life*?' The vast majority of people in the world are interrupted all the time. And actually, if we can't pray in that, and if we can't find

God in that, and if we can't shape our meaning and our way of seeing the world in that interrupted space, then really, what's it good for, beyond the few people who can be uninterrupted?

Al   Absolutely. That reminds me of one of my favourite child theologians, Bonnie Miller-McLemore, who wrote a book called *In the Midst of Chaos*,[1] some years ago, and it came out for me at just the right time in my journey of becoming a parent, when we had a young child. I think the bits of spirituality that I was reading were all about going and finding a space away somewhere to do the praying stuff and to do the reflecting stuff. But what Bonnie was saying in her book is actually, you know, deal with it. You're a parent, that ain't gonna happen. I remember early on when we had Rafi, retreating sometimes to the loo, and locking the door to try and just get a few minutes of quiet space. But even then, he would know where I was and be hammering on the door from the outside saying 'Daddy, Daddy!' And what I think Bonnie opened up with the possibility that actually working out how to engage with God in the midst of the demands and the interruptions and the chaos was actually not a second best, but was a possibility to engage in a more real and authentic and rich way than our assumptions of separation.

Ruth   Yeah. I think that's a really important bit of relearning for me, and it really does intersect with some of the dimensions we've been looking at. Gender, very obviously. The idea of being able to step away from all other responsibilities in order to engage with God feels to me a very male suggestion. But also class – like the idea of a quiet space. Certainly, for me, growing up, it wasn't a thing. Nowhere was quiet. When you live in a house where you can hear the neighbours cough through the wall, nowhere was ever quiet. I think that's where, for me, the Academy being interrupted by the rest of life is actually quite a positive thing to be happening. I remember the first time I sat in a library in Oxford, and I couldn't get over how quiet it was. I've never studied somewhere that quiet apart from during exams, ever before. I think the assumption that you need to cut yourself off in order to write something is a bit like some modes of theological education where the suggestion appears to me to be that you need to step back from parish life in order to be formed as a priest, and I find that quite a strange suggestion. I'm not sure uninterrupted is always the best option.

---

1 Bonnie Miller-McLemore, *In the Midst of Chaos: Caring for Children as Spiritual Practice* (San Francisco, CA: Jossey Bass, 2007).

Exposing existing realities

Al   I'd like to pick up on your point about what's been exposed about inequalities by the virus. We've talked about, and others have talked about, the virus and the interruption as being revelation, as being *apokalypsis* [Greek for revelation, or unveiling]. That sense of something being unveiled. And you've touched on some of those aspects of that already. But I wonder, what have you noticed being unveiled? Or being brought to more clarity?

Ruth   I think a lot of things that have always been true are just more obvious and more in-your-face. There's the really obvious inequality of wealth, and whether people can feed themselves. Some of the continuing inequalities around gendered division of labour in the home have been really noticeable. And I think massively, race. Racial inequality in the deaths that we're seeing from the virus, particularly among healthcare and other key workers, and just the obviousness of how stratified our economy and our society is by race and class, in terms of who is on the one hand really, really key in keeping the food on the shelves, but on the other hand, seen as expendable and worth risking. There's that paradox: these are the people who we can't live without, but also these are the people who we don't value enough to protect. That has always been true, it's just more obvious now. The speed with which we've gone from rhetoric around 'low skilled' to rhetoric around 'key workers', and we're talking about the same people very often.

Al   Absolutely. Yes. And it's been quite remarkable to see that shift, hasn't it? I guess one of the wonderings is how deeply that lodges in the public imagination and discourse. And how the temporary unveiling of some of our eyes in crises like this, how that can become more permanent, how we don't slip back into obliviousness.

Ruth   I think a really important part of that is just naming it and saying, 'this is what's happening'. This is what has always been happening, but now we're seeing it.

Al   I think alongside that, there's been a sense of just not being aware of certain people groups that have been undervalued, been overlooked, are currently and always more at risk, but also actually exposing our connections to each other, exposing our sense of connectedness and dependence on each other. I've been fascinated by the language over the last little while. Someone wrote an article recently,[2] reflecting on how the first stage of government response treated us as *subjects*. Government told us what to do, and most of us willingly did it. The second stage has shifted more to the language of the *consumer*. You know, 'if you can, you can do that'. But 'we need to make some choices, you need to make some choices'. It's all about the decisions that you make. And that glosses over the fact that some people are more able to make decisions than others. Some people have more choices open to them than others. We can choose to work at home on our laptops in our conservatory or our back garden, and many others of our neighbours don't have any choice but to go to work. But there's another possibility of language and thinking about who we are in it all, and that is that actually we're profoundly connected to each other and profoundly dependent on each other, as well as responsible for each other. It feels like our government at the moment don't really have that kind of language in their register.

Ruth   I think the reciprocal interdependence is what has been really noticeable for me. I think a lot of political language in the recent past (the last few decades, probably) has been about who is dependent on whom, and that somehow dependence is a bad thing. All the language around benefits and language around scrounging and being dependent on the state has been very negative for a very long time. And I think we've somehow allowed the idea that dependence is bad, that some people depend on other people, but not the other way round, to enter the public discourse. Yet suddenly, it's become so clear that that is just not true. Those of us who have an income that is independent of the state are not independent of our neighbours. We're just not. That's how food gets as far as our house. That's all just become really stark. And all the notions that go with that, of being self-made or independent. It's there in figures of speech when we say someone's 'of independent means'. There's no such thing. For me that ties in with something that we've touched on a bit around class, and the idea of independence, self-sufficiency, and 'getting out' and 'making something of yourself'. That is certainly a narrative that I encountered a lot when I was a working-class teenager, wanting something different from what I saw around myself. It was the only narrative, and I think it still is the only narrative for a lot of people. You can 'make something of yourself', you can 'get out',

---

2 Jon Alexander, 'Subject, Consumer, or Citizen: Three Post-Covid Futures', *New Citizenship Project*, 17 April 2020, https://medium.com/new-citizenship-project/subject-consumer-or-citizen-three-post-covid-futures-8c3cc469a984, accessed 8 May 2020.

you can do something different as an individual, if you work hard enough and you do well enough. I guess the unspoken goal of that is that you become independent of your community. But it's really made me reflect on what a damaging thing that is to be setting up as a goal for young people. You don't, you just become dependent in a different way. And you can't and you shouldn't be trying to be.

Al   I think one of the joys of this time living on the Firs and Bromford has been noticing around me how much interdependence is going on here and the expressions of neighbourly care and creativity. People sticking tables outside their houses and inviting people to put food on them for others to help themselves, just in a sense of sharing what we have, so that those who need something can get what they need. There is an immense resilience and creativity; for example, one of the local nans, going into the beautiful bluebell woods with her grandkids and decorating trees, making little fairy houses, bird feeders and the like, and even when they get broken, burned and removed, going back again and again, rebuilding, recreating, and making it more beautiful, more complex and more widespread than it was before. I think all of us who have been wandering through our neighbourhood in the last few weeks have been touched and sustained by this. And we are really actually very dependent on being able to do those walks and see those bits of beauty and creativity and resilience. That's some of the stuff that keeps us going.

Ruth   I think one of the things, to return to our 'what has been revealed?' question, one of the things that I think has been revealed is the gifts that are already present in our neighbourhoods. And actually, some of that resilience and creativity is perhaps present somewhere like the Firs and Bromford in a way that it isn't somewhere like where I live, where there are big gated houses, and you don't see your neighbours. And actually, what's being revealed is that there's a gift where you are that is lacking where I am. Whereas I think the prevailing narrative would be that the people who live in these massive houses around here have more, and materially of course they do, but actually, they don't; they're not more independent either. Because they are dependent on the people who stack the shelves at Sainsbury's, and load the Ocado deliveries. But it's not the same. Actually, I think they're missing out because they're not engaging in that mutual interdependence that you're describing.

Al   You've noted before how this crisis has exposed something about church and who we think we are as church and what we think we're about. Do you want to say something about that?

Ruth   I guess this picks up on what we were saying earlier about formation, and instinct, and habit (in a good sense). It's really revealed what our instinct says church communities are, which has been formed and developed by the way we've behaved. There are all sorts of differences – and we don't want to get too stuck into the nitty gritty of livestreaming versus recording and all those things – but one of the really interesting things to me is how much of the conversation has been about worship. And obviously worship is a really important part of what it means to be church. But how those conversations are taking place; whether the starting point for that conversation is, 'How do we engage as many people as possible?' or 'How do we create something really beautiful?', or (as I think it has been for us) 'How do we make sure this is inclusive of the people who are least well connected? And in ways that reflect the reality of life at the moment?' And none of these are bad questions to be asking. I think they reflect a different emphasis and a different sort of prioritization. Maybe all of them if they are taken too far can slip into some of those temptations that we've identified. I just think it's really interesting to see what assumptions are exposed by the questions we ask. Is your first question 'Who can participate in this?' Or is your first question 'What will this look like at the end?'

Al   I think you've touched on something that explains some of the heat that's going around in some of the exchanges between Christians, particularly on social media. Actually, a lot of the stuff is not about the presenting issues is it? It's about those deep underlying assumptions, it's about what we're about. I've been fascinated by the tension between, on the one hand, Church wanting to say, 'Actually, this is about keeping things as normal as possible, providing that sense of stability, continuity through the crisis, the sense that the Church is who you can rely on for that solidity.' And then at the same time, the language of the Church saying 'Actually no, there's something to be grasped here. There's a new reality at the other end of this and we need to seize the opportunity to shape that new normal. We can't go back to business as usual, and we shouldn't really be invested in sustaining it.' It feels to me like both of those in a way are power grabs, they're spotting an opportunity for the Church to say, 'This is the space. We are either in control of the space or wanting to grab control of the space, so that reality can be defined by us and how we do things.' I think that links to how we talked in the book about the 'three P's' as temptations to the power of the provider, the performer and the possessor. I think you've said in a previous conversation that all three of those have been intensified and more evident. Certainly, we've seen in the city here and more widely in the country, big voluntary organizations stumbling over themselves and each other to be the ones feeding people. But, also, actually being very public and vocal and *visible* about being the ones feeding people. And obviously, people do need feeding at the moment. There are people in our communities going hungry and that is a tragedy, which is a symptom of the underlying inequalities that have been exposed and intensified. But at the same time, as we've said in the book, actually that can be profoundly seductive, to be the provider in that relationship, and profoundly distorting of the relationship. I think something similar has happened with worship and church as well, actually, with the competition, even if it's not being explicit or conscious, but that sense of 'Are we doing a better job? Are we getting more people? Is ours slicker or more beautiful?' has been a really seductive temptation.

Ruth And I think all of that again is revealing what's already there. Because suddenly everything feels like it's being played out much more publicly. So, I don't think it's new that clergy are worrying that the church up the road might be doing something slicker that's attracting more people. But if your Facebook feed has got three people watching and somebody else has got 300 watching, it's really obvious, in a way that it isn't if there's three people in your church and 300 in the church up the road. Although it still doesn't matter, to my mind. But it's much more risky. It feels to me like it's all become much more high stakes. So, if you do something in your church on a Saturday afternoon, and nobody turns up, nobody knows that's what's gone on. But if you do something new on your Facebook, and nobody engages with it, it's a much more public failure. (Although I don't think it is a failure.) In the same way that you're getting that much more public power grab of 'we're the ones feeding people', which I agree is really problematic, and I think that's partly because it moves us away from that reciprocal interdependence. With worship, I've been quite disturbed by some of the ways that people have been analysing numbers of views on YouTube and Facebook and that sort of thing. I think all that data is not all that helpful in showing to what extent people are actually engaging with stuff. But also, I think it drives us in a particular direction. It's really easy to count Facebook likes or YouTube views. It's really, really measurable, and so the temptation becomes to do the things that are measurable. Whereas the worship we've been doing and encouraging people to do in their own homes, we have no way of measuring. Which I absolutely don't think matters. But I think there's a real temptation to do something measurable. Because we want to be making a difference, which isn't a bad thing to want to be doing. But it tips into that temptation to want to be seen to make a difference, which is a very different thing.

Al   I wonder if a lot of the driver of that is that in the midst of crisis, our insecurities have been amplified and intensified. And actually, when we're in that place of insecurity, of discomfort, we naturally reach for the things that stabilize us and make us feel like we've got some sense of control.

Liturgy, interrupted

Al   And I think this, for me, is one of the things that speaks of liturgical time, and the way liturgical time has been interrupted and reshaped in the midst of the crisis. It felt, even before we reached the date in the diary that was Easter, that there was something profoundly 'Holy Saturday' about this time, something about needing to dwell in that place of discomfort and disruption and pain and grief. And not to avoid it or resist it or want to jump out of it too quickly.

Ruth   I agree, and I think there's something about being in that sort of empty time as well. One of the things for me, in the particular liturgical tradition that I've spent most of my life in, is that Holy Saturday is when you don't do anything. There's stuff to do for Good Friday, and there's stuff to do for Easter Sunday, and Holy Saturday is the time when there isn't. I think it's profoundly important to have a day when we are useless, when there is nothing to be performed, and nothing to be provided, and we just *are*. That's been quite a helpful thought for me. And it's so tempting, isn't it, to want to rush on to the 'but there's something new coming, but it's going to be okay, but it's going to be something different'. I think for those of us who are excited by something different emerging and the possibilities of that, that's a huge temptation. Personally, I'm not all that tempted to try and cling to the old. I'm quite happy to let a lot of that go. But the temptation for me is 'something exciting might come out of this, and I want to know what it is'. But actually, I can't make it happen. That's not my role. It's not any of our role. And I won't recognize it if I'm not willing to sit with the not-knowing first.

Al   I think there's almost a paradox in that between on the one hand emphasizing the importance of opening ourselves to interruption and to be disrupted and changed. And on the other hand, committing ourselves to sit in that space, the between space, not clinging on to the old but not too quickly grasping the new as if it is somehow within our grasp and control. Actually, there's a requirement for enduring, for faithfulness, for presence in that space of being interrupted, that lasts.

Ruth Yes, and I think for me, that's tied with that other dimension of liturgical time, of being interrupted in that bit of the cycle of eucharistic living that comes in between the sending and the gathering. I'm very influenced by Godly Play and the idea of the Circle of the Eucharist, and we're still within that circle, but we've been interrupted in a particular part of that. So, by not at the moment participating in any form of communion in any of the ways available to us, I don't think we're not within that eucharistic cycle. I think we *are*, but we're acknowledging which bit of it we're in, which is the uncomfortable bit, it's not the bit we want to be in.

Al   It's precisely the bit that we can't control in the normal ways that we control liturgy. I was really struck by Julie Gittoes using Dan Hardy's phrase about the Eucharist – the *gathered* bit – being the interval in the midst of life, of a life lived eucharistically, but the gathered bit being almost just a brief interruption in the midst of the rest of it.[3] And actually what we're experiencing at the moment is that flipped. The interruption has forced us to engage with life outside the gathering in a much more unavoidable way.

Ruth It feels to me like for a long time the Church has been talking (in a slightly, to me, irritating buzzword-y way) about 'Monday to Saturday faith' and 'everyday faith' and all those phrases, and actually being interrupted in this way has really helped me to reframe that as part of the eucharistic cycle. And it has forced us into living more fully into that bit of life, which is most of life for most of us.

---

3 Julie Gittoes, 'Why I am fasting from the feast', *Church Times*, 17 April 2020, www.churchtimes.co.uk/articles/2020/17-april/comment/opinion/why-i-am-fasting-from-the-feast, accessed 8 May 2020.

Al   I think, and this is something that we've tried to pick up in the
       book, that when the Eucharist is more frequent, it's much easier
       to fall into the default position of 'the Eucharist is the thing that
       tops us up, that energizes us and equips us, to send us out in the
       world to go and do stuff'. The way that that we've chosen to work
       with Eucharist here in this time is to say that actually, if we can't
       gather, then we can't do Eucharist in that sense, and then actually
       where we are forced into the position of looking to encounter God
       in other places. I think, for me, for us as a household here, and for
       many of our neighbours, the paradox of lockdown is that we're
       stuck at home but actually we've been pushed out each day, to go
       and find some exercise supposedly. But I think that the fresh air,
       the openness, the being able to just breathe more fully, has been
       the thing that has been so important for us and many others. And
       actually noticing, noticing the world beyond the human doing
       its thing, getting on without us, and actually flourishing without
       us in many ways. I think that has been one of those profoundly
       nurturing forms of interruption of this time.

Ruth   I think that brings us to thinking about stuff that we've already
       touched on in the book quite a lot about orders of ministry and
       what we mean by that. Maybe, actually, the non-human world
       is our starting point, even before we get to thinking about our
       neighbours (starting with our non-human neighbours, I suppose).
       For so long the Church has been having these conversations about
       lay discipleship and lay ministry and 'setting God's people free'
       and all those sorts of things. And suddenly we're forced into the
       reality that people have to be able to live lives without ordained
       ministry being a regular feature of their experience of faith at the
       moment. And again, it's revealing what's always been there. It's
       always been true that people have had vibrant and important and
       essential elements of their faith that have absolutely nothing to do
       with any form of ordained ministry or organized Church. That
       has always been true. But it's more obviously true now, and the
       importance that is more obvious. And I think some of the anxiety
       and some of the temptation towards those 'three P temptations'
       that is evident among some ordained colleagues is a very under-
       standable anxiety of 'then what is the point of us?' Are we useless?
       And I think one of the challenges is to be able to say, 'Yes, we are.'
       And that might actually be exactly the point of us.

Al   Yeah. That might be the gift that we bring to the body.

Ruth   Yes, being able to say 'Yes, we are useless. And that's okay.' I
       think some of us, particularly in some more catholic traditions,

have paid quite a lot of lip service to that over the years – 'it's a stipend, not a salary', 'you're paid to not have a job', etc. – and yet, that's not actually been how we've lived, that's not been the reality.

Al   I've been particularly struck in the last few weeks – and it's slowly evolving in terms of how we find ourselves doing church here – that my main job, if there is one, has been one of gathering, and of asking questions. So, on the one hand, inviting people to engage in spaces where they might connect with each other, but also inviting people to contribute to something that might become a resource for people. But even within those gatherings that we've managed, the main thing to be done has simply been to ask the questions: 'How are you? How are things going? What are you thankful for? What are you noticing?' And actually it doesn't need an ordained priest to do that, and lots of people have been doing that independently, but if there's any kind of sense of priestly vocation at the moment, it feels like it's around that: inviting people to notice what's going on, inviting people to notice where they're encountering God, what's deepening for them. And to find ways of *gathering* those 'noticings', so that people in their dispersal are able to encourage each other in what they're noticing and what they're seeing going on.

Ruth   That's brought me back again to my favourite bit of the ordinal (which apparently is not most people's favourite bit!) When my DDO asked me which image of priesthood most resonates with you from this I with no hesitation said, 'Oh, it's the bit about *sentinels*, about being watchers and watching for the signs of God's kingdom.' And apparently that was not the usual response. But I think that feels very much like what the work (not only of ordained people, of course) but what part of the work is at the moment is, is watching. And that takes us back into that Holy Saturday space, because if you're the sentinel, the watcher, you can't make it happen. That's not what sentinels do. But you've absolutely got to notice when it is happening. So, it's about letting go of the control, but giving the attention and that really sort of intentional attentiveness to what's going on and what God's doing, where and how, and I think that's what those questions are about for me. And then maybe just suggesting, 'Is there a connection here? What about this? I wonder what that might be?'

Breaking down and building up

Al   I was reminded of a book [mentioned in Chapter 16] by a couple of black political theorists from the States that talks about the 'undercommons'.[4] There's a sense of the commons being those webs of connection and sharing, but the 'undercommons' being the same, but normally below the radar, below public visibility, particularly in those parts of society that structurally are *pushed* to the edges or *pushed* under the radar. I've been fascinated by those in the church who've become really enthusiastic about social media and the internet as being this new public space that they – *we*, I'll own myself as being part of that – have just discovered as a way of connecting between people, whereas particularly those with physical disabilities are saying, 'No, actually, we've been doing church this way for a long time. This has been our primary way of connecting, and good of you to notice, thank you. But don't try and start colonizing it, or telling us how to do it. And actually, if you want to open your eyes and ears, you might actually hear some wisdom from us about how we've been doing it for a while and what works and what doesn't, about what we've learned along the way.'

Ruth   Yeah, and I think it's the same as well in non-digital spaces. So, lots of my middle-class friends are suddenly saying, 'I talked to my neighbours, and they're actually really nice, and we had this chat, and they brought me round some cake …' And I think if we look to our neighbours on the Firs and Bromford they'd say, 'How is this new?!' But, again, there's that risk of colonizing, of turning this into something it isn't.

Al   It was fascinating here a couple of weeks ago when one of our neighbours said they wanted to put a table out to share food. One of the organizational responses very quickly was, but what about health and safety? How are we going to control this? How are we going to make sure that this is done in the right way? And actually, those of us who are local, who are neighbours, but also part of organizations wrestled with that for a little while, but came out the other end and said: 'It's not for us to control.' Actually, this is neighbours getting on with doing what neighbours do here. We just need to step out of the way. We need to let it happen. And we need to cheerlead, encourage and celebrate it. But not take it over.

---

4 Stefano Harney and Fred Moten, *The Undercommons: Fugitive Planning and Black Study* (Wivenhoe: Minor Compositions, 2013).

Ruth   I think the more we can find ways to embrace those little bits of disruption, the easier it will get, the more ingrained those habits become and then the easier it becomes to make those lasting changes. Because once we've done one thing, and actually it was fine that we weren't in control and it was okay, then maybe we can try something else. Maybe we don't need to be in control. It's a bit like, when I first was in a context where we were trying to get children more involved with liturgy, and we decided to let them lay up the altar. This was a really big thing. And I was really in favour of this, I really wanted to do it. And in the back of my mind, I was thinking, 'What's going to happen when they drop something? What is going to happen when they drop the sacrament?' And then one day, one of them did: a ciborium full of hosts, all over the place. And it was fine. It was disruptive. But ultimately, it was fine. And actually, sometimes being disrupted is what we need in order to stop worrying about the possibility of being disrupted.

Al   That reminds me, I'm listening to Brené Brown reading her book *Daring Greatly*[5] at the moment, and she's just been talking about the marble jar in the classroom where she uses it as a metaphor for trust and building trust. The jar is just there and the jar can be empty but slowly marbles are put into it and the more marbles that go into it, the more that level of trust is built up. And I think it struck a couple of chords for me. One is that in our community building work here we often talk about the pace, the speed of trust, something that can't be hurried, that has to happen slowly. But also, as you were talking, I wonder if actually one of the things that is going on with everything that we're talking about is not those of us with privilege working out ways to get others to trust us, but actually those of us with privilege learning to trust differently, so that we can let go.

Ruth   And again, it's that mutuality thing, isn't it, that interdependence that cuts both ways. Actually, we can't be in control of whether people trust us. We can behave in trustworthy manners, and obviously we should, but we can't be in control of whether other people trust us. We can be in control of whether we're willing to trust other people. That's the bit where we should perhaps be exercising some agency.

Al   Absolutely, yeah. I was just rereading this morning [as I was writing Chapter 15], a bit of Grace Jantzen's *Becoming Divine*, where

---

5 Brené Brown, *Daring Greatly: How the Courage to Be Vulnerable Transforms the Way We Live, Love, Parent, and Lead* (Harmondsworth: Penguin, 2012)

she talks about 'trustworthy community' as being a goal,[6] and I was quite struck by that image. It goes back to a bit of [one of our previous] conversations, about what we might say about cross and resurrection. And what we might hope for from the Roman centurion, and his relationship – or non-relationship – with the women watching at the cross. I wonder if one of the things that we're seeking towards is that idea of a trustworthy community, that possibility. It's less grand than reconciliation, I think. That possibility of: can we be in a place together where we can trust each other enough?

Ruth I think for me, that connects in really importantly with how we're responding to this current situation. It's about what sort of trustworthy are we trying to be. Because in one sense, the idea that the Church is the thing that's always there and is always reliable and dependable, is a form of seeking after trustworthiness.

Al Yeah, it's: 'Okay, lads, we've got this.' Yeah.

Ruth Yes. And that's very different from what I think we're trying to articulate here, which is more about being a community that reflects something that's true. For me, one of the really important things about suspending our participation in the Eucharist is that it's reflecting something that's true. I experience that absence of communion as deeply, deeply disruptive and rupturing not only to what I'm doing but really to who I am. But I think that's absolutely right. Because that's what's true. And liturgy should always be, I think, the ritualization of what is real. What is real at the moment is a profound sense of disruption, fracture, rupturedness and change. And so liturgy needs to be something that ritualizes that, and for me, what ritualizes it is the absence that comes from the absence of communion. And that's a different kind of trustworthiness. So, there's the trustworthiness of, 'Oh, don't worry, we'll look after it' or 'It's going to be okay.' That's a *different* kind of thing from the trustworthiness of 'We're telling the truth about this, and enacting the truth about this, and that's what we're sitting with.' For me, that's very often the thing that characterizes the church leaders who I find really attractive. Somebody like Nadia Boltz-Weber is a really good example of that. She's someone who just tells it how it is. What I find attractive about that is that it's very truthful and therefore trustworthy. I think the Church has not always been very good at being that kind of trustworthy. I think sometimes we've substituted the 'Come what

---

6 Grace Jantzen, *Becoming Divine: Towards a Feminist Philosophy of Religion* (Manchester: Manchester University Press, 1998), pp. 210–11.

may, the show will go on' kind of trustworthy for all the places where we're not able or not willing to be the 'We're willing to sit with the truth' kind of trustworthy.

Al   Yeah. I guess the case of abuse is probably one of the sharpest examples of this. Actually, the break of trust is two-fold. It's not just about situation of abuse, but it's about the institution then not being able to acknowledge that abuse has happened and to deal with the truth of that.

Ruth   Yeah, it's really fundamental. It's about what the Church is, that has in some sense been broken by that, and what the Church is that is reflected in our response to that. It's a really fundamental thing. Who are we, and what are we here for? The answer can't be: to preserve the status quo. That's a very Christendom answer. Which we're still quite enmeshed in, in so many ways. And it's a very tempting answer because we can control it. Or we can try to control it. Very evidently we can't. But we can try. And I think that's part of why the Church is so fixated on growth. And so unwilling to embrace the idea that constant growth isn't the only way of flourishing. And quite unwilling to accept some of the institutional death that we seem to be facing, one way or another, and the kind of the decay and the mess that goes with that. We've played around a bit before with this idea of decomposition ...

Al   Yeah. Say bit more about that.

Ruth: It's the idea [explored in Chapter 15] that breaking something down doesn't have to be a destructive act, it can be a creative thing. That's how ecosystems work in the natural world. You need decomposition, organisms that decompose things, they're a necessary part of that. And they may be nobody's favourite part, but they are necessary and the decomposition is necessary for the growth. And I guess it's an extension of the death and resurrection metaphor. But we're often very unwilling as a Church, as individuals, particularly as individuals with privilege within an institution that is extremely privileged. Maybe *we* are what needs to be decomposed. I think it's quite hard to embrace the decomposition and the agents of decomposition if you are the part of the ecosystem that needs to be decomposed in order for the new growth to happen.

Al   I was really struck again, when we talked before, when I wondered if our institutional resistance to death and to decomposition was a bit like a sort of twisted Gethsemane, with Jesus saying 'Take this cup away from me.' And you reflected back saying, well, how about *Peter*, in that situation, wanting to cling to his sword hanging on to that last vestige of power, even if it was pretty meaningless in the face of presumably a troop of Roman soldiers coming with superior weapons? But that sense of decomposition is something that actually happens really slowly as well. Maybe if we start down this road, then it begins to feel more possible as we go. Maybe if we start to accept, and let that happen, and celebrate decomposition happening, and if we notice where it's happening, then it begins to become more a part of our life that we embrace.

Ruth   Yes. I'm looking out into the garden as we're talking, and it's not that at one point all the decomposition happens and then at another point all the growing happens. It's both/and all the time. And sometimes you can see more of one and sometimes you can see more of the other. But it's both all the time. And I think maybe one of the things that this situation is doing is revealing some of the decomposition that's happening. I don't think it's necessarily making any more decomposition happen. But it's just pointing our focus more in that direction. I think, again, it depends what sort of instincts we've formed and allowed ourselves to be formed in as to how we react to that. Just like some gardeners favour a more neat and tidy approach to gardening and some of us favour a bit more of a chaotic, wild approach.

I think it's the same in churches, that we will react differently to that decomposition. There's a temptation to be like Peter with his sword. He didn't have any power or control in that situation. Whatever he had done with that sword, the outcome was going to be the same and Jesus was going to die. He didn't have any power or control. When Jesus told him to put down his sword, Peter isn't losing any power or control. He's losing the illusion of power and control. And it feels to me like that's what this situation is doing. We're not losing any power or control that we previously had. But we're losing the illusion of it. And if we allow ourselves to lose that illusion, if we allow ourselves to be interrupted in that way, then who knows what will happen? We don't know. But if we don't, if we just keep clinging on to something, then I can't see anything good coming of that.

Al   We started this conversation by saying that one of the perils of this work is that we that there's never a stopping point. I wonder if that is a good place to pause the conversation for the moment? Because I think there's a huge amount of promise and possibility that's actually beyond our thinking, talking and writing.

What is this thing that has happened to us? It's a virus, yes. In and of itself it holds no moral brief. But it is definitely more than a virus. Some believe it is God's way of bringing us to our senses. Others that it's a Chinese conspiracy to take over the world.

Whatever it is, coronavirus has made the mighty kneel and brought the world to a halt like nothing else could. Our minds are still racing back and forth, longing for a return to 'normality', trying to stitch our future to our past and refusing to acknowledge the rupture. But the rupture exists. And in the midst of this terrible despair, it offers us a chance to rethink the doomsday machine we have built for ourselves. Nothing could be worse than a return to normality.

Historically, pandemics have forced humans to break with the past and imagine their world anew. This one is no different. It is a portal, a gateway between one world and the next.

We can choose to walk through it, dragging the carcasses of our prejudice and hatred, our avarice, our data banks and dead ideas, our dead rivers and smoky skies behind us. Or we can walk through lightly, with little luggage, ready to imagine another world. And ready to fight for it. (Arundhati Roy, 'The pandemic is a portal')[7]

Questions for reflection

- What did you notice during the pandemic – about yourself, your neighbours, your community, your church?
- What surprised you? Is there anything you are aware of now, which you were oblivious to before?
- How did you feel about being 'interrupted' in this way?
- How do you think your response to this 'great interruption' has been shaped by your experience of privilege/oppression?
- What is there from this experience that you want to hang on to, and what do you need to let go?

Further reading

- Klaus Schwab and Thierry Malleret, *COVID-19: The Great Reset* (Geneva: World Economic Forum, 2020)

---

7 Arundhati Roy, 'The pandemic is a portal', *Financial Times*, 3 April 2020, www.ft.com/content/10d8f5e8-74eb-11ea-95fe-fcd274e920ca, accessed 8 May 2020.

Further Reading

At the end of most chapters, we have offered some suggestions for further reading that tie in specifically with that chapter's themes. Here we offer a few extras that resonate with the general direction of the book, and from which we have learned much along the way. You might want to compare and contrast the approaches these authors describe, to what we've tried to unfold in these pages.

- Mark Gornick, *To Live in Peace: Biblical Faith and the Changing Inner City* (Grand Rapids, MI: Eerdmans, 2002)
- Janet Hodgson, *Mission from Below: Growing a Kingdom Community* (Durham: Sacristy Press, 2018)
- Paul Keeble, *Mission With: Something Out of the Ordinary* (Watford: Instant Apostle, 2017)
- Chris Lane, *Ordinary Miracles: Mess, Meals and Meeting Jesus in Unexpected Places* (Watford: Instant Apostle, 2017)
- Sally Mann, *Looking for Lydia: Encounters that shape the Church* (2018)
- Anna Ruddick, *Reimagining Mission from Urban Places: Missional Pastoral Care* (London: SCM Press, 2020)
- Ray Simpson, *Church of the Isles: A prophetic strategy for renewal* (Stowmarket: Kevin Mayhew, 2003)
- C. Christopher Smith and John Pattison, *Slow Church: Cultivating Community in the Patient Way of Jesus* (Downers Grove, IL: IVP, 2014)
- Tim Soerens, *Everywhere You Look: Discovering the Church Right Where You Are* (Downers Grove, IL: IVP, 2020)
- Paul Sparks, Tim Soerens and Dwight Friesen, *The New Parish: How Neighbourhood Churches are Transforming Mission, Discipleship and Community* (Downers Grove, IL: IVP, 2014)
- Andre van Eymeren, *Building Communities of the Kingdom: How to work with others to build great spaces and places* (Northcote: Morning Star, 2016)

While we have done everything we can to make this book as accessible to as wide a readership as possible, *Being Interrupted* has grown out of the same soil as Al's PhD thesis, which has also been published by SCM Press. If you want to engage further with some of the deeper theological underpinnings explored here you might want to read:

- Al Barrett, *Interrupting the Church's Flow: A radically receptive political theology in the urban margins* (London: SCM Press, 2020)

We also want to point readers to two vital areas that we've not been able to cover here.

On Christianity through LGBQTI+ lenses:

- Christina Beardsley and Michelle O'Brien (eds): *This is My Body: hearing the theology of transgender Christians* (London: Darton, Longman and Todd, 2016)
- Andrew Davison (ed.), *Amazing Love: discipleship, sexuality and mission* (London: Darton, Longman and Todd, 2016)
- Elizabeth Edman, *Queer Virtue: What LGBTQ People Know about Life and Love and How it can Revitalize Christianity* (Boston, MA: Beacon, 2016)
- Ruth Hunt (ed.), *The Book of Queer Prophets: 24 Writers on Sexuality and Religion* (London: William Collins, 2020)

On Christianity through the lenses of dis/ability:

- Nancy Eiesland, *The Disabled God: Toward a Liberatory Theology of Disability* (Nashville, TN: Abingdon, 1994)
- Jennie Hogan, *This Is My Body: A story of sickness and health* (Norwich: Canterbury Press, 2017)
- John M. Hull, *On Sight and Insight: A Journey into the World of Blindness*, 2nd edition (London: Oneworld, 1997)
- Thomas E. Reynolds, *Vulnerable Communion: A theology of disability and hospitality* (Grand Rapids, MI: Brazos, 2008)
- Frances Young, *Arthur's Call: A Journey of Faith in the Face of Severe Learning Disability* (London: SPCK, 2014)

Suggested Reading Plan For Groups

We are hoping that as individuals, groups and church communities, you will be able to engage with this book, and the thoughts, feelings, questions and actions it provokes in you, in ways that are most appropriate to your own contexts, experiences and challenges. But we also know (from personal experience!) that sometimes it can be helpful to have some suggestions that break down a big meal into more digestible mouthfuls! So, this is just that: simply one way that you might work through this book in 'slow time', particularly within the context of a church community that follows the liturgical seasons. Many other approaches are also possible!

Part 1: Where Are We?

Chapter	Suggested timing
Act 1 and Introduction	2nd Sunday before Lent to Sunday before Lent
Chapter 1 – Who are 'We'?	Sunday before Lent to Lent 1
Chapter 2 – Finding our Place in Brexit Britain	2nd week of Lent (Lent 1 to Lent 2)
Chapter 3 – What are We Not Seeing?	3rd week of Lent (Lent 2 to Lent 3)
Chapter 4 – The Church's Privilege Problem	4th week of Lent (Lent 3 to Lent 4)
Chapter 5 – A Tale of Two Economies	5th week of Lent (Lent 4 to Lent 5)
Chapter 6 – Getting on the Wrong Side of Jesus	6th week of Lent (Lent 5 to Palm Sunday)

Part 2: Being Interrupted

Introduction and Chapter 7 – On the Road	2nd week of Easter (Easter 2 to Easter 3)
Chapter 8 – At the Edges	3rd week of Easter (Easter 3 to Easter 4)
Chapter 9 – At the Table	4th week of Easter (Easter 4 to Easter 5)
Chapter 10 – With Little Children and Act 2: Children Writing the Script	5th week of Easter (Easter 5 to Easter 6)
Chapter 11 – Amid the Trees	6th week of Easter (Easter 6 to Easter 7)

Part 3: Reimagining

Act 3: From a Homeless Church … and Chapter 12 – A Third Economy	Ordinary Time week 1 (from Trinity Sunday)
Act 4: A Street Party and Chapter 13 – Life at the Edges	Ordinary Time week 2
Act 5: The Community Talent Show and Chapter 14 – From the Outside, in	Ordinary Time week 3
Act 6: Unheard Voices and Chapter 15 – At the Cross (1st part: up to the end of 'Structural repentance: two examples')	Ordinary Time week 4
Chapter 15 (2nd part – from 'Relinquishing – revisited')	Ordinary Time week 5
Act 7: An Easter Eve Encounter and Chapter 16 – Resurrection (1st part: up to the end of the two examples of 'Remaining')	Ordinary Time week 6
Chapter 16 – Resurrection (2nd part: from 'Recycling') and Act 8: An Easter Day Walk	Ordinary Time week 7
Act 9: A Walk in the Woods and Epilogue, in Conversation	Ordinary Time week 8

Acknowledgements

Al and Ruth want to say thank you to:

- David Shervington, Rachel Geddes and your colleagues at SCM Press – for the speed and grace with which you have brought this book to publication, in the middle of a global pandemic; and for your patience (especially with Al) with a book that arrived on your desk slightly less than a year after its deadline!
- Anthony, Lynne and Rachel – not just for being willing to write this book's Forewords, for the parts each of you have played in the evolution of this book, and for your various and profoundly prophetic voices in leadership in church and world – but also for the ways in which you have accompanied and encouraged, stretched and challenged Al, and his theology, ministry and ways of seeing the world.
- Ally Barrett – for responding enthusiastically to our last-minute plea to work on some illustrations for the book; you have not just captured in stunning, powerful images what we've been trying to say in words, but you've enriched and expanded our imaginings with the creative, disruptive grace of the Spirit.
- Rafi Barrett – for your last-minute artistic expertise, creating the fabulous diagrams for the three 'economies'.
- Those who have read drafts of this book, and have offered encouraging and helpful comments on it – among them Jack Belloli, Joy Curtis, Paula Gooder, Keith Hebden, Jo Howard, Hannah Malcolm, Sanjee Perera, Jane Perry, Cormac Russell.
- The congregation members of Hodge Hill Church, and our neighbours on the Firs and Bromford – from the youngest to the oldest, from Phil to 'Faith', from Sonny in the chippy to the dancing triceratops – who continue to teach us so much about love, faith, church, community, resurrection and God, through your abiding presence with us, your creative interruptions, and all the immense wisdom that has been emerging among you over the years.

Al wants to say thank you to:

- Ruth – for initially agreeing to write a chapter, and ending up sharing so much of the journey of bringing this book to birth, for your companionship and conversation along the way, and the ways in which you have embraced the possibility of interrupting, challenging and disrupting me in ways that have encouraged, taught, stretched and converted me; and for your ministry among us in Hodge Hill, and the ways in which you have listened to us and led us, from the youngest to the oldest, with grace and authority.
- My colleagues and friends in Hodge Hill (the ministry team of Hodge Hill Church and the TogetherWeCan community-building team), who have all graciously and encouragingly borne with me as I've attempted to write this book alongside my ongoing work and ministry here – not least among you Jenni Crewes, my curate colleague for the last three years, who has taken on so many of the responsibilities of 'making church happen' since my sabbatical, and through the lockdown period of the Covid-19 pandemic; and Tim Evans, Sally Nash, Genny Tunbridge and Paul Wright, for your wise, passionate and generous companionship in exploring, experimenting and reflecting over many years now.
- Mark Pryce and Bishop David Urquhart, for encouraging and enabling me to take a sabbatical in the summer of 2019, in which I'd originally intended to finish writing this book, but which became instead a space for rest and recovery, a space to breathe and read, and a space to journey to South Africa and into ecotheology, which have all made this book clearer and more interesting than it would have been otherwise.
- All those who have invited me to lead workshops and residentials, give lectures and write articles, within which much of the thinking of this book has emerged – from the Church of Scotland's Priority Areas gathering, justice-and-peace-seeking Quakers and Roman Catholic religious, to the Council for World Mission's 'liberating whiteness' working group and the Common Awards research programme (and many more).
- All those countless others who have reflected with me over the years, whose wisdom and insights have ended up here (attributed or otherwise!) in our local neighbourhood, in local and wider church, in academic networks and communities of practice, and elsewhere.
- A few who have been companions, mentors and co-conspirators on this particular journey for the longest, and/or who have consistently encouraged and challenged me to 'press on' and go deeper: Keith Hebden, David Hewlett, Sanjee Perera, Jane Perry, Sharon Prentis,

Dean Pusey, Anthony Reddie, Cathy Ross, Cormac Russell, Richard Sudworth and Keith White.

- Those three people who have had to share this journey most intimately, who have heard me to speech, taught me patiently, and brought their own creative interruptions to the process most often – Janey, Rafi and Adia – your love, and the ways in which you engage with and make sense of the world, are priceless gifts which never cease to surprise me.

Ruth wants to say thank you to:

- Al – for inviting me on this journey, and for your companionship along the way; for hearing me to speech, and trusting in my wilder ideas even when I don't; for being willing to be interrupted, and for challenging me to do likewise; for all the 'yes, and…'s, and the joy of improvising together; and for modelling a way of living interruptedly which gives me hope for the future.
- The community of The Queen's Foundation, among whom I have learned and am learning so much: my fellow students, especially those who have listened attentively and sometimes critically to my developing ideas, among them Jodie Brown, Ruth Edmonds, Belinda Stanley and Kate Tingle; and the teaching staff, especially those who have encouraged me to believe (when I have often struggled to do so) that I have something to say and a voice worth hearing, among them Nicola Slee, Rachel Starr, and Helen Stanton.
- The women of the Saturday Morning Breakfast Group: Becks Hickman, Jo Howard, Heather Stanley and Soobie Whitfield, for their steadfast companionship, friendship and love, and for being 'church' for/with me in ways which challenge, nurture and sustain me.
- The community of On Fire Mission, in which I have found a home, and by whom I am continually reminded afresh of the surprising, expansive, disruptive, life-giving work of the Spirit, and encouraged to be open to the unexpected callings and promptings of God.
- All the children and young people I have had the pleasure and privilege to minister with and among, at Hodge Hill Church, at All Saints, High Wycombe and beyond. You have taught me so much about interrupting and being interrupted, and about looking at God and the world in ways that are fresh, real, often unexpected, and sometimes uncomfortable.
- In particular, the young people of Engage: Ben Atkinson, Sarah Dagnall, Kirsty Dunn and Will Knights who, by the honesty and integrity with which they wrestle with questions of faith, have encouraged me to be deeply dissatisfied with the Church as it is, and to long, dream, work,

and pray for something radically different and more like Jesus. Thank you for interrupting me so well!

- My beloved partner Rachel, who has supported and encouraged me in more ways than I could possibly list, not least by being open to all the interruptions this book and the process of writing it has brought to our life together.

Index

Christian Climate Action 202
Christianity
 dominant worldview and 54–5
 see also churches; Jesus of
  Nazareth
The Christlike God (Taylor) 68,
 69
Church Mission Society 68
Church of England *see* churches
Church Urban Fund, Web of
 Poverty 25
churches
 children and 58–9
 class culture and 57
 economies 63
 in edge-places 142–3
 gathering 155–7
 gender issues and 57–8
 McDonaldization of 65–7, 71
 missiological challenges ix–xi
 oblivious to abuses 207
 orders of ministry 160
 other-than-human
  creation 59–60
 in a pandemic 227, 233–5
 post-imperial melancholia 72
 powers in giving 68–72
 race and 56
 social media and 239
 speaking out 155–7
 third economy 130–1
 white majority 56
 wilding/planting 131–3
St Clare of Assisi 144
class
 within Church xii–xiv
 Church culture and 57
 Grenfell Tower and 43–5
 identifying with the divine 80
 inequalities in pandemic 231–2
 listening to others and 40
 McGarvey and 180

negative labels 44–5
perception of failures 198
recognizing 21–2
whiteness and 30–2
climate change *see* environment
Climate Psychology Alliance 202
Coles, Romand
 edge-places 144
 intercorporeal illumination 149,
  150
 wormhole hope 213
colonialism/imperialism
 Britain and 56
 challenge for today and ix–xi
 missionary gaze 149
 post-imperial melancholia 32–4,
  72
 relinquishing 176
Coming Back to Life (Macy and
 Brown) 214–15
communications technology, place
 and culture and 30
communion, neighbours and food
 158–9
community
 connectors 146–7
 the deacon and 162–3
 disruption 239–40
 edge-places and 145–6, 209–10
 gifts of the neighbourhood 133–6
 the kin-dom of God 194–6
 neighbours and food 158–9
 in pandemic 230–2
 on the planet 213–14
 thrown together 209
 trustworthy 211
 Web of Poverty 25
 see also Firs and Bromford
Copeland, Cynthia 203
Council for the World Mission,
 'Legacies of Slavery' hearings
 181